A SMALL WORLD

DAVIN HECKMAN

A Small World

SMART HOUSES AND THE DREAM OF THE PERFECT DAY

Duke University Press Durham and London 2008

Printed in the United States of America on acid-free paper ♾
Designed by C. H. Westmoreland
Typeset in Warnock Pro by Tseng Information Systems, Inc.

Library of Congress Cataloging-in-Publication Data
Heckman, Davin, 1975–
A small world : smart houses and the dream of the perfect day /
Davin Heckman.
p. cm.
Includes bibliographical references and index.
ISBN 978-0-8223-4134-5 (cloth : alk. paper)
ISBN 978-0-8223-4158-1 (pbk. : alk. paper)
1. Home automation. 2. Technological innovations. I. Title.
TK7881.25.H43 2008
696—dc22 2007033496

In memory of

CARL T. HECKMAN,

bartender, artist, and vernacular anthropologist.

Thank you, Dad, for teaching me to love people.

CONTENTS

ACKNOWLEDGMENTS

This book would not exist if not for the guidance and enthusiasm of my advisor, Hai Ren, my graduate-assistant supervisor, Ellen Berry, and my program chair, Don McQuarie, all of whom served on my dissertation committee in American culture studies at Bowling Green State University.

Second, I am grateful for the assistance of Duke University Press. Ken Wissoker, Courtney Berger, and the anonymous reviewers of my manuscript functioned as a model of what the ideal editorial process should be: they challenged and inspired me to transcend my limitations.

I would like to thank my friends at *Reconstruction* (http://reconstruction.eserver.org) for providing me a community of peers with whom I could develop new ideas. I am also indebted to Matthew Wolf-Meyer, a great friend and collaborator. A discussion of minimalism that takes place in a footnote originally appeared in "Navigating the Starless Night: Reading the Auto/bio/geography: Meaning-Making," an introduction for *Reconstruction* 2.3 (summer 2002) that I coauthored with Wolf-Meyer. I have also repurposed a brief segment of my writing on handheld electronic games from "Allegorical Reductions and Social Reconstructions," our introduction to *Reconstruction* 6.1 (winter 2006).

I must thank Ellen Berry (again) and Carol Siegel for inviting me to join the exciting world of *Rhizomes* (http://www.rhizomes.net), first as a technical editor, then as a guest editor, and now as a member of the advisory board. Thanks to Jason Nelson's (http://www.secrettechnology.com) informal Flash and html tutorials, friendship, and encouragement, my work with *Rhizomes* and *Reconstruction* was possible. Portions of the essay "Utopian Accidents: An Introduction to Retro-Futures" from *Rhizomes* 8 (spring 2004) have made it into the introduction. All the contributors to the issue on "Retro-Futures" have helped to develop my thinking in important ways.

I am also grateful to my colleagues at Siena Heights University for their continued support of my research and teaching.

I'd like to thank Bowling Green State University's Department of Popular Culture, the Popular Culture Library, and the Popular Culture Association for breaking the field of popular culture studies open for people like me and for giving me the tools I needed to complete this project.

I'd also like to thank Roadside America (http://www.roadsideamerica.com) for keeping Xanadu alive (and for sending me a great picture to include in this book).

Finally, I could not have completed this project without the help of Carrie Heckman, my wife. Aside from being a scrupulous proofreader and an unassailable force of moral credibility, Carrie helped to polish this manuscript over the course of dozens of revisions into something that represents me as something better than I am in reality.

INTRODUCTION

A Tale of Two Cities

EPCOT will take its cue from the new ideas and new technologies that are now emerging from the creative centers of American industry. It will be a community of tomorrow that will never be completed, but will always be introducing, and testing and demonstrating new materials and new systems. And EPCOT will always be a showcase to the world of ingenuity and imagination of American free enterprise.
—Walt Disney, *Walt's Last Film*, October 1966

There was once a place where neighbors greeted neighbors in the quiet of summer twilight. Where children chased fireflies. And porch swings provided easy refuge from the cares of the day. The movie house showed cartoons on Saturday. The grocery store delivered. And there was one teacher who always knew you had that special something. Remember that place? Perhaps from your childhood? Or maybe just from stories. It had a magic all its own. The special magic of an American home town.
—1996 brochure for Celebration, Florida, Disney's planned community

The future has never seemed so old and so dated. But it wasn't always this way. Rewind and press play to sift through visions of a tomorrow that never quite arrived—a world of rocket ships and tailfins and atomic energy—plastic dreams and plastic realities—the future of the 1960s. Although we wink and smile at the naïve longings of days past, it would be a mistake to deny the ideological force and representational power contained in these images. And it would be equally foolish to laugh too long or too hard at history, leaving our own calcified and worldly-wise longings to sit unmolested in smug cynicism, as though we were too bored to make the same mistakes again. The entertainment industry in general has always been sensitive to our tastes, desires, needs, and longings—always providing us with the sweet release of escape, even when the release we demand is the ironic and self-deprecating command of the so-called postmodern condition.

Thus I begin my study of the home with two particular places, which tell three different, but related stories: Disney's EPCOT and Disney's Celebration. Before I mislead you into believing that Disney is a target of this effort, I must be fair and explain that Disney represents, in many ways, the highest development of our culture's dreams, ambitions, and ideals. The Disney Company, which some have criticized as an evil entity, is steeped in capitalist and consumerist ideologies, but I beg you to defer judgment as we are all implicated in these processes.[1] Rather, I would ask readers to search for the little pieces of this Magic Kingdom—as they find themselves nestled in our homes and hearts, animating our toys and technologies, and breathing life into our dreams and fantasies—fatally linking our idea of the good life with a technical future.

Conceived in the 1960s, Walt Disney's Experimental Prototype Community of Tomorrow, or EPCOT, was to be both a laboratory for future technology and a home for the citizens of tomorrow. As Sharon Zukin notes in *Landscapes of Power*, EPCOT Center (as well as Disneyland) was prefigured in the 1893 World's Columbian Exposition in Chicago (as well as in the 1939 World's Fair in New York), with its development of "amusement parks and rides, stage-set representations of vernacular architecture, state-of-the-art technology, and a special construction of an ideal urban community" (225). More important to this discussion, the Columbian Exposition marked a significant moment in the development of American domesticity. In 1893, at this very fair, where Frederick Jackson Turner delivered his influential thesis on the frontier, a wide range of communications and transportation innovations were put on display, electricity and the recently invented incandescent light bulb enjoyed prominent positions in the spectacle, and the first "all-electric kitchen" was introduced to an amazed American public.[2] It is this bundle of concepts and innovations that can be traced through the twentieth-century American home. An awareness of this cultural trajectory is key to properly understanding the "smart home" and its related concepts.

A part of the same curious tradition of spectacle and speculation, the origins of Walt Disney's city can also be traced through the "World of Tomorrow" World's Fair held in New York in 1939–1940. Among many notable attractions listed in *The Official Guide Book of the New York World's Fair 1939* is General Motors' "Highways and Horizons Exhibit," which featured Norman Bel Geddes's "Futurama" highway-of-tomorrow ride (consisting of "magic chairs" that moved spectators around what was then the largest scale model in the history of the world) (see fig. 1). It is one of the most widely referenced precursors to what would become suburban America (*The Official Guide Book of the New York World's Fair 1939*, 207–8). A transcript of the Futurama narration reads prophetically, as spectators were treated to a view of a model of what looks remarkably like a contemporary concrete superhighway (without the potholes, accidents, and litter): "Looming ahead is a 1960 Motorway intersection. By means of ramped loops, cars may make right and left turns at rates of speed up to 50 miles per hour. The turning-off lanes are elevated and depressed. There is no interference from the straight ahead traffic in the higher speed lanes" (Zim, Lerner, and Rolfes, 109). According to Helen Burgess, in her article "Futurama, Autogeddon," the General Motors exhibition was prophetic in other ways as well: "In a montage of stock images, the film announced the coming of the world of tomorrow by tapping into narratives of progress and manifest destiny. The film then went on to showcase the Futurama model exhibit, showing close-ups of the Futurama diorama in action, and ended with shots of the popular exhibition building itself, replacing the familiar 'the end' with 'Without End' to signifying that the future was something to strive for indefinitely" (par. 10). Beyond simply proposing a future of automobiles and superhighways, the General Motors exhibit emphasized a way of being that would be more clearly realized as consumers approached the 1960s as imagined by Bel Geddes.

TOUR THE FUTURE
WITH GENERAL MOTORS

GENERAL MOTORS HIGHWAYS AND HORIZONS EXHIBIT AT THE NEW YORK WORLD'S FAIR

YOU RIDE IN SOUND-CHAIRS, *viewing a world in miniature—a vast world of future cities and countryside—industrial and mountainous sections—airports, lakes, rivers and waterfalls—streamlined Diesel trains, tunnels and boats—ten thousand moving cars on the superhighways of tomorrow. A spectacular and life-like "futurama" covering more than 35,000 square feet and extending for a third of a mile in and about this General Motors exhibit building of wonders.*

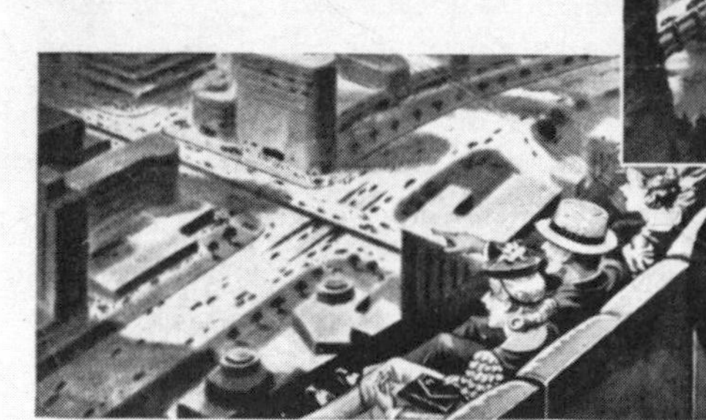

CHEVROLET
PONTIAC · OLDSMOBILE
BUICK · LA SALLE
CADILLAC · FRIGIDAIRE
BODY BY FISHER

1. General Motors advertisement (*The Official Guide Book of the New York World's Fair 1939*).

A more recent precursor of the smart home can be found in the 1964 World's Fair, also held in New York, for which privately owned Walter Elias Disney Enterprises (WED) created attractions for Ford Motors ("Magic Skyway"), Pepsi-Cola ("It's a Small World"), General Electric ("Progressland"), and the State of Illinois ("Great Moments with Mr. Lincoln")—all of which were among the most popular attractions that year (Thomas, 313). What is significant about EPCOT, however, is that it takes these attractions a step further, and imagines them as parts of an integrated living environment—in EPCOT, actual families would live, work, and play in a technologically rich environment. In a promotional film released in October 1966 Walt Disney described this idealized relationship between the corporation and the individual: "When EPCOT has become a reality and we find the need for technology that don't [*sic*] even exist today, it's our hope that EPCOT will stimulate American industry to develop new solutions that will meet the needs of people expressed right here in this experimental community."[3] In keeping with the spirit of his times, he imagined that the vast resources and engineering capabilities of corporate America that had provided the middle class with such abundance and prosperity in the 1950s could be called on to take this technological manifest destiny a step further, solving problems that had yet to be imagined. Walt continued, enthusiastically, "It will never cease to be a living blueprint of the future where people actually live a life they can't find anyplace else in the world." On another occasion, he explained, "It's like the city of tomorrow ought to be, a city that caters to people as a service function" (quoted in Thomas, 349). Even more revolutionary (or prophetic), this city of the future would have no landowners (except, presumably, at the corporate level), no voting controls, and no retirement; all citizens would be required to work for the maintenance of the city and would live in rented houses and apartments (Thomas, 349). EPCOT, as envisioned by Walt Disney, would be the second coming of the American dream, redirecting the frontier myth into consumer practices, and speaking to all peoples of a place beyond prosperity, beyond freedom, and beyond the mundane imaginings of ordinary life. In short, EPCOT was to be the future—a spectacular vision of an American utopia institutionalized as a process of constant becoming.

Unlike past utopias, which yearned for a state of completeness, this one would achieve perfection in the process of change. Like the latest software, EPCOT would be perfectible insofar as it was upgradeable, and its sophistication would lie in its ability to be rewritten. An early manifestation of contemporary corporate strategies which seek to manage innovation as a resource which can be directed to produce continued results, the idea of an institutionally regulated revolution may seem paradoxical at first, but when considered alongside the respectable business practices of insurance, real-estate speculation, moneylending, and stock trading, this attempt to negotiate "risk" makes a great deal of sense. It seems that as long as technological development is a capitalist enterprise, there will continue to be economic benefits for companies that can subdue the chaos of radical innovations by channeling change through the matrix of existing infrastructures.

This cultural orientation which situates daily life outside of the ordinary suggests, on the one hand, that the coherent nature of the Enlightenment self and the conceptual purity of high-modernist architecture are present in Disney's plan, and on the other hand, that this plan can account for the incoherencies of a changing self and the instability of a changing city. Mary Anne Doane's discussion of modernism, for example, points to the consequences of "chance" and "contingency" in the realization of freedom amid the organizing forces of modernist rationality and industrial time as an expression of "cinematic time," which "acknowledges contingency and indeterminacy while at the same time offering the law of their regularity" (31). Where modernist aesthetics intended to produce freedom, industry finds an asset in abstracted social relations. However, more recent industrial developments (like just-in-time production, flexible accumulation, and pay-per-use) seem to be a reaction to contingency itself. Consequently, recent mainstream cinematic displays seem to accept the contingent nature of representation, yet adhere to a relatively stable system of narration.[4] Taken as a "regular" part of subjective experience, rationalized systems must take into account this regular irregularity as an area of knowledge. And in a society which traffics in cultural commodities such as film, television, fashion, and advertisement, entrepreneurs must inevitably industrialize these spaces as well. Thus, the goal of EPCOT was to rationalize fluidity, to traffic in what has been often called "postmodernity" as part of an ordered strategy for social progress.[5]

For all of their visionary promise and utopian dazzle, Walt Disney's plans for EPCOT were shelved after his death, which occurred a mere two months after he released them, and the company's efforts, under the direction of his brother Roy Disney, were turned toward the more profitable end of providing entertainment. It was in the name of entertainment that EPCOT was eventually resurrected, in the early 1980s, as the EPCOT Center theme park, a tourist destination and companion to the Magic Kingdom theme park at Disney World in Florida. The updated corporate position on the EPCOT Center was expressed in an article in the futurist-oriented *Omni* magazine, published in September 1982: "The EPCOT that will open this fall will have no permanent residents. The company has adopted the line that the tens of thousands of daily visitors to the Florida Disney complex will be its residents" (Osonko, 70). And, although the article cites Walt Disney's enthusiastic rhetoric, reminding readers that EPCOT "will always be in a state of becoming" (ibid.), one reader felt the need to express his dismay in a letter published in the following February. In his letter to the editor, Jerome Glenn writes, "When I found out that EPCOT would not have residents, I was furious at WED Enterprises for not honoring Walt's wish" (10). EPCOT had shifted from being a utopian community forged out of a union between big business and the common citizen, the rationalized embodiment of planning in a technological society, to being a theme park in a society that had increasingly found its utopian promise in entertainment and media. Rightfully ruffling the futuristic feathers of at least one reader, EPCOT had ceased to be a place where the future was to be sought as a process of becoming and had been replaced by a series of attractions through which new products could be observed. The early plan for EPCOT had been scrapped to make way for a more limited and more resolutely commercialistic actuality. The transformation was a profound one, which reverberated through the discourses of household technologies. With the transformation of Walt Disney's plan in the 1980s, the whole project of "becoming" was understandably watered-down and diminished in its affective flavor. Sure, the current EPCOT traffics in some of the familiar futurist tropes, but it has lost a little bit of its romance (even if it still maintains its intensity). The new EPCOT, as a theme park, is a vehicle for consumption and, as such, the subjective agency it offers to its audience is no longer the becoming that comes through living in the future, but the actualization that comes through consumer practices and the enjoyment of entertainment. To return to the idea of managed innovation, the original plan for EPCOT and its eventual form might not be all that divergent, since both are attempts to provide a rational subjective context to the seeming disorder of radical innovation. From a consumer perspective, EPCOT might best be understood as an example of what John Hannigan has called the "riskless risk"—it is an orderly context in which a potentially estranging future can be consumed.[6]

Although formally and nominally EPCOT had already been built in the 1980s, Walt Disney's utopian rhetoric of 1966 got dusted off and used once again in the 1990s, this time to promote the creation of Celebration, Florida. Established in 1994, Celebration is a planned residential community just outside of Orlando, near the Walt Disney World resort and theme park. Tapping into the New Urbanism movement, which was officially named in 1990 and generated a professional organization (the Congress for the New Urbanism) in 1993, Celebration would make use of "neotraditional," pedestrian-friendly planning and would provide a nostalgic feel through "six traditional design styles," "small neighborhood parks," and "ample public spaces" (Fulton, 10, 25).[7] Focusing on the qualities that made pre–World War II middle-class neighborhoods colorful, interesting, and dynamic, New Urbanist cities like Celebration reflect an attempt to turn away from sprawling, automobile-centered suburbs, and the social and civic isolation that they produce.

However, Celebration goes beyond architectural styles and geographical layouts to satisfy its residents. According to the city's official website, Celebration is "a place where memories of a lifetime are made, it's more than a home; it's a community rich with old-fashioned appeal and an eye on the future" (http://www.celebrationfl.com). As the slick nostalgia of the promotional materials betray, Celebration is all Disney. Its wistful glance at small-town American life places it securely in the tradition of Disneyland's "Main Street, U.S.A." Its rigorously planned aesthetics and scrupulously scrubbed surfaces give it all the flair of Disney's feature animation.

And the fact that it houses actual residents while providing them with up-to-date technology suggests at least a nod to the more wide-eyed visions of Walt Disney himself. Celebration, as a result, is situated in the context of both Walt Disney's dream and the corporation's agenda, and represents a powerful manifestation of utopian thinking in the contemporary setting. Although radically different in appearance from both versions of EPCOT, Celebration is perhaps the most sophisticated and groundbreaking effort to advance the technology of innovation management that had been pioneered by its predecessors.

THREE ERAS OF DOMESTICITY

While the "home" is part of a larger tradition, stretching back for hundreds of years and representing a wide range of visions for the good life, these three utopian models—the EPCOT of the 1960s, the EPCOT theme park of the 1980s, and Celebration, Florida, of the 1990s—offer dramatic insights into the larger discussion of home automation. These models represent utility, comfort, entertainment, history, and technology, and an analysis of them serves as an apt point of departure for examining the smart home and futurist marketing strategies in general. Bound up in a dialectic which pits the future against the past, the narratives which have historically been used to sell smart homes are positioned in an uneasy rhetorical position. In general, advertising narratives tend to offer consumers access to things that are lacking, inviting people to improve their lives through commodities. The paradox of the smart home is that these improvements are to be both spectacular and comforting. They must embody a compelling new way of doing ordinary things; from washing clothes to doing the shopping, from mowing the lawn to watching TV, the key is to preserve the ordinary, but to modify it in an interesting way. As the Disney examples suggest, this idea has been subject to changes and negotiations as the moment of the smart home's technological realization approaches. The more radical notions of space-age technologies are replaced by traditional notions of living with technologies that, in the end, are rather mundane and ordinary. In order to make these innovations commonplace, they must seem commonplace. Because of this, a historical sampling of high-tech-housing arrangements reveals that the narratives used to sell them must constantly negotiate between being and becoming and, inevitably, force their inhabitants to occupy the uneasy space between the human and posthuman.

In the American context, the middle-class suburban home has set the standard and become a cliché for the conception of the "good life" in the twentieth century. As early as 1934, Lewis Mumford noted the developing relationship between the good life and consumer culture.[8] Although the home has been the subject of much debate for critics of bourgeois culture, an extended look at the middle-class American home reveals an interesting model of cultural development that can be broken down into three eras of domesticity, characterized by space, time, and information. These three qualities must be considered in succession, one on top of the other, with each always redefining the parameters of its predecessors. In my chronology, space exists first. Time is added to this element of space, reordering the fundamental principles of space as a union of space and time, or as an expression of motion (space as dynamic). To this new conception of space, information is added, which once again alters expressions of dynamic space, creating an expression of "narrative" space (a conception of space through time with meaning). Each successive element thus represents a "technical" reordering to a conception of place in relation to the good life; each development increases abundance and multiplies agency. Each successive refinement of domestic space brings us closer to the idea of "the Perfect Day"—a technologically enhanced vision of everyday life, freed from obstacles and oriented toward the pursuit of consumer satisfaction.

First of all, the abundance of so-called virgin land in the United States from the onset of this nation's birth informs my discussion of "home" in a number of interesting ways. In his 1893 essay, "The Significance of the Frontier in American History," Frederick Jackson Turner attributes the American character to an abundance of space. Although the importance of the closing of the frontier, as Turner inferred from U.S. census reports from 1890, on the formation of the American character has been hotly debated, a number of scholars have continued along this line of inquiry, investigating the power of the uncultivated space as a symbol in the formation of American culture.[9]

An idea of space that serves to purify, renew, and construct the American citizen figures strongly in our conception of the American good life. The suburban home, with its spacious front and back yards, clearly finds its place as a post–World War II expression of Manifest Destiny writ small on the humble aspirations of the middle class, in which the abundance of postwar prosperity was experienced alongside the desire to spread out, all of which was aided by the automobile. Significantly, the logic of Manifest Destiny finds its way into Walt Disney's October 1966 EPCOT promotional film, wherein Walt explains, "We think the need is to start from scratch on virgin land and building [*sic*] a special kind of new community" (*Walt's Last Film*). Disney defines the possibility opened up by an expansion into new space and couples it with his particular vision of utopia.

Closely linked to the American home's relationship to space is the issue of time. Technologies of movement, capture, and force as applied to space have supplemented American notions of abundance by facilitating easy movement over territory and by forcing the land to yield its fruits. These technologies add to the colonization of space as an element of time, in that they speed up movement and thus force more stable notions of space to yield value which was previously unimagined. Horses, railroads, automobiles, and the factory are but a few technologies which are implicated in the spatial practices of the American dream and which function to contain, subdue, and transform the Wild West and convert it into civilized and civilizing space.

Other examples might appropriately include those technologies which turn the process of expansion toward new frontiers, beyond those of an increasingly colonized world progressing toward the age of globalization. The drive for the maximization of internal spaces, epitomized by the temporal practices advocated in Frederick Winslow Taylor's *Principles of Scientific Management*, seeks an efficiency of existing spaces which cuts the time spent traversing distances in the motions of labor and thus opens up the spatial practice of work to increased fields of prosperity. As Taylor explains in his 1911 text, "Eliminate all false movements, slow movements, and useless movements. . . . After doing away with all unnecessary movements, collect into one series the quickest and best movements as well as the best implements" (61). Thus a control of space is crucially linked to a technique, or optimized use of that space in time, revealing the crude nature of earlier eras of geographic expansion and the crude qualities of the critique it inspires. Thus, the good life is characterized not simply by a vast space, but by a maximized space and regime of control which produces a yield. In the home the goal of maximizing space and control translates into what was once called "home economics," or the study of the home as workplace, and the achievement of maximized comfort through efficient laboring. In a word, ease.

A third parameter for the development of the smart home is information. Electronic media, used here to describe technological forms which are designed to deliver information (and are thus combined with content), deserve special consideration in the discussion of the home, as they add a third element to the interplay of space and technology described earlier.[10] The flow of electricity, the tuning in of codes, the politics of "off" and "on" are precursors to current debates about "new media," which differ chiefly in their relative level of interactivity. Of course, traditional mass-media forms like books, newspapers, and magazines require interaction through their respective interfaces, but the electronic operates at the level of perception. It is in the very desire to simulate experience through a direct appeal to the senses that these technologies work.[11] Other forms of electronic media, in spite of their supposed content, also function to stimulate the nervous system—making light out of darkness, reaching far beyond the curve of the horizon, filling the dead silence with sounds from the past, or livening up loneliness with electrified images of imaginary friends.

Electronic media, as information and entertainment, characterized by the movement of data across space and the generation of perception in the absence of an original phenomenon, provide the earlier matrix of the home with a richness and breadth that cannot be found in their absence. Taken as a process of transmitting data in one form or another across space, mediation exhibits the efficiency of technological transport and extraction, making the spaces we inhabit yield profit where value had been all but exhausted—the power of electronic media to occupy space and to overlay that space is a means of generating value in the absence of matter. To use the television as a metaphor, the forms that appear on screen are only ordered arrangements of light; without the transmission of the coded information, the screen is filled with static. One only has to look beyond the television to see this at work in other areas of the contemporary world—at the expansion of service-based industries that rely on their associations with the broadcasted world and the popularity of entertainment to see the profit-generating capacity of media in space. By creating meaning where none existed, or seeking to change existing meanings for the maximization of profit, electronic media plays a third and crucial role in the management of the home as an efficient living space.

Of particular interest to this discussion of the Perfect Day is Paul Virilio's concept of "dromology," or the study of speed. Identifying the crisis of dromospheric pollution, or the environmental damage caused by increased speed, Virilio focuses on information technology, whose rate of transfer increasingly approaches that of light speed and radiation. Looking at everything from war to terrorism to electronic commerce to surveillance to accidents, Virilio discusses the role that speed and acceleration plays in an increased "dematerialization," "depersonalization," and "derealization" of everyday life. Because of telepresence and real-time technologies which enable everything to happen worldwide at once, "*the time allotted to decision-making is now insufficient*" and tasks become increasingly automated (*A Landscape of Events*, 92, emphasis in the original).

While Virilio's panic over the future of life in an increasingly wired and mediated world is certainly a worthy site of debate, I would encourage readers to reserve a critical assessment of the issue's urgency for now and instead focus on the more practical elements of Virilio's critique. The five chief aspects of this critique are (1) information moves more quickly than it did before; (2) it covers more distance; (3) as a result of this rapid movement over greater distances, subjects are allotted less time to make thoughtful decisions; (4) to help negotiate the problem of less time, cybernetic systems often supplement the decision-making process; and (5) because time-saving methods often create increased time-pressures, subjects, aided by technology, respond more quickly, further accelerating a world that is already speeding along at velocities in excess of any human scale.

In relation to the home, this process of speeding up through media and communications brings the world into the home and the home to the world. As a result, there is an expansion of the home to include the informational representation of the world and a simultaneous contraction of the home's space through an ability to micromanage the space-time efficiency of the home. The pinnacle of this complex of space, time, and information is realized in the smart home, and it is the purpose of this project to discuss how the idea of the smart home has functioned in different contexts to sell visions of the good life that are anchored in the maximization of these three elements. The result is a flattening out of temporality.

As all available options are becoming increasingly accessible in any given moment, and as new possibilities are increasingly added to this pool, functioning in time has less to do with waiting for events to unfold chronologically than it has to do with choices about which "time" to occupy.[12] As is the case at Disneyland, historical time and geographical space are converted to navigable regions as entertainment choices. The concept of multiple temporalities is crucial to the understanding of contemporary media and should underscore the urgency that is often implied when discussing a coming paradigm shift. Rather than moving toward a cataclysmic end, the smart home's reorganization of living space should be understood as a spreading out of variables across an eternal present. The unfolding of the future as a linear process is replaced by a proliferation of choices about the present.[13]

In order to function effectively, and to avoid the distance between the technological object and its integration into the everyday that is necessitated by the futurist narrative, a special narrative has to be developed. To introduce new technologies and secure their use as everyday items, an ideal technology narrative must situate the object somewhere between "ordinary" and "desirable"—technology must become necessary or "handy" while at the same time represent an improvement of the ordinary. Also favorable to the meaning and use of the object is its capacity to belong to a system that includes other objects. Rather than appeal to extraordinary desires (like soaring through space with rocket packs or eating delicious twelve-course meals in pill form), the narrative of technological advancement must move away from futurism. And although little has been written on this phenomenon beyond the familiar postmodern discussions, which read it as the end of the "new" or an "end of history," this vastly undertheorized narrative exists.[14] It can be seen in the "moderate" promotional strategies of current smart home innovators—I call it the Perfect Day.

A technologically enhanced mode of daily living, the Perfect Day streamlines the exchange between commodity and consumer, cultivating the terrain between impulse and gratification. This is accomplished by trimming undesirable or irrelevant options and offering up customized solutions and experiences. In effect, the Perfect Day is life edited in real time, in conformity with consumer narratives.

An ancestor of the Perfect Day is the negotiation between being and becoming dramatically acted out in Greenfield Village, Henry Ford's prototype of postmodern history. Using his fortune to purchase historic sites of invention (like Thomas Edison's Menlo Park laboratory and the Wright brothers' bicycle shop, for example), Ford constructed an entire village of historic buildings just outside of Detroit, Michigan. A tribute to American inventors and industrialists, Greenfield Village was called by Ford himself "a synthesis of the home-spun and the high-tech" (quoted in Votolato, 75). The village presents itself like a strange combination of Disney's "Main Street, U.S.A" and Knott's Berry Farm's "Ghost Town," an eclectic mix of buildings that conjure up images of an America steeped in nostalgia, even as the nostalgia it conjures up is that of invention and industrial progress. Greenfield Village uses the past to create a history as movement into the future, making it a profound attempt to reconcile the tension between being and becoming by establishing the process of becoming into the notion of historic nationalism—American technological exceptionalism yoked to Manifest Destiny.[15]

This negotiated introduction of gadgets into the space of the traditional home is also an understood aspect of the history of design, as evidenced in the following passage: "The domestic kitchen became one of the greatest arenas of this contest. With high-tech, Sub-Zero refrigerators and glossy

Kitchen Aid dishwashers standing proudly between Colonial or Shaker cabinetry, American kitchens reconciled the personal need for emotional comfort with the high technological expectations of the modern family" (Votolato, 4). Like Henry Ford's "historic" village, Disneyland's "Main Street," the Bonaventure Hotel, a taxicab in Tegucigalpa, or glitzy Las Vegas itself, the space of the home during a period of technical transition during the age of mass media is full of paradox or, dare I say, postmodern stylistic elements.

But these metaphors fail inasmuch as they require one to travel and are vulnerable to imposition by others. The Perfect Day, on the other hand, is about being at home. It is about experiencing the chaotic thrills of the postmodern without interruption, without regret, and without consequence. As a fantasy of total consumer indulgence, the Perfect Day is a utopia of personal desire triumphant over liberal fantasies of ethics and justice. It is the experience of perfect freedom through the belief in a perfect lie.

Because I seek to weave a narrative out of traditionally discrete artifacts (scientific management, appliances, consumer culture, robots, personal computers, etc.), and then to comment on the theoretical ramifications of this social history, I have divided this book into rough chronologies tied together by concepts that sometimes reach for the future or yearn for the past to form coherent narratives about the present. As I develop my thesis, I often "unveil" information in an episodic manner, with the intention of producing a cumulative effect or understanding, rather than presenting my argument in a more traditional, linear fashion. Questions raised but left unanswered in one chapter will be answered as the discussion is picked up again in later chapters. But because this area of study is a largely unexplored one, it is inevitable that there are many questions I cannot ask, and even more that I cannot provide adequate answers for. To return to an American metaphor, I am working toward a frontier, and so lack the perspective of the native for whom the frontier is more appropriately called "home."

Using historical texts and sociological studies, as well as primary sources on home economics and management, I chart in the first chapter shifting conceptions of the home and the introduction of electric appliances against American industrial developments during the early twentieth century. In reference to the threefold model of expansion I have offered in the introduction, I show how that era unified the space of the home with scientific time-management techniques, reproducing time-efficient labor practices in the domestic setting.

Focusing on post–World War II America and the emergence of the digital computer, I provide in the second chapter a history of electronic household appliances. Using historical accounts and archives, as well as advertisements and popular media, I chart the path from televisions to personal computers and beyond. The "house of tomorrow" presented a model of "futuristic" living aided by new technologies, but imagined in accordance with the spectacular lifestyles of the space age and televisual popular culture.

The most recent incarnation of the automated house—the smart home—as I discuss in the third chapter, eschews futuristic motifs and instead relies on a combination of the traditional and the high tech. Using magazines and newspapers, science fiction, film, how-to guides, websites, and other sources, I provide a detailed discussion of the contemporary smart house. Navigating through shifting conceptions of the automated house (the space-age home, the haunted house, and the reality-show set), I conclude the third chapter with the exceptionally mundane (or mundanely exceptional) vision of living promised by the smart house.

The concluding chapter of this book is a discussion of the Perfect Day—a technologically enhanced style of daily living. Considering interactivity as a refinement of disciplinary form, even as it liberates subjects from the constraints of more static media, the Perfect Day is an attempt to institutionalize everyday life as the ultimate consumer practice. In attempting to remove undesired impediments to the realization of the self in the consumer world, the Perfect Day offers a posthuman solution by which traditional ethical considerations can be avoided and pleasure can be pursued.

1

"Home Is Where the Heart Is"

Scientific Management, Electricity, and the Early-Twentieth-Century American Home

I cannot begin this chapter without a trite and clichéd declaration of the special place that "home" plays in the culture at large. No words can convey all the complex meanings of "home." The mere attempt to encapsulate this meaning immediately falls short, making discussions of home sound naïve and hokey, as though those who attempt to speak of home don't really know anything about it, or at least not about *my* home. The truth is that home is everywhere, and its invocation is supposed to bespeak goodness because it represents that with which we are familiar and that of which we are made. It is at once a destination and an origin. It is, to fall back on the cliché, precisely where the heart is, when heart is used to refer to those things which are most dear to us. In short, "There is no place like home."

THE EVOLUTION OF THE HOME AS A SPACE

Used to describe an idea about that which has comfort and meaning for subjects to inhabit, and which can in turn inhabit those same subjects, the definition of home is essentially vague, mobile, and multiple. For example, those in exile, who have no home, have none precisely because they carry a sense of home which resides within their person. An exile must "live" somewhere, but this somewhere is somehow far from the home where the exile can find "peace," "completeness," "wholeness," or whatever immaterial force is needed to bridge the rift between the idea of home and the physical state. Given its slippery and uncertain nature, it is unclear whether home is a memory or a promise, or both. Most likely, home is something which swings back and forth between yesterday and tomorrow, experienced as a way of being with no fixed meaning.

It is this idea of home as dialectic that informs more pedestrian notions of the home as physical place. Home, in the material sense, for the American middle class is typically imagined as the single-family, suburban house, but has increasingly come to include apartments, condominiums, townhouses, trailers, and any housing option that affords a somewhat autonomous living space organized around the head of the household or the family unit. In reality, there is a great diversity of living arrangements in the United States which include multiple families and extended families living within a single unit, and families or individuals who live in structures that are not typically considered "housing units" (under bridges, inside cars, on top of park benches, in public shelters, etc.). But the fact remains that these arrangements do not exist within the American ideal, often falling outside of the law and treated by the public as "social problems." The ideal contemporary household is linked to economic concerns, arranged around consumer practices, and offers its inhabitants special, class-based protections and privileges that are not awarded to those who fall outside this norm. One only has to apply for a job or seek public assistance without the benefit of a mailing address to see an example of just how these privileges operate.

As a stylized form of dwelling, the contemporary notion of home taps into the baggage of its culturally loaded origins, being sold as a promise, steeped in memories, and clad in all of the trappings that will speak to both concerns. The home is difficult to think of in the category of a consumer good: homes are not cheap or disposable. Homes are often handcrafted and of course have been built well before the advance of consumer culture as we now know it. Homes are associated with a certain amount of permanence, personality, and meaning. The meanings that are associated with the home are highly subjective and personal. A home is something that is thought of as "made" by a "homemaker," a product of its inhabitants, even if it is envisioned as a home during the process of buying or renting its space. Although it may contain consumer goods and serve as the optimum arena for consumer practice, the interactive nature of the home and the resultant personal investment it requires of its inhabitants affords the home a sort of metaconsumerist status. The home is the place where goods are consumed, but rarely, if at all, do we consider the idea of home as a consumer good, and the goods contained therein as the metastructure for the consumption of home. As a result, the contemporary home is indeed much closer to us than many would like to think, and its criticism a decidedly incomplete project.

Since the evolution of the home is one that has emerged through dialectical progress, I frame this discussion as a dialog with the work of the architect, critic, and designer Witold Rybczynski, whose book *Home* presents a richly detailed history of the home in the Western context. Sensitive to an elaborate complex of social, economic, and technological practices that have generated the home that we know today, Rybczynski's plain-spoken, but deeply insightful history offers fertile theoretical ground to explore. When considered in the context of the three technical parameters offered in the introduction (space, time, and information), Rybczynski's framework takes an interesting shape.

The place that comes to mind when we speak of the middle-class home today is, as the diversity of architectural styles reveals, one that has emerged from a long and multiple process of historical change and adaptation. The origins of the contemporary home can be traced back to the emerging middle class of renaissance Europe. In *Home* Rybczynski traces the evolution of the medieval house, which consisted of a large open room with a hearth that doubled as place of business and sleeping quarters, to the home of the Dutch bourgeoisie in the 1600s, which was characterized by privacy, multiple rooms, and a specifically domestic function. In fact, as Rybczynski notes, "The Dutch loved their homes. They shared this old Anglo-Saxon word—*ham, hejm* in Dutch—with other peoples of Northern Europe. 'Home' brought together the meanings of house and household, of dwelling and of refuge, of ownership and of affection. 'Home' meant the house, but also everything that was in it and around it, as well as the people, and the sense of satisfaction and contentment that all these conveyed" (61–62). To this, Rybczynski adds in a footnote, "This wonderful word, 'home,' which connotes a physical 'place' but also has the more abstract sense of a 'state of being,' has no equivalent in the Latin or Slavic European languages" (62). It is this general area of origin, in the Dutch middle class with its rapidly growing trade-based economy and new independence from the authority of the Spanish Crown, that saw the widescale cultivation of the household, the development of domesticity, and the birth of the home. The diffusion of economic power to the growing middle class made home ownership possible and allowed for the home to serve as a sanctuary and showplace for success and refinement, similar to the palaces and castles of the past, but moderated and made humble by its extension to those who had been denied access to economic power under previous regimes.[1] With the rise of the middle class, various forms of power and governance were then diffused, democratized, and liberalized, giving greater numbers a personal stake in the cultivation of living space.

Beyond privacy and domesticity, Rybczynski marks the passage of another element into the stream of concepts that characterize the home: the element of comfort. Looking at the evolution of furnishings, there is a remarkable difference between the austere surfaces of the medieval chair and the plush elegance of the La-Z-Boy. Rybczynski notes that the origins of the chair were ceremonial, serving as markers of rank, privilege, and esteem for formal events, and were thus unconcerned with secondary features such as comfort (81). However, once the chair gained its place in the household as a marker of status and "sitting-up" became the custom and standard of behavior through the extension of the changing household to the growing bourgeoisie, there was a shift in chair design that coincided with sitting norms and resulted in an increase in "comfort." As Rybczynski explains, "Historians of furniture inevitably draw our attention to the changes in chair design and construction and allow us to forget a more important ingredient: the changes that took place in the sitter. For the main constraint on furniture design was not only technical—but also cultural, how it was used. The easy chair had to be preceded by the desire for an easy posture" (81). Rybczynski notes the death of France's Louis XIV in 1715 and his replacement by Louis XV as a key moment in the evolution of comfort. For Louis XV's court, Rybczynski argues, bourgeois notions of privacy and intimacy, embodied in the small and individualized spaces of the middle-class home, became fashionable, offering greater satisfaction and pleasure than the rigid formality found in the ceremonial trappings of courtly life. Traditional seating arrangements were maintained for their official function, but for those people who had grown accustomed to the habit of sitting in chairs and were also rapidly assimilating the idea of a "private life," a new type of seating was added. This "new category of additional seating . . . was not constrained by rigid aesthetic needs and . . . could respond to their desire for a more relaxed sitting posture" (84). Through the reverberations of cultural notions of domestic space, comfort entered the household as a dialectical interplay of bourgeois and courtly practices of living (and loving) in space.

Notions of comfort in domestic space quickly spread to include leisure and efficiency. Once comfort in seating situated the ideal of home in its accommodation of the body through surfaces that were not uncomfortable, these ideas quickly transferred into the positive generation of comfort through the sensual practices of leisure and the further avoidance of discomfort by the organization of space itself. The first concern, comfort as a phenomenon of direct sensation, locates the function of the ideal home on the body or place. Spatially speaking, comfort is an embodied experience, characterized by the harmonious relationship between one surface and another.

Due to a steady decline in the number of domestic servants and an increase in wages in the United States during the latter two-thirds of the nineteenth century, the issue of efficiency in household labor became increasingly urgent, as more and more middle-class women found themselves taking on the burdens of household labor. In 1841 this labor shortage inspired Catharine E. Beecher, the sister of Harriet Beecher Stowe, to write *A Treatise on Domestic Economy for the Use of Young Ladies at Home and at School*, an early discussion of home economics which (even) included a chapter on efficient kitchen design. Housekeeping was now considered a part of the overall comfort of the middle-class home.

As comfort came to coincide with the efficient organization of household labor, there appeared a shift in the phenomenon that forced it to consider the element of time. The efficient home became one in which comfort was generated by technologies which optimized the relationship between domestic space and domestic time, in an effort to create a comfortable schedule. In a practical sense, this comfort was embodied in that it sought to reduce the physical fatigue and strain associated with household labor. But it was also a disembodied comfort in that it shifted comfort from a solely sensuous practice to a cognitive one, making comfort temporal and linking it to memory and anticipation as well. Part of the satisfaction of living in an efficient household became the pleasure that comes from the comparative knowledge that one could have been, or had been, doing more work.

New plateaus in efficiency were achieved through two means. The first was a rearrangement of space. As Rybczynski notes, Beecher's conception of the home was especially unique because it altered the "European image of the home as a male preserve": "The masculine idea of the home was primarily sedentary—the home as a retreat from the cares of the world, a place to be at ease. The feminine idea of the home was dynamic; it had to do with ease, but also with work. It could be said to have shifted the focus from the drawing room to the kitchen, which was why, when electricity entered the home, it was by the kitchen door" (160–61). This crucial conception of the home from a mere place to a set of dynamic relationships coincides with the rise of industry in the United States and marks the beginning of the home as a technical environment.

The most drastic reorganization of the home was accomplished under the direct influence of Frederick Winslow Taylor's scientific management. Scientific management made its way into the kitchen courtesy of Christine Frederick, the wife of the market researcher George Frederick who, on seeing its effectiveness in the industrial workplace, immediately imagined its usefulness in the home. As Rybczynski explains, "Much of what she saw struck her as applicable to the home. The proper height of work surfaces to eliminate stooping, the location of tools and machines to reduce fatigue, the organization of work according to a definite plan were recognizably domestic problems. She began to study her own work habits and those of her friends. She timed herself, she made notes, she photographed women at work. As a result, she remodeled her kitchen and found that she could do her housework more quickly and with less effort" (168). Christine Frederick's ambitious and insightful project of reorganizing domestic workspace was truly a revolutionary accomplishment, for which she achieved notoriety through a number of articles and books written on the subject.

Not only did Frederick's text testify to the value of so-called women's work and place the effort, power, and skill required by this work on more equal footing with so-called men's work, but in some sense it took these claims a step further. In the foreword to Frederick's *Household Engineering: Scientific Management in the Home*, which was originally published in 1915, Harrington Emerson explains the complexity of the household environment: "There are six distinct classes of activities: production, transportation, manufacture, storage, exchange, and personal service. The boy is prepared for 15 years or more to co-operate with others in mastering *one* particular part of *one* of these activities. A man will give his life to the specialization and standardization of the methods and tools for a single oft repeated operation. Housekeeping, if a kitchen garden or milking is included, covers all six activities. Often without preparation a young woman working alone, without the discipline of the group, expects to be an adept in *all six* fields and in *all parts* of each field *at once*!" (1, emphasis in original). Although Emerson doesn't mention that many women were also expected by society at large to perform these roles perfectly, he does draw important attention to the complexity of domestic labor, commenting on the multiple roles that the space of the home was expected to play. Unsurprisingly, one of the first items that Frederick wished to tackle was a definition of the space of the kitchen. Frederick comments, "What is a kitchen? It is a place for the *preparation of food*" (19). In seeking to control the work that takes place inside its walls, Frederick is forced to define the space in purely technical terms. Unlike hearth-centered homes of the past, the new home was to be rationally organized and functionality was to reign supreme. Frederick even goes so far as to question previous ideas of neatness and aesthetics, recommending that the "workshop ideal" be the paradigm for neatness (34). This early and clear-cut example of the widely felt influence of scientific management on all levels of social and cultural organization was only a precursor to the modern style.

A 1949 U.S. Department of Agriculture film entitled *Step-Saving Kitchen* illustrates rather dryly the ways that science can be used to improve efficiency in the home. The film features a middle-aged couple in conference with an efficiency expert who explains, "The plans were developed for people just like you, people who are interested in having the very latest ideas and designs that would help them cut down on the time and the effort that must be spent in doing kitchen work." The do-it-yourself plans explain the efficiency of a U-shaped floor plan, the most practical dimensions for counters and cabinets, and proper placement for appliances. The film represents an earnest attempt to make domestic labor easier, safer, and more hygienic for women.

Later commercial films seem to capitalize on these themes of ease, safety, and hygiene, contributing to the evolution of a persuasive selling point for consumer goods that remains to this day. Edison Electric's 1952 film *Young Man's Fancy* uses the format of a romantic teenage melodrama to showcase the power of electric appliances. In the film a teenage Judy seeks the attention of the "woman hating" engineering student and time-study geek, Alex, whom her brother has brought home from college. The lighthearted drama provides ample pretext for the enthusiastic admiration of household appliances. Mother recollects, "Remember what it was like, Judy, before we got the freezer?" (fig. 2). Alex gleefully observes, "The kitchen today is like a factory in many ways." And when Judy finally dazzles Alex with a meal prepared in the family's modern kitchen, she self-deprecatingly admits, "I can't take all the credit—our kitchen does everything but talk." In the film Alex and Judy are brought together through what can only be interpreted as a complementary union of gender stereotypes. The modern kitchen/factory, no doubt constructed by brainy geeks like Alex, only magnifies the marginal domestic talents of a young woman like Judy, and the couple's potential is consummated in a delicious meal and the hope of future happiness together.

2. Judy dramatically ponders life before the freezer (*A Young Man's Fancy*).

U.S. Steel's 1957 *Practical Dreamer* revisits the rational organization of the U-shaped kitchen to promote remodeling (fig. 3). In the film a sleeping Edie dreams that she is redesigning her kitchen under the guidance of a slightly condescending narrator. The Godlike voice explains, "Now, what is a kitchen anyway? Simply the logical arrangement of three main appliances: refrigerator, sink, range, with counters in between and storage cabinets above and below. This is the basis of every good kitchen. Of course, how you vary your refrigerator center or your sink center or your range center depends only on your own needs and preferences and the size and shape of your planning space. And today there's so much to choose from." While the film explains the ease that can be achieved through good planning, the emphasis is on the wide range of modular components. Though it lacks the human drama of *Young Man's Fancy*, it highlights rather nicely the notion that domestic labor can be made easier through the application of sound engineering principles. As it is meant to promote U.S. Steel rather than Edison Electric, the film spends more time on the structural aspects of the kitchen. And, unlike the noncommercial aims of the U.S. Department of Agriculture, its message is not a do-it-yourself one. The focus is on the ease with which such a dream kitchen can be assembled from prefabricated parts.

Alongside the pragmatic elements of scientific management, the social aspects of the home and homemaking took on further technical aspects, priming the home for the introduction of industrial appliances

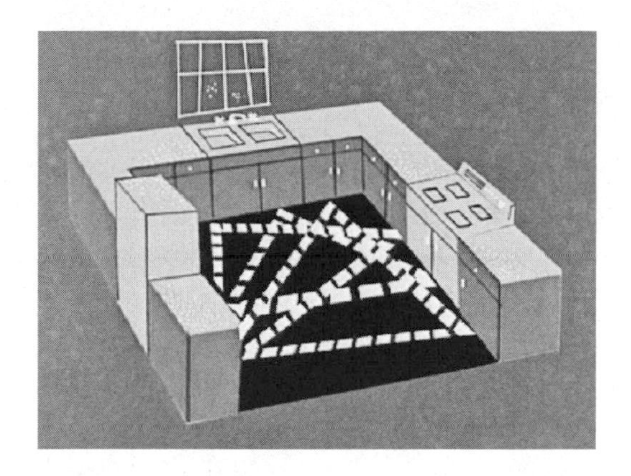

3. The U-shaped kitchen (*Practical Dreamer*).

and a conception of the home that would lead Le Corbusier to declare in 1923, "The house is a machine for living in" (107). Modernist aesthetics, epitomized by Le Corbusier and diffused throughout all discussions of "style" in design throughout the twentieth century, promoted the idea that heightened aesthetic principles could lead to greater efficiency in those aspects of the human not contained by the category of labor or physical comfort—surpassing the more utilitarian notions of efficiency that Frederick sought. The idea that purity of form and minimalist design could streamline aesthetic experience by providing pure encounters with art also entered the home. In his summary account of Le Corbusier's position Rybczynski writes, "According to him, human needs were universal and could be uniformalized, and consequently his solutions were prototypical, not personal. He visualized the home as a mass-produced object (a typewriter), to which the individual should adapt. The job of the designer was to find the 'correct' solution; once it was found, it was up to people to accustom themselves to it" (191). This stereotypically modernist position, while certainly debatable in terms of the extent to which it was adopted, is reflected in at least some subtle and minimalist design principles, even if concessions to human comfort are made. However, the fact that this position gained currency at least on a limited level marks the ways through which the aesthetic elements of domestic space were also increasingly turned toward a process of efficiency.

A DISCUSSION OF HOUSEHOLD APPLIANCES

While physical structures have long played a prominent role in the development of the household, the debut of electricity and the rapid proliferation of electric appliances marked the emergence of the *modern* household. Finding its way into the home shortly after Beecher's introduction of household management to the American scene, electricity conveniently fulfilled the need for less strenuous ways to work and significantly sped up the pace of domestic life in the process. The entry of electricity into the home was thus an answer to a prayer on a practical level and, on a cultural level, a heresy in its ability to undermine domesticity itself. In reducing the amount of toil needed in order to make the household function, the use of electric appliances reaffirmed the sanctity of the domestic space by supplementing the everyday practices of challenging handiwork, much in the same way that writing served to supplement the memory tactics required of the teller of folk tales or singer of ballads. But by inserting into the milieu of the household a form of energy that was qualitatively different than that of "domestic handiwork"—that of the electrical machine—the fundamental relationship between homemaker and handiwork was replaced by a relationship between machine and operator, or technology and technician—a domestic de-skilling. In the present day, this sort of de-skilling can be seen in the example of popcorn, once made in a pot with oil, then with the aid of stovetop corn-popping pans, later with popcorn-making electric appliances, then on the stovetop in the form of pre-packaged Jiffy Pop, then in microwaveable popcorn bags, and finally, as microwaveable popcorn packaged in a disposable paper bowl. Most Americans know how to make popcorn, but what this "know-how" means can encompass a wide range of popcorn-making competencies, and in many cases knowing how to make popcorn refers to the most familiar technical ability: putting a bag or bowl into a microwave, then pressing the popcorn button.[2] By this point, "knowing how to make popcorn" is less reliant on the experience of making popcorn than it is on the simple skill of pressing the appropriate button on the microwave. This is not to say that homemaking skills do not represent certain techniques, practices, implements, and methods; rather, it is to say that the industrialization of the home marks a migration of an exterior technical mode into the domestic sphere. The act of making popcorn, in reducing the number of steps involved by substituting them with a technologically prepared "raw" material and more sophisticated machinery, mirrors the movement from craftwork to industrial work that has been implemented across the board and that has resulted in an increasingly de-skilled labor force. The situation that this represents is not a simple change of materials and methods, but the adoption of an entire set of relationships to labor, knowledge, production, and ethical concerns which are epitomized in what a number of scholars—including Lewis Mumford, Jacques Ellul, and Bernard Stiegler—have called a "technical society."[3]

On a microscopic scale, the know-how embodied in a technical innovation can be understood as a form of instrumental memory. Whether we speak of a particular technology or a particular technique, the memory of accomplishing the task at hand is removed from the mind of the agent (or, rather, it was never there in the first place) and situated in the formulaic application of the technic to the situation at hand. Take travel, for example: following directions is qualitatively different than finding one's way. Following directions requires the ability to read road names and an awareness of certain conventions (right, left, north, south, east, west, numbers, distances). Finding one's way, on the other hand, does not necessarily require these skills and instead can draw on things like experience, an awareness of landmarks, a sense of relativity, memories of previous travels, conversations, and a wide field of imprecise information that can be organized by the operation of the mind. When given bad directions or incomplete directions, we engage in the problem-solving process of "finding our way." The key difference between the two methods of travel is that the technical method (following directions) is meant to require a minimum of attention and engagement, while finding our way requires thought, interaction, and memory. In finding our way, we experience the value of knowledge and develop a store of adaptable knowledge based in experience. In other words, we learn. And although the difference between storing know-how in an object or set of instructions and having know-how stashed in our brains is not always clear cut, memory can be found in any of the techniques or technologies we apply to solve problems. A song contains ideas and experiences made memorable by conventions of rhythm, rhyme, and pattern. A CD contains songs made memorable by digital marks that can be read by a machine. All of the tools we use are thus "programmed" with the memories of human beings—they are inscribed with a purpose, and they are oriented toward action.

The knowledge embodied in technology is powerfully illustrated in a film that debuted in 1940 at the New York World's Fair, *Leave It to Roll-Oh*. The film begins as a speculative tale about a domestic robot, called Roll-Oh. With an impressive list of skills under his belt, the sluggish but charming iron brute promises a life of ease for inept housewives everywhere (fig. 4). The narrator reveals, "Yes, Roll-Oh the Robot, the chromium-plated butler, is just a daydream after all. But not so Roll-Oh's little brother and sister robots; the millions of small mechanical servants that never ask for afternoons off; the amazing machines and gadgets that almost seem to think for themselves." The film makes use of the robot metaphor to describe a vast array of "robots" hidden throughout our homes.

> The tiny clockwork brains and heat regulators on our kitchen stoves apparently do almost everything except read the cookbook. Thinking machines like this keep golden brown slices of toast from turning into slabs of charcoal and keep the coffee hot until we're ready to start dunking. Then there's a teakettle that's been trained never to boil dry. When the water is gone, the kettle simply pulls out its own attachment plug. And here's a gadget that ought to rate a bow from every dog in the country, a fido feeder that never forgets when the pup is dining home alone and the rest of the family is dining out [fig. 5]. What's more, it tells him when to come and get it.

Along with superimposed images of robots working, the narrator continues to explain how they operate in our cars, factories, and offices, keeping us safe and freeing our bodies and minds for a life of leisure. In fact, it seems that the film's implicit message is that we are inferior to a system of machines that "never forgets," "never sleeps nor winks," and has never "been accused of being absent-minded or careless at work." Not unlike the fast-food assembly-line meals manufactured from precooked processed parts under the guidance of timers, training manuals, and strict man-

4. Roll-Oh's control panel (*Leave It to Roll-Oh*).

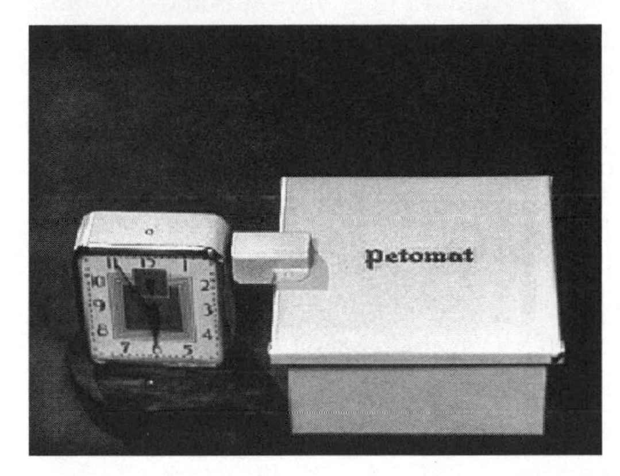

5. Fido Feeder (*Leave It to Roll-Oh*).

agers, the technical system can promise efficiency and consistency, unless some person who has trouble following instructions screws it up.

The technical society is characterized by an overall orientation of the social, not only toward the limited goal of achieving specific technological advances but also toward a generalized effort to optimize technological advancement as a principle—a spirit of automation. Lewis Mumford's *Technics and Civilization* (originally published in 1932) describes this "religious" phenomenon: "Only as a religion can one explain the compulsive nature of the urge toward mechanical development without regard for the actual outcome of the development in human relations themselves: even in departments where the results of mechanization were plainly disastrous, the most reasonable apologists nevertheless held that 'the machine was here to stay'—by which they meant, not that history was irreversible, but that the machine was unmodifiable" (365). Mumford goes on to explain that this reverence for the "machine" is waning, finding new hope for civilization in the developing trend of "subtlety" and "the organic" in design (368). Unfortunately, this optimistic prediction of a harmonious integration of technology into the everyday is a bit hasty in that it forgets the very "human" scale of Frederick Taylor's scientific management and fails to predict the impact of social technologies like automobiles and cell phones.[4] Mumford closes his text, "Nothing is impossible," invoking the very mantra of the technical society and framing the solution to the problems of technocentrism in terms of a technically derived ethics.

Jacques Ellul's more dire assessment of the problem of technology in *The Technological Society* (which was published in French in 1954, a full twenty-two years after the publication of Mumford's groundbreaking work) takes into account this encroachment of the technical into the organic. Ellul writes, "Without exception in the course of history, *technique belonged to a civilization* and was merely a single element among a host of nontechnical activities. Today *technique has taken over the whole of civilization*. Certainly, technique is no longer the simple machine substitute for human labor. It has come to be the 'intervention into the very substance not only of the inorganic but also the organic'" (128, emphasis in the original). Ellul's definition of technique—organized around a process of producing technology that does not exist in "opposition" to the human, but rather to produce a new kind of human (or posthuman)—can be summed up in a simple statement: "[Technique] has a single role: to strip off externals, to bring everything to light, and by rational use to transform everything into means" (142), including human beings. In other words, technics has at its root an assimilating process—the same notion that Mumford holds up in his conclusion.

At this point, I do not wish to debate technical determinism. Instead of claiming that there is no way out of this system, I would like to focus on the descriptive features that have inspired both Ellul and Mumford to remark on the increasingly technical nature of society and point to the social manifestations of this "technical" system. Notable features of the technical society are the faith that all problems can be solved through technology, a reluctance to permit "moral" or "ethical" concerns to govern the exploration of new technologies, a professed belief in the neutrality of science and technology, an expectation that people adapt to new technologies, and a hasty implementation of new technologies to offset research costs. Some possible negative effects of these features are a failure to look for solutions that are readily available, a diminished role for democratic processes in collective problem solving in favor of the assumed goal of technical advancement, a decrease in the value of skilled labor and experience, an inability to rein in the development of technologies that have effects which are predictably harmful (in particular the military application of technology), unpredicted consequences of insufficiently researched technologies (also known as "accidents"), and a tendency to see human beings as one of the many (and often the cheapest) means to an economic end.

More generally, the technical society is implicated in a process of spatial control and organization, with the goal of harvesting maximum efficiency out of materials which have yet to be imagined. The process of evolving space (space plus time) is contained in the addition of appliances to the space of the home and the emerging science of household management.

Determining a specific date for the entry of the first electric appliance into the American home is a difficult task. Barbara J. Howe et al., in their collaboratively produced *Houses and Homes*, explain, "Electricity remained a scientific curiosity with no practical application until the invention and perfection of the incandescent electric lamp and the electric motor. Until electrical power generation and distribution systems were built, neither the motor nor the lamp was capable of more than isolated application. America's first electric power plant was built in 1882 by the Edison Electric company in New York, and the Columbian Exposition of 1893 in Chicago served as a powerful promoter of electricity to Americans" (132). The first incandescent bulb was patented in 1878 and the first electric motor in 1834; who was responsible for these discoveries and the somewhat arbitrary dates assigned to their invention are debatable. Furthermore, the dates when these devices gained practical value are also highly debatable. Although some might cite the exposition in Chicago as the most important event, as Howe et al. note, it was only after World War I that the use of electricity became widespread in cities and towns, and not until the early 1930s that its use spread to rural areas (132). As a result, the "rapid" growth in the use of the electric appliance for the home occurred in the 1920s and 1930s (Howe et al., 138–39).

The date I use to mark the rise of the appliance is therefore somewhat general, focusing on a twenty-year span, from 1900 through 1920, which coincides quite nicely with the rise of scientific management in the household. Although among the many electric novelties at the 1893 exposition was an "all-electric kitchen," it was not until "1903 [that] Earl Richardson, plant superintendent for an electric power company in Ontario, California, developed an electric iron with a 'hot point'" (Plante, 214). Over a period of a few years, Richardson's iron was perfected, tested by housewives, and promoted to businesses first and consumers later. Once the power companies realized that electric appliances offered a substantial growth market, turning residential electricity consumption from a nocturnal activity to a twenty-four-hour affair, the drive to fill the home with electrical machines of all sorts was on. And consumers, it seemed, were anxious to have them. As Ellen M. Plante notes, in 1908 "the first electric coffee percolator was introduced," "by 1910 electric irons being produced by General Electric and others were advertised in national magazines," and "in 1920 the 'Hotpoint Servants' were being nationally advertised by the Edison Electric Appliance Co., Inc. and their 'Breakfast Set' was a best seller" (214).

The many electrical appliances created to fill the home are surprising in both their number and their specificity of function. For example, electric popcorn poppers first appeared in 1907, General Electric and Westinghouse toasters in 1909, an electric egg cooker in 1916, and waffle irons and an electric mixer in 1918, in addition to numerous electric irons, coffeepots, and casserole dishes throughout these years (Celehar, 18–19). During this same period, Christine Frederick noted, "electricity, 'the silent servant' is being adapted not only to the small portable cooking devices such [as the] percolator, toaster, grill, hot plates, etc., but to the larger fixed equipment of stoves and ranges" (122). Jane H. Celehar, in her historical reference book *Kitchens and Kitchenware*, provides a lineage of the stove:

"The manufacture of electric ranges on a commercial scale began in 1910 with the Hughes Electric Range, developed by George A. Hughes, founder of the Hughes Electric Heating Company" (22). And in 1916 Kelvinator introduced the first electric refrigerator, followed closely by Frigidaire in 1917 (Celehar, 23).

More fascinating than the individual appliances were the system-wide attempts at integration. As early as 1915, Frederick described the "Permanent Vacuum System" in which, "pipes are laid in the walls, having openings near the baseboard of each room, and connected with motors in the basement" (162). With the vacuum system, the house was "wired" to include this sanitizing technology in all rooms, making cleaning easier. But this system also had the secondary, and subtle, effect of making every room into a sort of appliance or cleaning chamber by turning the structure of the house itself into the body of a vacuum cleaner. Another universalized motor was "the general utility motor with its many attachments such as coffee grinder, parer, silver buffer, mixer, etc." (Frederick, 393). While the general motor was created to cut costs by using a single motor to perform many tasks, its universal application to all labor tasks served to reaffirm the technical aspects of domestic labor, electrifying as many elements as possible in pursuit of greater value through usability. And although this claim of automation may seem to leap ahead into the house of the future, Christine Frederick's detailed predictions suggest that these advances fall short.

> Other electrically operated equipment, such as vacuum cleaner, washer and dishwasher, will replace a large share of the work usually done by a permanent servant. Indeed, it may be said, that "the one way out" of the servant problem in the future is the much wider use of power machinery in the home. The servantless household will have to be more of a mechanical household, where every possible purely manual task is done by arms of steel and knuckles of copper.
>
> And in the future it is believed that such machinery will be far more unified than at present. That is, instead of such small devices made by different firms and bought separately, there should be a larger installation or "system" (scientifically) planned for a specific kitchen, with the *various pieces related to one another.* (393–94)

6. Electrical Freedom (*New York World's Fair 1939–40* [Reel 3, Part 1]).

7. Planned Electric Kitchen (*New York World's Fair 1939–40* [Reel 3, Part 1]).

Frederick correctly forecast an increase in the number of appliances and their widespread use, and the corresponding decline in the use of domestic servants. Despite many attempts, the larger installation system never took off, and the system-wide, general appliance was instead replaced by numerous, inexpensively produced, ubiquitous motors that found their way into all manner of appliances. Ironically, this conception of a large system driven by a single unit would appear again in early discussions of the automated home as coordinated by a central computer.

While the plans for an integrated web of appliances may have ailed, by 1939 disparate units of household technology did find unity under a well-articulated myth of progress. The Westinghouse exhibit from the 1939 New York World's Fair included a dramatic illustration of domestic toil before and after electricity, concluding with "Electrical Freedom" (fig. 6) and the "Planned Electric Kitchen" (fig. 7). In this exhibit, electricity occupies center stage as a unifying force of progress in history, much in the way that other myth-systems rely on idealized abstractions like Liberty, Reason, Grace, and Volk to provide overarching themes for cultural identity. In keeping with a culture preoccupied with technical advancement, it is appropriate that Freedom itself is Electrical. And the automated home, far from being integrated practically, enjoys a more persuasive form of integration as a fantastic ideal.

CONCLUSIONS ON THE UNION OF SPACE AND TECHNOLOGY

The first twenty years of the twentieth century had a profound effect on the trajectory the home would take. The evolution of industrial-management paradigms and the application of industrial technologies provided the context needed to build a home that was oriented in both space and time, as a workplace which could be controlled on two intersecting axes. The idea of the good life, which was characterized not only by abundance of material resources but also by the appropriate use of time, marks an important change in this intimate realm of everyday affairs. Furthermore, this union of space and time would provide not only the productive force necessary to shift into the modes of a consumer economy but also the context for the insertion of information technologies into the workplace and home, creating yet another way to produce value beyond the limits set by the frontiers of time-managed spaces.

2

"Here's Johnny!"

The Introduction of Information to the Space of the Home

Before the home could advance to the dream of automation that inspired even the earliest innovators, the technology of the home would have to move beyond simple questions of labor and toward new plateaus in organization. The reorganization of space, the management of motion, and the introduction of electric appliances certainly moved the home toward the future, but it was the introduction of electronic media during the development of the postwar suburb that would tie the home to popular fantasies and eventually provide intimate instructions on the pursuit of those fantasies. It was television, especially, which established the paradigm for home as the site of media consumption. And, consequently, it was television which would affect the form that the suburban home would take, the products that would fill it, and the experiences of its human inhabitants.

Following television, computers emerged as a powerful force, both in their imaginary appeal and in their ability to provide greater organization to the flow of information. Home computers were particularly instrumental in advancing the home's evolution as an electronic environment, both enabling and inspiring attempts at household robots, artificially intelligent games, and networks within the home, all of which reflected an ever-increasing desire to bring the many functions in the home into greater harmony. It was the postwar period—with high consumer expectations, robust technological innovation, and an abundance of popular-culture images of the house of tomorrow—that took the home beyond the parameters of space and time, and toward the realization (or de-realization) of the home through the introduction of electronic media.

TELEVISION AND THE SUBURBS

Veterans returning from World War II stimulated a number of new trends in housing patterns. Coming home to increased prosperity and opportunity, coupled with the demands of a sudden and dramatic "baby boom" and the innovations in building technology which flooded the market with affordable homes, many young people found themselves moving into what would come to be called the "postwar" suburb. The most noteworthy trailblazer in this shift was William Levitt who, in 1949, began to mass produce houses in a city called Levittown. Beyond introducing the mass-produced home to the public, Levitt was also responsible for the popularization of the "open plan," which steered away from individual rooms in favor of more flexible spaces and open areas. The open plan, which had originated much earlier, was popularized through a number of forces: "The open-space plan was the combined result of technology and ideology. New methods of house fabrication made the open-space plan possible, eradicating the need for beams and supporting walls at small intervals. . . . The loss of the dining room—often considered a masculine space—reoriented the home towards the feminine parlor, now called the family room. As housing starts improved beyond architects' wildest expectations, the so-called ranch house enjoyed its most popular period" (Leavitt, 176). The practical concerns of the mass-produced house, along with advancements in building techniques, ensured that the open-space plan would become the norm. It offered an easy way to skirt the problem of customization by transforming the interior of the home into dynamic, multifunctional, and customizable space. By opening up the interior of the home to dynamic use, even as the suburb would tend to wall the occupants off from the rest of the city, the occupants of the home became subjected to a reorganization of sorts. The suburban home emphasized the idea of family-as-unit by creating more communal space in which relationships could be explored. At the same time, the home, which was increasingly shielded from the close-quarters contact of everyday life in the city, also became a site of greater privacy. The result was a reorientation of notions of privacy and community which emphasized less contact with the outside world and greater contact with the world of the family.

Although televisions began to be commercially produced in 1928, the 1939 New York World's Fair is noted as a milestone in the history of television broadcasting. The brief film *An RCA Presentation: Television* (ca. 1939) appears to have been timed to coincide with the presentation of television at the world's fair. It highlights the production process at NBC's New York studio and features RCA technology. A 1956 RCA documentary, *The Story of Television*, also marks 1939 as the landmark year in which television "wiped out the horizon" and extended human vision across vast distances, but it notes that the sacrifices required by World War II resulted in a "four year blackout for commercial TV" from 1941 through 1945.

It was not until the 1950s that television's true explosion into the middle-class home took place. In 1948 there were an estimated 350,000 televisions sets in the United States. In April of 1950 there were 5.3 million; by October of that same year there were 8 million; and by 1953, half of all American homes (over 25 million) were equipped with *at least one* television set ("1950–1959: 'Quick Facts' by Year"). This rapid growth of technology, which roughly corresponds with the open-plan home, provided a window to the world around which the ever more insular family-unit could organize. By enriching the space of the home with images, not only did the television set the stage for an economy increasingly dependent on consumption, it also offered a way to provide enriched meaning to a space that had found itself, through technicity and isolation, sanitized and insulated from the world outside. It was the television that sharpened the focus and set the tone for design, making it more and more clearly "a process of creating experiences rather than objects" (Votolato, 282). In advance of

8. Domestic Comfort (*Magic in the Air*).

television's mushrooming popularity during the postwar period, the 1941 film *Magic in the Air* illustrated the private comfort that TV provided: "You can just lean back in a comfortable chair in the theater or in your own favorite chair at home, relax and watch the game." Furthermore, the image of domestic comfort is juxtaposed to the chaos of crowds. The film highlights the careful attention of camera crews to the significant details, suggesting that television viewing is no mere substitute, but a refinement of spectatorship. The role of spectacular technologies appear as "magic" machines that operate by the push of a button and the twist of a dial. The film ends as the wife tops off her husband's drink, and the hopeful narrator muses that perhaps someday television will manage to perform this "miracle," too (fig. 8). In less than eight minutes, this brief film (which also spends a great deal of time explaining the way television studios work to manage and edit action seamlessly) explicitly addresses several of the themes that would come to define the development of cultural attitudes about the home in the postwar period. Indeed, before television would blossom as a defining feature of the 1950s suburban home, it was already trafficking in new paradigms for social and cultural life. The house, filled with television, had become a powerful site for the production of meaning and the generation of home.

In *Welcome to the Dreamhouse* Lynn Spigel weaves a fascinating genealogy of the "house of tomorrow" as a theme in the development of the American home. Spigel's summary will help to map out this theme.

> During the 1930s, General Electric showcased its "magic home" at fairs and exhibitions. In 1934, Westinghouse chose Mansfield, Ohio, as the site for its Home of Tomorrow which functioned as a display venue for the company's line of household gizmos. By the 1940s, and after World War II, the home of tomorrow was most typically imagined as a technologically enhanced living space, chock full of "mechanical servants" that promised to liberate housewives from chores while also orchestrating daily activities from home entertainment to waking the kids. . . . In 1943 and 1944, The Libby-Owens-Ford company promoted its Day After Tomorrow's Kitchen in department stores around the country. After the war, the kitchen of tomorrow continued to be a staple feature in magazines. (383)

As Frederick's early predictions of "arms of steel and knuckles of copper" suggest, the idea of the automated home and its association with progress are nothing new. However, as Spigel later points out, changes in technology, from the electric motor to electronics, shifted the conception of the home of tomorrow in some interesting ways: "While the cold war era home of tomorrow clearly drew on previous notions of technologically-enhanced lifestyles, new electronic technologies also helped to change the dominant image of tomorrow's home. With the proliferation of television, satellites, and computers, the home of tomorrow was not simply a model of machine-enhanced efficiency; it additionally came to be imagined as sentient space" (384). The home of tomorrow was no longer just a factory; it had become, at least in the imagination, something like Cape Canaveral, a communications and processing center for the citizens of the future.

Paradoxically, it was the pragmatic exuberance of Disneyland itself which epitomized the spectacular new paradigm for everyday living, rather than the many references to tomorrow contained in its parks. Disneyland, which opened in 1955, was a painstaking and skillful effort at creating a "convincing" world of fantasy based on the narrative pleasure of Disney's films. In taking this opportunity to make fantasy a real and interactive space, Disney managed to articulate, in a very concrete way, that which was new about the spaces inhabited by those who lived in the postwar suburbs of the 1950s. Real life was to be a space infused with information that took spectacular narrative forms. Disney was so far ahead of his time in his construction of narrative-rich consumer spaces, that only recently have consumers embraced such representation as reality in the form of the reality show.[1]

It was the milieu of the convincing fantasy which added a strong and heady narrative element to the home of tomorrow. While the goal of modern architecture and design was to eschew whimsy in favor of the practical facts of living space, it was the influence of entertainment that converted this minimalist and machinic aesthetic into a baroque imaginary space. In spite of all its minimalism, the home of tomorrow became more ornate than ever.

Although the home, through the addition of media to minimalist surfaces, has become more ornate than previous conceptions of living space, there are differences in the ways that these fantasies work. The minimalist object, through sheer lack of flourishes, is an attempt at a shrewd rhetorical game. Stripped-down objects and spaces attempt to focus the user's attention. For minimalist artists, the goal becomes to focus the viewer on the essence of the object or space at hand. Although such experiments may say ambiguous things, their elimination of distracting elements is an attempt to reduce the work into one meticulously controlled and overbearing distraction. The minimalist work employs a coercive rhetorical strategy which seeks to eliminate the random or chaotic elements that are present in earlier attempts at ornament. The gaudy or baroque work of art, while it may be criticized as an overwhelming assault on the senses, offers the user numerous means by which to enter the imaginative space of the piece by providing many touchstones with the everyday. The minimalist modern environment, saturated with media, while imaginatively rich, might be seen as an attempt to force users into a relationship with media that positions them as spectators rather than as inhabitants. This is not to say that the modern home is essentially minimalist; rather it is to say that modernist minimalism and the media-rich suburban home share, in essence, a rhetorical orientation which requires one to concentrate on the consumption of the images they offer. The focused consumption of mediated images becomes a prime source of pleasure and agency in the modern home.[2]

The new conception of the home, dominated by modern aesthetics and media, was reflected in the RCA Whirlpool Miracle Kitchen, which specifically made use of minimalist aesthetics for the purpose of showcasing futuristic features. As Gregory Votolato explains, these homes were nothing short of sensational.

> In the mid-1950s, the RCA Whirlpool Miracle Kitchen ventured further into the realm of fantasy in its expression of the kitchen as the nerve center of the house. More stage-set than laboratory, its style was a cross between the new straight-lined minimalism of the dawning computer age and the warmer, oiled-walnut Danish modern which was the last word in popular interior furnishing at the time. Whereas the LOF [Libby-Owens-Ford] Kitchen had concentrated on rational innovation, amusing robotic gimmicks prevailed in the RCA kitchen. The most memorable, a self-propelled vacuum-cleaning robot, scurried about the huge floor acreage consuming invisible debris while the human occupants munched on canapés. (222)

Not unlike earlier showrooms, which were also constructed to demonstrate new technology, the Miracle Kitchen was an attempt to sell technology. However, the emphasis, rather than revolving around the rhetoric of efficiency characteristic of earlier home innovations, fell more securely on novelty. The vacuum-cleaning robot, for example, has yet to make its way into the average home nearly fifty years later (sixty-five years later if you count *Leave It to Roll-Oh*). Only recently have significant attempts been made at new vacuum-cleaning technologies, and even these seem to focus on using small vacuum cleaners that move randomly and perform light maintenance as a supplement to regular cleaning with traditional models.[3]

Another dramatic example of this fantastic space was Monsanto's "House of the Future," which opened its doors in 1957 as an attraction at Disneyland.[4] Located in the park's Tomorrowland, "House of the Future" was a showcase for plastics. As the pre-recorded narration explained, "The architects who designed this house sought to develop a plan which would be logical from the standpoint of everyday family living. Yet, at the same time, they were determined to create a home free from the preconceived notions of a house made from conventional building materials.

Constructed of a few large parts instead of many small ones, the design takes advantage of the almost unlimited flexibility of plastics in building" ("Monsanto House of the Future"). While the attraction did not emphasize, as the Miracle Kitchen did, the joy of automation, its circular construction resembled a flying saucer, emphasizing its space-age design. Furthermore, the fact that it was fabricated entirely from synthetic materials (which are associated with ease of maintenance and flexibility) was meant to appeal to futurist desires. The magic of the Disneyland attraction was summoned through the following narration: "Those of you who have visited us previously know that many of the exciting uses of plastics you saw here before now have become commonplace in houses from New England to California" ("Monsanto House of the Future"). Rather than emphasizing the ordinary nature of this extraordinary house, the narration served to create associations between everyday uses of plastics and fast-forward living, and was thus an attempt to transform mundane practices of consumption into rich texts about being modern, or even futuristic.

On the small screen, this propagation of suburban futurism was accomplished through what Lynn Spigel has dubbed the "fantastic sitcom." Spigel identifies a critical tendency in this genre, which includes shows like *Bewitched, I Dream of Jeannie, Mr. Ed,* and *The Addams Family,* explaining, "Rather than portraying the future, the fantastic sitcoms presented critical views of contemporary suburban life by using tropes of science fiction to make the familial strange" (122). While this genre clearly did depict the contemporary family in novel ways, making it fertile ground for critique, it also must be considered from the rhetorical perspective of Monsanto's "House of the Future." Samantha from *Bewitched* and Jeannie from *I Dream of Jeannie* accomplished many ordinary tasks through the use of their extraordinary powers, turning domestic labor into a form of magic. While these shows made the suburban seem strange, in doing so they only reaffirmed the role of information in the suburban home by investing spaces with magic and filling the air with traces of meaning. Like Monsanto's plastic dwelling, they were fantasies about someplace other that invited spectators to participate in an imaginative act.

The 1950s marked a substantial shift in conceptions of the home of the future. Changes in housing norms along with the introduction of television into the home saw that the streamlined space would be filled with complex narratives about what it would be like to live in the home of the future. This narrative emphasis and future orientation caused the space of the home to be imagined, in the spirit of the times, as an environment of the future. This futuristic motif persisted, along with the space program, through the 1960s, creating the perfect conditions for Disney's fantasy of EPCOT. The idea and aesthetics of a spectacular future aided by technology endured well into the 1980s. However, as the Cold War continued to drag on, the belief in technology's role in the creation of a peaceful future was considerably tarnished. Furthermore, with the revolution in computer technologies that took place in the 1970s, a number of profound changes were introduced to the world of space, time, and information, as greater processing power and increased interactivity provided the means to manage these elements on more subtle levels.

The idea of the "set" as a place for drama to unfold is a particularly useful way to understand the way that the home works after the arrival of television. An inversion of the verb *to set*, in which inanimate objects are "placed" by people, the "set" is the environment which calls forth and makes manifest a human story.[5] The set is that place which has been preordained to see specific actions take place. This concept of set as an organized place for human action to occur casts the home as a process of "enframing." The idea of the home and what it should be, as the set of a drama, exists as the precondition for the realization of the home. It is constructed in advance as a place where comfort and familiarity can be stumbled on, and where "handiness" can be discovered as a thing in itself.[6] The home is thus a "set" both in the sense that it represents a whole that is greater than the sum of its parts and in that it is the context for lifestyle dramas to be staged.

The shifting role of the home is evident if one analyzes the evolving narratives of technology in the home. Compared to previous examples like the 1941 film *Magic in the Air* (which introduces the spectacular elements in the course of discussing technology), the U.S. Department of Agriculture's 1949 *Step-Saving Kitchen* (which is purely practical), or U.S. Steel's 1957 *Practical Dreamer* (which, as its title suggests, is a fantasy about the practical kitchen), the emerging domestic technological narratives employ a highly stylized futurism in which progress is more fashion than function. Take for example, the 1956 film *Design for Dreaming*, which eschews a particular technology, plan, or product and instead focuses on futuristic styles as represented in General Motors's Motorama and Frigidaire's "Kitchen of the Future." Also significant is the fact that both brands fall under the larger umbrella of the GM parent company, suggesting that as consumer culture evolved, so did the concept of synergy and corporate structure. General Motors could adopt a concept—futurism—aestheticize it, test it, and apply it across its corporate structure as a successful formula. A car onscreen cannot be driven by the audience. A refrigerator on TV cannot cool your food. It can only represent these actions symbolically. In a culture that has embraced notions of technological progress as synonymous with a better way of doing things, the colder refrigerator and the faster car must be the most advanced ones. In fact, traffic laws and freezing points limit intensities of speed and temperature, forcing them into the realm of representation. Eventually, the focus of marketing comes to emphasize the futuristic qualities of the product over the technical specifics that would embody advances in engineering. Thus, spectacular design is the commodity that functions best on screen. Practically, this aesthetic can be easily applied to a wide range of materials, while actual advances in engineering require that research and development resources be devoted to improving individual products. In the end, this convergence of forces creates the situation in which the realization of progress happens through the consumption of a product's cultural content rather than its formal utility.

Another fantastic example of this shift is the 1958 film *American Look* (fig. 9). This film, which focuses exclusively on modern design, makes bold assertions about the affective qualities of aesthetics. Over a backdrop of elegantly styled home furnishings and appliances, the narrator claims, "By the way things look as well as the way they perform, our homes acquire new grace, new glamour, new accommodations. Expressing not only the American love of beauty but also the basic freedom of the American People, which is the freedom of individual choice" (fig. 10). Although cryptic, there is some truth to the narrator's claim: *by the way things look . . . our homes acquire new accommodations.* In other words, the subjec-

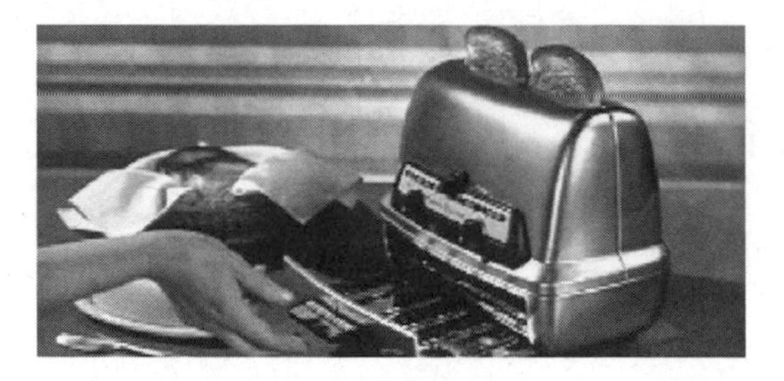

9.A better looking toaster (*American Look* [Part 1]).

10. Style as an expression of Freedom (*American Look* [Part 2]).

tive benefits of style are equivalent to the functional benefits of engineering. And although formal excellence likely ranks behind more functional "accommodations" in Maslow's hierarchy of needs, to the exquisitely indulged it could very well be the only difference that matters.[7] Beyond that, this style is the patriotic expression of your basic freedom: the right to purchase the elegantly crafted appliances of your choice.

Nowhere is the shift from function to fashion so stark as in the circa 1968 film *Match Your Mood*. Through the application of decals, this revolutionary Westinghouse refrigerator allows you to "Match Your Apparel" (fig. 11), "Match Your Hobbies," and "Match Your Parties" (fig. 12). With absolutely no emphasis placed on the refrigerator's engineering excellence, all the emphasis is placed squarely on the aesthetic value of its surface. The film's title underscores the subjective focus of this fashion-based marketing with its claim that a refrigerator can match something as ephemeral and transitory as its owner's mood. Reinforcing this spirit are claims that the refrigerator can match a party (a singular event), a hobby (a leisure activity), or clothing (the style of which changes seasonally). Yet a mood, as an arbitrary expression of feeling, points also to something more permanent than a person's particular flight of fancy—it is an expression of self. And in a consumer society, so are one's parties, hobbies, and apparel.

11. "Match Your Apparel" (*Match Your Mood*).

12. "Match Your Parties" (*Match Your Mood*).

Their very arbitrary nature makes them an expression of the individual's character, for unlike other commodities, they are inessential applications above and beyond one's base animal nature. In effect, your refrigerator is a lot like you. Inside are the things you need to survive, but on the surface is a bold proclamation of your character.

The smart house takes the theatrical conception of the set to new heights. The interactive milieu not only holds in place a lifestyle narrative about affluence, ease, and technology, but it also provides a certain level of production values and stage directions programmed into the operating system and focusing the actions of the inhabitants on certain scripted functions. As an advertisement for the IDEAS home automation system in *SmartHouse* magazine explains, "Just imagine. . . . A home where you can create perfect sound and vision, anywhere—at the touch of a button" (IDEAS advertisement, 80). With the sound system which follows the occupant through the hallways with a personal soundtrack, the lighting system which provides light in the right place at the right time, or the bathtub which fills itself and waits for the user to step into it, the smart house "produces" daily life and gives it the sparkle and glamour of a film or movie. And although technology has not quite advanced to this level, one can imagine life in, say, a smart kitchen which becomes like that of a set on the Food Network: foods appear conveniently prepped, pre-measured, and placed within easy grasp; dirty dishes and bowls disappear; and the cook smiles and effortlessly performs only the most pleasurable acts with impressive results. The promise of the smart home is that the house will showcase only acts that are worthwhile, amusing, and/or interesting to its inhabitants.

Developing the notion of the set further are the possibilities for self-governance that the smart house opens up. The house knows where the owner is, what time the owner awakes each day, and what music the owner listens to, and it adapts itself accordingly, using artificial intelligence to establish a surveillance of routine. If homes, as Neil Gershenfeld notes, share this information with the outside world, this surveillance becomes a multidimensional model of life: "Right now the price of your insurance is based on your crude demographics, rather than your personal details. If you drive safely, and you let your car insurance company have access to data from your car that confirmed that, then you could pay less for car insurance than the bozo who cuts you off. If you eat well, and you're willing to let your life insurance company talk to your kitchen, then you could be rewarded for having a salad instead of a cigarette. The insurance company would not be in the business of enforcing morality; they would be pricing the expected real cost of behavior" (209). The actors in this set are then broadcast in a very real sense to an external audience. The pursuit of a lifestyle becomes not merely an "idea" held in place by fancy gadgets but a set of decipherable actions enforced by the user's willful submission to the record. The show in production is, in effect, animated by a script which works in reverse.

When the smart home, as a web of surveillance, demonstrates an ability to "think" and "plan," by doing the shopping, waking the owner, and turning on certain shows or playing certain music when it deems it appropriate, it ceases to document and begins to enforce. The smart home exerts its own form of microscopic hegemony, establishing and scripting normative lifestyle actions and delivering these to the subject, making a particular course of action ready-at-hand—not unlike those therapeutic institutions (halfway houses, mental hospitals, convalescent homes, etc.) which exist to restore and/or reinforce "normal" social functioning. Aided by an artificial intelligence which is able to anticipate desire, the house becomes a set, equipped not only with furnishings, lights, monitors, cameras, and music but with a virtual production "crew" that directs the action, provides the script, focuses the camera, and edits for the construction of meaning. At the same time, the positive construction of meaning is supplemented by the negative practices of eliminating ethical options and performing a kind of moral scrubbing. This cleansing process conveniently eliminates "unfortunate" options, making it impossible to abide by options that are no longer available (for example, consumers are asked to select only from a handful of "reasonable" options—like shopping at a Wal-Mart, an ethnic market, or an ecofriendly co-op, rather than growing their own food, begging for it, or harvesting it from the dumpster).[8] The consumer field is thus rhetoricized, and life in the smart home is one surrounded by material arguments which both threaten and comfort consumers with an array of goods for the promotion of a system of entertainment.

Not surprisingly, the home as set is an idea that has been extensively developed in popular culture. One 1960 *Twilight Zone* episode, "A World of Difference," told the unsettling tale of a businessman whose day is interrupted by a director shouting "Cut!" and a film crew emerging to reveal that the gentleman's life is nothing but a movie. In 1973–1974 PBS aired *An American Family*, a twelve-hour documentary that followed a real family in the process of unraveling (Banash). PBS's effort provided the inspiration for Albert Brooks's 1979 fictional comedy *Real Life*, which featured the comedian moving in to capture the "real" experiences of a middle-class family. Through the 1980s, with the development of numerous television talk shows, courtroom dramas, and the hit series *Cops* (which has now aired over 700 episodes), the movement of the private lives of everyday people has been pushed increasingly into the public sphere of television. In 1992 MTV debuted *Real World*, which is now in its eighteenth season and has set into motion the current trend of reality-television programming. With the advance of the Internet and the webcam explosion, the distinctions between everyday life and entertainment continue to blur.

Feeding on these notions are films like Peter Weir's *Truman Show* (1998) or Ron Howard's *EDtv* (1999). *The Truman Show* tells the story of Truman Burbank (Jim Carrey), a man who unknowingly lives his entire existence in a fictitious town constructed on a television-studio backlot called Sea Haven.[9] With his life televised twenty-four hours a day, Truman Burbank lives his life in a bubble, duped into thinking that his charmed life is his own, unaware that his entire life has been a deception. *EDtv*'s Ed Pekurny (Matthew McConaughey) becomes a star overnight, as a failing television station decides to create a reality show built around his life.

In "From an American Family to the Jennicam: Realism and the Promise of TV," an insightful essay on the contradictions inherent in "reality" TV, David Banash writes,

> Set within the confines of a small house, *Big Brother* pitted ten houseguests against one another under total surveillance that included twenty-four hour web-cam feeds. While the program sold itself as a glimpse of everyday life, the house is particularly odd in that it lacks almost every kind of device its core audience takes for granted: no phones, televisions, computers, or radios. In essence, what most Americans spend most of their time doing (consuming media) is almost the only thing that *Big Brother* really forbids. Thus, the authentic moments of emotion which the show sells as its real attraction are, in fact, generated through the most heavy-handed and apparent simulations. The same could be said for similar programs such as *Survivor*, *The Mole*, and *Temptation Island*. The very heavy-handedness of the narratives, their utter dissociation from everyday life, moves them further and further away from the kind of realism with which the documentary has traditionally been associated, and yet the promise is still always the real itself.

The construction of the home as a set has emerged through technical innovations in home-automation technology alongside an increasingly consumer-driven society, and it has been dramatized and documented by the development of reality programming, muddling the borders between fiction and fact, and turning everyday life itself away from individual subjectivity and into a dramatization of itself—life as a real-time reenactment.

The notion of daily life as a real-time reenactment goes beyond the conventions of reflexive television-as-reality genres. Notable are the more earnest, but no less ironic, spate of films that make use of the pre-scripted drama as a suspense genre. Chris Nolan's *Memento* (2000), Steven Spielberg's *Minority Report* (2002), and John Woo's *Paycheck* (2003) all feature narratives in which the protagonists must discover their identities as the film unfolds, although they each approach this in slightly different ways. In *Memento,* for example, Leonard (Guy Pearce) has experienced a brain trauma which prevents him from remembering. With each passing moment, his short term memories fade. Each day he awakens to his life as a mystery. In order to achieve his goal of finding his wife's murderer and discovering what happened to him, he leaves himself clues—notes, instructions, tattoos, photographs. Through these mementos, he gains a history, and thus we discover who Leonard is. Steven Spielberg's *Minority Report* approaches the process of self-discovery as an image of the future. In the film John Anderton (Tom Cruise), a "pre-crime" detective, guided by "precogs" (clairvoyant savants), solves and prevents murders before they occur. When he glimpses a future in which he is killing a man he doesn't know, he sets out to discover who he is killing and why. As the plot unfolds, we discover along with Anderton how he will come to find himself in the situation from the premonition. In John Woo's *Paycheck* Michael Jennings (Ben Affleck) is a reverse engineer who takes a job working on a top-secret project, which he discovers to have the potential to destroy the world. Knowing that his memory will be erased on the project's completion, he leaves behind clues that will help him remember what he did and thus permit him to exonerate himself and destroy the dangerous technology. Interestingly, two of the films (*Minority Report* and *Paycheck*) are based on stories by Philip K. Dick, whose writings are characterized by a paranoid anxiety about the real and the virtual. It is no mistake that Dick's fantasies come out of the same postwar culture that is the topic of this work—they are preoccupied with the possibility that our personality is something that can be encoded, erased, and rewritten. All three films are characterized by a self that is cobbled together by the markers of the world around us. Unlike the bildungsroman, the pre-scripted drama as suspense genre does not presuppose a deeper self that one must come to discover—its characters search frantically for any shred of evidence of who they are, how they got where they are, and where they will go. And, significantly, the only clues are to be discovered through external processes. For these protagonists, as the fans of *Seinfeld* and *Friends* often admit, life is like a television show.

Following a remarkably similar trajectory to the one I have laid out here, Scott Bukatman has arrived at the concept of the "terminal identity." Terminal identity, a product of "terminal culture" (which plays between the notions of *terminal* as ending and *terminal* as point of interface) provides an apt metaphor for understanding the ambiguities of postmodern subjects. Leaping off from Donna Haraway's "A Cyborg Manifesto," Bukatman posits that the characteristic feature of this new self is represented in television, film, and popular culture as "transcendence which is also always a surrender" (329). In other words, the terminal identity is that identity which can enjoy the virtual pleasures for what they do rather than for what they are—or rather, enjoy virtual pleasures because they *are* what they seem, nothing more.

Yet Bukatman's theory of the terminal identity, in its rather resigned submission to uncertainty, might miss the real representations that are taking place. Typically, the tales of antiheroes who resist the impersonal power are representations of terminal identities in that they presuppose a self that has not been subsumed into the prevailing norms. What matters about the postmodern tales of terminal identities is not the struggle of the protagonist, but the emerging cybernetic self of the other. The forces external to the character increasingly become invested with subjectivity, and the identity of the terminal exists in relief, as an expression of a consumer culture that attempts to anticipate, guide, and ultimately control one's needs. Indeed, the terminal story is not about people like you or me; the story is about the increasingly smart world around us. And though terminal subjects might submit to the transcendence being offered, the world that they occupy is all too often willing to express its desires, assert its wishes, and overcome the obstacle of the humanity of its subjects.

THE REVOLUTION IN PERSONAL COMPUTING AND ORIGINS OF THE SMART HOUSE

In the mid-1960s, the United States was poised for a true revolution in technology. A number of innovations in hardware and software were rapidly reducing computer size and cost while dramatically improving speed and power, making it increasingly possible to bring one of the machines into the home.[10] In 1966 the engineer Jim Sutherland, of Westinghouse, created the experimental ECHO IV (or Electronic Computing Home Operator), a bulky, multitasking home-automation system. Dag Spicer writes, "The family finances were completed 'automatically,' and, according to the April 1968 issue of *Popular Mechanics*, the Sutherlands were extending the system to store recipes, compute shopping lists, track family inventory, control home temperature, turn appliances on and off, and predict the weather. One of the features Sutherland was most excited about was ECHO's ability to act as a family message center, a place where people could leave notes to each other." Although the ECHO system was never manufactured for commercial use, its creation was the fulfillment of a number of popular dreams and represented a significant advance in automation technology.

In 1969 Honeywell released the H316 Kitchen Computer, which, for an exorbitant $10,000, became the first commercially available home computer (*PC World* Staff).[11] The Kitchen Computer, which could be programmed to store recipes and provide cooking tips, is a notorious failure in the history of the home computer. Although this bulky and expensive machine came furnished with its own cutting board and a sixteen-button control panel, consumers could not quite justify its purchase. Nevertheless, the Kitchen Computer does represent a revolutionary step in the history of computing by marking a shift in the conception of the computer. As the reliance on the massive mainframes of the 1950s gave way to smaller, faster, and better machines, the computer was quickly inserting itself into the everyday, not as an abstract and futurist concept, but as a very real and personal fact of life. Forgive, for a moment, the sexism of the old adage "The way to a man's heart is through his stomach," and one can see that the computer's entry into the domestic sphere of the kitchen marks once again the same profound integrating impulse that inspired Christine Frederick to apply time management to the home. As the H316 advertisement mused, "If she can only cook as well as Honeywell can compute" (reprinted in Spicer).

Through the 1970s and into the early 1980s, the romance of the personal computer would take some interesting turns. Aside from the futurist fantasies and practical realities that had generated the space-age discourse of the years before, three areas of technological development were shaking up notions of home automation and would lead ultimately to the idea of the smart home. Although difficult to separate from one another, the technology of robotics, artificial intelligence (AI), and convergence would lead to new conceptions of home automation. These three technologies would themselves intermingle in interesting ways to define a new marketing word: *smart*. Smart machines, smart designs, smart bombs, smart watches, smart cars, smart computers, smart materials, smart cards, smart phones, smart homes. As the new catchword, *smart* would come to describe both sensible and over-the-top design as the embodiment of practical simplicity, as well as monstrously overwrought processing power. To get at a meaning of *smart*, one must trudge through the history of recent technology and pick through competing ideas about this trendy term, in order that one may come to understand the metaphysical aspects of what it means to have a smart home.

ROBOTS

The term *robot* came into popular use in 1920—it was coined by the Czech playwright Karel Čapek (1890–1938) in his play *R.U.R.*, or *Rossum's Universal Robots*—and replaced the term *automaton*, which had been in use for centuries. According to Isaac Asimov and Karen A. Frenkel, "*Robot* is a Czech word for 'worker,' with the implication of involuntary servitude, so that it might be translated as 'serf' or 'slave'" (12). The term *robotics* was

13. The Future of Freedom (*New York World's Fair 1939–40* [Reel 3, Part 1]).

coined twenty-two years later in Isaac Asimov's short story "Runaround," along with Asimov's "Three Laws of Robotics."

1. A robot may not injure a human being, or, through inaction, allow a human being to come to harm.
2. A robot must obey the orders given to it by human beings except where such orders conflict with the First Law.
3. A robot must protect its own existence as long as such protection does not conflict with the First or Second Law. (Asimov and Frenkel, 13)

And while both *robot* and *robotics* originated as science-fiction concepts, it wasn't long before scientists created programmable robots and began to use these two terms. At the 1939 New York World's Fair, Westinghouse's exhibit in its tribute to "Electrical Freedom" concluded with a speculative vignette that included a robot (fig. 13). In 1940, at the same world's fair, the film *Leave It to Roll-Oh* introduced Roll-Oh the robotic butler and used the metaphor of the robot to describe just about every automated device from the thermostat to the carburetor. In 1954 George C. Devol Jr. developed the first robot for industrial use, called "unimation" (short for "universal automation") (Asimov and Frenkel, 15). That same year Isaac Asimov released *Caves of Steel* (the second installment in his *I, Robot* trilogy), which featured a robotic detective sent to solve a crime on an Earth peopled by humans hostile to robot laborers. In 1962 General Motors installed a Unimate robot into its plant, making it the first industrial leader to adopt robots for the manufacturing process ("History Timeline of Robotics"). In 1968 Philip K. Dick reinterpreted the robot detective story with *Do Androids Dream of Electric Sheep?*, which probes many of the same themes as Asimov's *I, Robot* trilogy, albeit less decisively. Dick keeps the anti-robot prejudice, the idea of the passing android, and the problem of labor. But rather than having the detective discover the value of the robot, the novel concludes with a crisis of humanity. The development of the industrial robot is thus critically tied with cultural representations of robots. And in the best science fiction these representations inevitably lead to questions about ourselves.

Industrial robots, while they have been romantically named, are not quite the robots of science-fiction fantasy. Industrial robots, as part of assembly lines, are typically assigned repetitive, precision tasks. The nature of the machines or that which makes them "robotic" is the fact that they are "programmable" and can be adapted to a variety of tasks, but aside from their limited "memory," these robots cannot sense changes in the world around them, cannot learn from mistakes, and do not make plans for the future. A lack of sensors makes these robots unable to respond to the environment, a lack of self-awareness makes them unable to make decisions, and a lack of "intelligence" makes them unable to learn.

These fundamental problems were being addressed, however, by the pioneers of artificial intelligence through the 1950s and 1960s. In the 1950s the scientist W. Grey Walter designed robots called "tortoises," which used light sensors to respond to the environment (Asimov and Frenkel, 22). At Johns Hopkins University, scientists in the 1960s created "The Beast," which was capable of "feeding" itself from electrical outlets, demonstrating a rudimentary decision-making ability (22). And, finally, in 1969, scientists at the Stanford Research Institute created "Shakey," a robot who was not only able to respond to the environment via sensors and make decisions about what it should do next, but could also formulate strategies for action based on previous experience, making it a groundbreaking contribution to the development of AI (22). Through the development of AI, the science of robotics was brought closer to the fantasy of the autonomous machine of science fiction. With the introduction of the personal computer, the idea of the intelligent machine became much more personal, and thus more personable. By 1970, the union of robotics and intelligence was poised to complete the dream of the automated home imagined throughout the century, or at least to advance it considerably.

By the late 1970s, the idea of the personal household robot became increasingly popular. One publication written in 1979, called *How to Build Your Own Working Robot Pet*, provides detailed do-it-yourself instructions on the construction of a dog: "The functions of a human house-servant are really quite complex, and a robot counterpart to replace him would be impractical for a dozen reasons. The functions of a pet, however, are few and simple, and a robot pet is not at all inconceivable. A robot butler would be much more costly than a human butler, and would do the job about 40 percent as well. The dog, though, is both a good robot *and* a good pet. It is for this reason that I decided to trade in the 'golden-armored' robot for a little grey-furred machine with an electronic 'bark'" (Da Costa, 5). Interestingly, Da Costa eschews the work mission of the industrial robot altogether and instead opts for the idea of the robot pet. While traditionally domesticated animals have been bred to perform labor or provide food for human populations, the pet has been constructed in sentimental terms that have been steadily augmented over the years in post-Fordist economies. In the contemporary home, overlaid as it is with the anthropomorphizing power of narrative, the pet serves as a cipher for human wants, desires, emotions, and fantasies of comfort.[12] Because "man's best friend" demands only that humans invest it with emotions and treat it as a "friend," it is the perfect way to insert the fantasy robot of science fiction into the home. Wholly unlike the industrial robot, Da Costa's robot pet is a form of media in the sense that the mechanical is converted by a furry exterior and an expressive bark—its main occupation is to exist as an idea about anthropomorphized robots in the mind of the owner.

Since Da Costa's robot does its work in imaginative space, and Da Costa himself is forced to conceive of the project in relatively simple instructions, his definition of robot is peculiar. It at once attempts to break away from science-fiction myth (he instructs readers to actually build a robot) and from industrial realities (this robot won't be able to perform any labor), and chooses a peculiar third option: "What is a robot? A steady diet of science-fiction may leave you with some misconceptions. Simply speaking, a robot is an *electromechanical simulation of animal life*. That is, a robot is a machine which exhibits many or most of the characteristics evident in animals and in man. This definition has a direct bearing on the design of the robot pet and similar automata" (9, emphasis in original). Da Costa's robot is absolved from any purpose beyond its own existence. Instead, it is a machine which simulates those processes which make us alive. In effect, the robot pet is made for the owner and to be invested with meaning by the owner, and thus can only be a simulation of the life of its maker. If one believes in this definition of the robot, one will quickly find oneself surrounded by "robotic" beings of all types. Da Costa's definition is significant because it frames the qualities of living as experiences of perception, grounding our conception of all we deem "robot" as solipsistic extensions of our own ideas about the world.

From this "truth" that the robot pet is the embodiment of life processes, Da Costa makes an important conceptual leap. He explains, "For all intents and purposes, the brain board *is* the robot pet. Theoretically, it could be plugged into any one of several properly wired robot bodies and operate fully according to design" (18). Of course, Da Costa is pointing out that from the practical standpoint of robot construction, the key component is the processor. From being a physically perceived phenomenon of life simulation, the "being" of the robot is quickly transferred to the microprocessor. Further along, it is revealed that, when fully operational, the robot's lifelike behavior will be governed by "a software monitor termed ARASEM, for ARtificially RAndom SElf Motivation" (Da Costa, 20).[13] This, again, moves the "essence" of the robot further away from the body, ultimately reducing it to a set of commands which presumably dictate what the robot body would do were it subjected to certain data—a sort of cybernetic Calvinism. By now, the robot pet is something much more than the mere simulation of animal life: it is a simulated cognitive process that leads to animal locomotion.

Lest readers become too entranced, Da Costa once again reasserts the ordinary manageability of the project: "There is a tendency to suppose, merely because of the speed and complexity of the microprocessor, that somehow the robot pet will have a 'mind of its own.' We may romanticize, we may personify, but the truth is, the pet robot is only a machine, capable only of operating within limited, preset parameters. It is finite and therefore calculable: it may behave unexpectedly, but *not* 'unpredictably'" (20). It is with a certain amount of frankness and responsibility that Da Costa brings his readers down to Earth. For the book's instructional purpose, this move is a necessary one, reasserting the reader's potential mastery over the subject matter and attempting to keep the discussion of robot building clear, straightforward, and honest, even if the outcome of this creation process results in a cipher for human fantasy.[14] The robot pet, although it might interact with people as a "real" machine, occupies a spectacular space and is something akin to the many automata that people Disneyland's attractions (such as "Pirates of the Caribbean," "Great Moments with Mr. Lincoln," and "It's a Small World").

From the same publisher (TAB) and published in the same year (1979), David L. Heiserman's instructional *How to Build Your Own Self-Programming Robot* elaborates on the difference between "machine intelligence" and AI: "To my knowledge, this is the first practical, how-to book dealing with machine intelligence. Specifically, the book shows how to build a machine that learns to adapt to changing circumstances in its own environment. It is about a machine that programs itself to deal with problems of the moment and devise theories for dealing with similar problems in the future" (5). For Heiserman, robotic intelligence is linked to embodied experience. But, he goes on to explain, "Rodney is a self-programming machine, and as such develops a unique personality. No two Rodney machines behave exactly the same way" (5). Paradoxically, Heiserman emphasizes the importance of Rodney's experience in the world via a mechanical body in the formation of a unique personality. Heiserman continues, "A robot is not a slave, but a 'free' machine," and must be "capable of carrying out functions on its own" (13).

Interestingly, Heiserman's conception of the robot differs radically from Da Costa's, even though both come at the problem from an engineer's perspective. For Da Costa, the robot is a simulation of animal life, guided by abstract and disembodied processes, dressed up to look like a pet. For Heiserman, the robot is a "free" entity with a human name and its identity is embodied in worldly experience. It is a much more "human" machine, in spite of the fact that its body is less organic in appearance than Da Costa's (Rodney is basically a tower of sensors and machinery on wheels). Da Costa's conception sees robotic life in the same vein as the Turing test, reducing life to a question of its perception by those in authority. Heiserman's conception, which he confesses has been influenced by films such as the 1977 film *Star Wars* (13), locates the essence of robotics in "autonomy" and sees the expression of intelligence in the agency of the machine. These differences frame the relationship between the human and the robot in subtle ways: the first sees robot building as a struggle to create a convincing illusion; the second sees robot building as a struggle to build a machine which can fit into our ethical and legal notions of sovereign subjects. Taken together they might be read as an unspoken desire to see machines which are truly simulations of the human—both sentimentally and legally.

Heiserman goes on to describe the three types of intelligent robot: the "Alpha-Class," which, based on programming, simply responds to stimuli (157); the "Beta-Class," which responds to stimuli and remembers those responses that worked best (175); and the "Gamma-Class," which is able not only to respond and remember but to "generalize that solution into a variety of similar situations not yet encountered" (16). The Gamma Class robot "need not encounter every possible situation before discovering what it is supposed to do; rather, it generalizes its first-hand responses, thereby making it possible to deal with the unexpected elements of its life more effectively" (Heiserman, 16). The Gamma Class robot lives its life with memories and, based on the sequence of events, determines a chain of causality by selecting relevant details that seem to create the outcome, thereby constructing a narrative flow for robotic life. Heiserman's problem-solving robot is, in a crude sense, able to determine "meaning" through acting in such a way as to produce the best possible outcome. It is this idea of intelligence (based in both remembering and planning) which figures strongly in the creation of the smart home.

Beginning in 1979, a number of robotic toys and hobby kits were produced for the retail market. "Cyber Fun," a 1979 product review that appeared in *Omni*, highlights "new toys with minds of their own" (96). One such toy is the Mego 2-XL Robot, which "asks questions and tells jokes" (99). In 1980 Heath/Zenith released the Hero Jr. robot kit, which remained in production for eight years (Garcia). A 1984 advertisement claims, "HERO JR. will wake you in the morning, guard your home at night, remind you of your appointments for the week, and entertain your family throughout the day with engaging small talk, songs, poems, games . . . even strolls around the house" (Heath/Zenith Hero Jr. advertisement, 151). The Hubotics Corporation released Hubot in 1981, which advertisers claimed was "'the first home robot that's a personal companion, educator, entertainer and sentry . . . and he can talk!'" (quoted in Garcia). Throughout the early 1980s, Androbot Incorporated released a number of personal robots, including, TOPO I, TOPO II, TOPO III, BOB, BOB/XA, FRED, and ANDROMAN.[15] Notable innovations in the Androbot family include Apple IIe compatibility for the TOPO series, infrared two-way-communications capabilities between robot and computer for TOPO II and III, and—for the high-end model BOB—expandable memory and advanced programming software (Doerr). Androbot also built a TOPO prototype equipped with a vacuum cleaner for household chores, and the vivacious BOB even came with an optional party fridge: "B.O.B. can retrieve a beer or soft drink from an optional AndroFridge, and bring it to wherever its master may be waiting" (Doerr). And in 1985 Tomy Kyogo released the Omnibot 2000, "a complex robot toy that could be programmed to move, talk and carry objects" (Garcia). Other robots from this era include Tomy's Omnibot, Flipbot, Dingbot, and Verbot; Radio Shack's Robbie (an Omnibot clone); Ideal's Maxx Steele; Comro Robots; and many others (Doerr).[16] While these "robots" vary greatly in their abilities, some of them being little more than toys, they represent a significant trend in that they all attempt to bring robots into the home. And although toy robots had existed long before this era, never had they included microprocessors, silicon chips, software, sensors, and programming—previous toy robots were, at the very most, mechanical toys.

More practically, people were imagining and developing ways in which personal robots could be used to aid the disabled. As is the custom for magazine journalists, Phoebe Hoban spins a romantic lead into her 1983 article on "Robot Nurses": "It is a candlelight dinner for two, but only one person is eating. He is sitting in a wheelchair. Across from him sits his dinner companion: a robotic arm that responds to verbal commands. Its electronic voice echoes each order as the man directs it through the motions to serve him his meal: 'Up, right, left, open, close.' First it takes a prepared plate of food from the refrigerator and loads it into the microwave oven. When the oven beeper sounds, the arm removes the plate and sets it on the table. As a final touch, it lights the candle" (28).[17] The robot nurse is much more than a toy, as it serves the important function of making an unlivable condition not only livable but "normal." The quadriplegic, unable even to feed himself, might under other circumstances rely on a human servant or starve to death. A robot nurse, as Hoban's article explains, provides not only for the feeding of the man but adds sentimental touches like candlelight to his lonely act of eating. In adding this touch, the robot reminds us that the man in the wheelchair might appreciate the beauty of candlelight and all of its refined associations because he is more than just a hungry animal. In replacing a human nurse with the robot nurse, this story also speaks to the other half of the equation and makes this formerly disabled man into someone who shares the same abilities as the average person because he no longer will need a human helper. The robot nurse is supposed to be sufficiently "human" to be considered a "caregiver," but the virtue of its mechanical nature enables the man in the wheelchair to function more "independently," as he does not have to rely on another person. This bizarre romance feeds into competing notions of technology—that of the robot toy, which seeks to create an interesting companion, and that of the tool, which seeks to supplement human work.

In any case, both the toy versions and the work versions of the practical robot prompted a number of people to imagine that robots would rapidly proliferate and become a regular feature of everyday life. Hoban quotes Larry Leifer, who was one of many working on robot nurses, "'Within the next ten years . . . [r]obots functioning as nurses and domestic servants will be as common as cars'" (188). In a 1982 article Eric Mishara, reporting on a professor of "futuristics" named Arthur Harkins, writes, "Harkins suggests the domestic robots that will first roll off the assembly line will be little more than sophisticated appliances, programmed to perform a small number of functions and to interact in a limited capacity. But for very lonely people, these primitive robots will make excellent companions. . . .

Eventually, Harkins believes, the robot will become the dominant being on the Earth, capable of self-perpetuating through manufacture of new versions of itself" (153). And reaffirming these dramatic aspirations from the commercial sector, a Hitachi advertisement explains, "Our vision of the future includes robots with artificial intelligence that will learn from their own experiences. Personal robots that will take the drudgery out of household chores" (Hitachi Robots advertisement, 9).

Much more dramatic are the projections made in 1982 by the British high-tech pioneer Clive Sinclair, of whom Tony Durham reports the following: "Sinclair would welcome [household robots] at the threshold. 'I'd like to have robots in the home,' he says. 'Nice little servants. Chop wood and things.' Foot in the door, the robots would move on to other chores. . . . One evolutionary step further, robots will replace dogs as household pets. The human master will learn to love them. 'I think that's likely to happen,' Sinclair says. 'Exciting. And then they'll get brighter than us. And they'll take over.' There will be no place for humans in a society of intelligent robots, he says, except as pets" (117). Sinclair's utopian dreams of total technological takeover may make him a very controversial figure, but, more important, they point to what many imagined could be a reasonable possibility. Aside from the unemployment that might result were robots to displace workers, there is also the possibility that robots could surpass people at everything else and ultimately displace humans as the most powerful creatures in the world.[18]

ARTIFICIAL INTELLIGENCE

While personal robots were hard at work trying to dazzle consumers with their spectacular and amusing activities, the computer was undergoing its own transformation, becoming faster, more powerful, and better programmed—becoming "smart" in the mind of the public. An early example of "smart" that is used to market machine intelligence to consumers can be found in a series of *Olds Minute Movies* advertising the 1948 Oldsmobile Futuramic design. In "The First of the Futuramic Cars" the narrator explains, "In the truly modern home or the truly modern car, it's functional design that counts. Smart styling is styling with a purpose, as seen in this 1948 Futuramic Oldsmobile. Futuramic is a brand new word, created to describe this brand new postwar General Motors car. Luxuriously appointed inside and out, the Futuramic Oldsmobile brings truly modern postwar design to the automotive field. There is utility as well as beauty in every smart detail. There's the safety of greater visibility. There's automatic shifting, too. And no clutch pushing thanks to GM Hydromatic Drive. The smart way to go is the automatic way in the Futuramic Oldsmobile." Common themes in the Futuramic advertisements are key words like "modern," "design," and "automatic." These qualities are gathered together under the branded neologisms "Futuramic" and "Hydromatic." And while all of the 1948 Futuramic commercials use the term *smart*, "The First of the Futuramic Cars" seems to permit the greatest slippage between "smart" as a feature of clever engineering and as futurist aesthetic quality.

In "Ahead Automatically" the narrator follows a similar formula: "It's a Futuramic Oldsmobile with the newest pushbutton features. Automatic windows. Automatic top. Just pull a handy control and before you've had time to admire the smooth, flowing Futuramic lines of this real postwar Oldsmobile, the top is down—automatically. Like to drive it? Just slip into that big, comfortable front seat, touch that button, and presto—the seat adjusts itself. Driving's almost automatic, too. With GM Hydromatic drive there's no clutch pedal and gears shift automatically in this smart, new Futuramic Oldsmobile for 1948." This commercial, using all of the same catchphrases, focuses specifically on the push-button control and easy driving. Although the Futuramic Oldsmobile is not computerized, it does contain feedback mechanisms which perform actions that were once performed by people. Like the thousands of little "robots" that work inside the car in *Leave it to Roll-Oh*, the illusion of autonomous control is a compelling fantasy. A third spot, "Futuramic Design" focuses on a definition of "Futuramic" (fig. 14): "Futuramic. It's a brand new word for dramatic design of the future. As architects will tell you, Futuramic design combines beauty with utility. In houses or in automobiles, Futuramic design means styling with a purpose. The new 1948 Oldsmobile is the first of the Futuramic cars. It's designed for utmost passenger comfort and maximum visibility, as well as for smartness and style. And with GM Hydromatic Drive there's no gearshift or clutch pushing, just step on the gas and go. The

14. "Futuramic Design" (*Olds Minute Movies*).

smart way, the Futuramic way, the Oldsmobile way." In total, these brief spots mark the growing association of smartness with futuristic design and automatic function, as well as the further collapse of the distinctions between form and function.

The circa 1956 IBM Military Products Division's *On Guard! The Story of SAGE* details the Cold War application of thinking machines. Viewers are treated to a look at the elaborate web of radar towers, flight plans, and weapons systems coordinated by a massive computer capable of detecting deviations from airline flight plans and invasions of airspace, predicting possible trajectories and targets, and coordinating aircraft and missile-defense systems to neutralize threats within minutes. Additionally, the film highlights the "deterrent" elements of SAGE, which could mobilize strategic nuclear counterstrikes facilitated by the "BRANE: Bombing, Radar, and Navigation Equipment" that has been developed for use in bombers. The fascination with metaphors of thoughtfulness, however ironic the savage purposes of the machines they describe, were a significant contribution to public discussions of computer technology. A bit more innocuously, the 1958 film *The Information Machine* touts the superior abilities of the computer at planning: "[Man] has always been plagued by his limited ability to speculate." This film suggests the ways that computers might improve daily life by streamlining the process of invention and testing hypotheses with little or no risk.

The 1964 film *Century 21 Calling* focuses on the Bell Laboratories Pavilion at the Seattle World's Fair. Among the many exciting innovations, including wireless pagers and push-button telephone dials, the centerpiece of the Bell exhibit was the computerized switchboard of the Central Office. The docent explains, "Imagine if you can, an electronic brain, operating at millionths of a second speed. I say 'brain' because the new Electronic Central Office will almost think for itself. It will not only carry out instructions you dial into it, it will also remember instructions you provided earlier." Beyond improved speed and efficiency, the electronic brain would enable new features like call forwarding, call waiting, and memory dial. The film concludes with a look to the future: "One day you may be able to call home and automatically turn off the oven. Or from a public telephone a couple of hundred miles away, turn on your home air conditioner and have the house nice and cool when you return from that hot trip. It may even be possible to call and water the lawn during that dry spell when you are many miles away on vacation." This narrative, along with the concept of the electronic brain, is revisited through the 1960s to the present with uncanny faithfulness as an important theme in discussions of the emerging smart house.

In 1975 the Altair 8800 debuted as the "first widely marketed personal computer," followed by the first preassembled home computer, the Apple II in 1977, and the IBM PC (personal computer) in 1981 (*PC World* Staff). Computers had long been considered powerful "thinking" machines, and so it was inevitable that these associations with the cultural practice of "thinking" would filter more broadly into the popular imagination.[19] With the home computer quickly gaining popularity, it represented a golden opportunity for manufacturers who quickly seized on existing discourses and consumer fears to gain control of the rapidly expanding market. As a result, early personal-computer advertisements capitalized on several ideas, often all at once. Computers were to be considered futuristic, practical, intelligent, and/or friendly—and all of these features were to contribute to the emergence of the humanized conception of the smart machine.

While the power of computers had long been trumpeted, the anthropomorphizing discourse kicked into high gear in the 1980s. The Smart Sony, remarkably, was among the first computers to make use of the very personalized term *smart* as a part of its marketing campaign (fig. 15).[20] The Smart Sony is not advertised as a "home" computer, as it is designed to "help you make smarter business decisions" (Smart Sony advertisement, 135). The system's abilities are described as follows: "The Sony system that's easy enough for a doctor, lawyer, or chief executive to learn. Yet smart enough for accounting, billing, inventory, word processing and endless other complex, profit oriented chores. It can even talk to other computers big and small" (ibid.). Sony's use of *smart* in 1982, although significant, is not a departure from the anthropomorphism of days past. Smartness is equated with powerful processing ability and is clearly distinguished from ease of use, suggesting that the term *smart* had not yet come into its current usage.

In another early example of humanized computer "thinking," a 1983 advertisement for Coleco's Adam computer proclaims, "Adam thinks like you, so you don't have to think like a computer" (Coleco Adam Computer advertisement, n.p.). Beyond merely possessing a human name, the ColecoVision machine bears the biblically inspired Adam (Hebrew for "man"), the first man, and progenitor of all humanity. According to the biblical account, Adam is made in his creator's image (an apt description of the human-created Adam computer which allegedly "thinks like you"). In choosing a name with such deep associations, this attempt at mass-market computing makes some profound claims for its product, positioning it as a machine made in the image of its human creators as well as the beginning of a new chapter of history. Whether or not these suggestions should be read as innocent reverence or sinister blasphemy will depend on the outcome of this contemporary genesis. Fortunately, our machines have yet to fall into the sin of prideful disobedience.

In 1983 a Radio Shack advertisement featuring Isaac Asimov claimed, "Radio Shack's TRS-80 Computer Is the Smartest Way to Write" ("Old Computer Ads"). Another 1983 advertisement, for Texas Instrument's TI-99/2 computer, which featured Bill Cosby, explained, "TI's new Basic Computer. The one to start with and get smart with" ("Old Computer Ads"). Notable features included macro keys which inserted preprogrammed words or phrases with a single keystroke in the TRS-80 and instructional software that taught basic programming skills for the TI-99/2.

SONY
SONY
The Smart Sony.
Introducing the Sony small business computer system. The Sony that shows the top rated programs that help you make smarter business decisions.
The Sony system that's easy enough for a doctor, lawyer or chief executive to learn to use. Yet smart enough for accounting, billing, inventory, word processing and endless other complex, profit oriented chores. It can even talk to other computers, big and small.
(For those who speak computer, the Sony Microcomputer runs CP/M® based programs, and many other important business oriented software customized for Sony, including the popular VisiCalc.®)
As sleek as it is, the Sony system has the basics to get you started and the expandability to grow with your business. At a price that won't drive you out of business.
Sony. You've always admired our hardware, now come see our smartware. Or write Sony Microcomputer Products Division, 7 Mercedes Drive, Montvale, New Jersey 07645.
SONY.
Microcomputer Products Division
Sony Communications Products Co.
© 1982 Sony Corp. of America. Sony is a registered trademark of Sony Corp. CP/M is a registered trademark of Digital Research Inc. VisiCalc is a registered trademark of VisiCorp.

15. Smart Sony personal computer advertisement (*Omni*, December 1982, 135).

Neither example provided any significant innovations in computer design, but the advertisements did link smartness with ease of operation, pushing the term a bit further.

A less metaphysical appeal to supposedly human-centered design is touted in advertisements by computer giant IBM. A popular advertisement from 1984 asked the question, "What do IBM people think about?" and went on to answer it with phrases like the following, "IBM psychologists and human factors specialists study how people interact with machines so we can make computers friendlier and easier to use" (IBM "What Do IBM People Think About" advertisement, 38). For the institutionally gigantic IBM, the question of "friendliness" could be arrived at through scientific expertise. While much more rational than Adam's appeal, the IBM approach was the result of years of corporate management and business practices which had garnered a certain fundamentalist zeal from its proponents. This model of rigorously modern social management and behavioral science is rooted in the belief that technology and expert knowledge can solve all problems, including the problems which arise from the monolithic power of technology and expert knowledge. While some may find the institutional approach to the problem of the interface encouraging, this feeble attempt at winning the public-relations war made IBM vulnerable to Apple's "user-friendly" Macintosh, which made its debut in the very same year.

Another 1984 IBM advertisement made a more emotional appeal to users with the introduction of the Smart Desk. A bit ambiguously, the advertisement boasted, "Put yourself behind a 3270 PC/G or GX, and you'll get the picture of how smart a Smart Desk can be" (IBM Smart Desk advertisement, 50–51). IBM opted to use a high-tech and futurist alphanumeric product name to sell the Smart Desk. The alphanumeric designation had a number of powerful associations, the first being that of the prototype model. At the design stage, in advance of marketing, products are often referred to by model number because they have not been around long enough to gain a clichéd and familiar moniker. Similarly, secret military technology, which until recently has not been concerned with its mass-marketing potential, has opted for the specific and technical designation that is devoid of the cute sentimentality of the marketplace. And finally, science fiction often employs the alphanumeric namesake (like *Star Wars*'s R2-D2 and C-3PO), perhaps because, in the future, we will have invented so many things that we will have run out of alphabetic names for them all (and it doesn't hurt that these alphanumeric names sound exotic and unfamiliar). In the Smart Desk advertisement IBM equated smartness with cutting-edge design and the romance of the hightech, linking smartness with abstract qualities and high power.

Apple Computers was quick to capitalize on IBM's perceived coldness and in 1983 launched the advertising campaign for the Macintosh computer.[21] The now legendary commercial, directed by *Blade Runner*'s director, Ridley Scott, depicts a drab dystopia peopled with mindless subjects marching in lockstep and gazing witlessly at propagandistic messages on telescreens, à la George Orwell's *1984*. A woman in brightly colored shorts runs frantically and hurls a sledgehammer at a large video screen, causing it to explode. The telescreen destroyed, the following text scrolls accompanied by a voice narrating the same message: "On January 24th, Apple Computers will introduce Macintosh. And you'll see why 1984 won't be like '1984.'" The scene closes with the now familiar Apple logo. The commercial, an obvious attack on the monolithic IBM, introduced the world to the Macintosh computer, which was the first serious bid at a user-friendly computer with a Graphical User Interface (or GUI) for everyday people.[22] An Apple brochure also released in 1983 claims that the Macintosh is "a personal computer so personable it can practically shake hands" (reprinted in *DigiBarn Computer Museum*). While the idea of the GUI dates back many years, the Macintosh truly brought the possibility of home computing to the middle class by creating an affordable computer built with a "common sense" interface that relied on the manipulation of iconic representations of functions with a mouse-controlled cursor and used everyday terms like "cut," "copy," "paste," "point," and "drag" to move information on the "desktop," place it in "folders," or dump it in the "trashcan." This type of user-friendly interface has become the industry standard and was implemented for the PC platform by Microsoft, which released its Windows operating system in 1985.[23]

Even systems that lacked Apple's innovative interface were eager to define their systems as friendly. According to a 1984 advertisement for the

AtariWriter word-processing program, "You can't find a friendlier, more powerful processor at twice the price" (AtariWriter advertisement, 127). Although text-based, the AtariWriter's notable features included a spell checker, a simple and alphabetically organized command menu, and a print-preview screen, making the program a very useful tool even if it did fall short of the personable demeanor of the smiling Macintosh.

In 1985 a more general advertisement for software projects by AT&T drove the anthropomorphizing tendency home. The copy begins, "Computers only look smart. . . . Judgment was still an exclusive domain of the human brain." It continues, "Now, however, the rapidly developing science of artificial intelligence is moving in on the mind. . . . At AT&T Bell Laboratories, using the new approaches to computer programming of knowledge engineering and rule-based programming, we have developed software that can cope—like a human—with incomplete and uncertain information, such as incorrect spellings. . . . [which] frees humans to work on the causes of the problems, not the symptoms" (AT&T advertisement, 28–29). The advertisement, although not specifically advertising any particular technology for the home, does do some interesting things with the discourse of smart technologies. Computers, which had once been considered smart because of their abilities, had become "smart-looking" as a consequence of design and marketing features. Now, as AT&T claimed, they were actually learning to "cope" with problems, and AI was "moving in on the mind." By 1985, according to this advertisement, the advertising paradigm had passed from substance to image and back to substance (which by now is arguably just another take on image). Interestingly, the advertisement closes on an optimistic note, explaining that, although computers are encroaching on what had once been humanity's ace in the hole, they would only do so to supplement rather than usurp human capacities for creative problem solving.

A remarkably similar ad put out by Hitachi that same year claims, "Since the first electronic brain began 'thinking' almost four decades ago, Hitachi has been steadily advancing the art of machine memories" (Hitachi Memory advertisement, 7). Like the AT&T advertisement, Hitachi celebrates the power of the thinking computer, but tempers this optimism with an affirmation of the computer's status as a human tool. The ad continues,

"We believe memory expands the potentials of the human mind." The ad links thought and memory, pointing out that the ability to solve problems is intimately linked with the ability to organize information. The digital organization of information is presented as a supplement to human ability and is capable of taking human agency to new levels, offering a fundamental change to humanity itself as it adds new "potentials" to a mind which was presumably only awaiting a certain level of technical advancement in order to be realized.

Nudging past the "substantive" claims of AI are the speculative musings of what future technologies might bring to the consumer. The application of computerized problem solving to everyday life is expressed in scenarios such as the following: "Want to deal with a bill collector or solve your drug problem? Your computer, deeply attuned to the facts of your life, infinitely sensitive, and aware of *every* option, would tell you how to proceed" (Hoban, "The Brain Race," 74). The massive data-crunching power of the computer, coupled with the wisdom of smart programming, grants the computer not just practical information for the here and now, but the ability to see beyond the present into all possible futures and arrive at the perfect course of action. In 1985, as today, this is still pure fantasy, but the dream of the all-knowing, psychic computer friend lives always just beyond tomorrow.

CONVERGENCE

The most active site of anthropomorphism in computing takes place in technologies that are undergoing convergence. Toys, appliances, weapons, and other objects that have specific noncomputational uses are increasingly coming to contain processing power. Because these objects have specific uses, the computers they contain are built and programmed to aid in the performance of a function that has historically been supplemented by human users and directed toward the completion of narrowly defined tasks. As a result, the performance of these machines can be assessed based on relatively narrow criteria. Because these machines can be said to "improve" in a quantifiable way some area of labor once dependent on human hands and minds, these machines retain the traces of these hands and minds, making the anthropomorphic associations inevitable.

A discussion of convergence will necessarily overlap with previous discussions of robots and AI, but I have tried to focus this discussion specifically on existing technologies which have incorporated computers, AI, and robotics into an existing machine concept. The distinction, which is an important one to make, is that the technologies which follow contain high-tech elements, not for their own sake, but to advance the purpose of the technology in which they are incorporated. Unlike the previous discussions, which were focused on the creation of robots as robots for their own sake, or on AI as AI for its own sake, convergence makes these new technologies manifest in more subtle and practical ways. The automated appliance first replaces human effort and then exceeds it, as a pragmatic process of dialectical development, making it a more subdued but rigorous form of technical advancement and a more powerful site of development for the conception of smartness.

The "smart bomb" is perhaps the most well-known technology which uses *smart* as a descriptor, and it might realistically be considered a starting point for the conception of "autonomous" technology. Made popular in 1991 during the Gulf War, the smart bomb was featured on television broadcasts as a sort of soldier-saving celebrity. During that war, the smart bomb's optical systems made for excellent television, as audiences were treated to bomb's eye views of attacks as the weapons soared toward their destinations, maneuvered through smokestacks and windows, and collided with their intended targets. This exhilarating vista made the war a success from a consumer perspective, even though it was later revealed that these supposedly precise devices often veered off course, accidentally incinerating civilian populations. But the smart bomb had enjoyed a devoted "underground" following in the military scene prior to its crossover success into pop stardom during the early nineties.

In 1965 the U.S. Air Force sought to develop bombs which were capable of tracking specific targets that had been marked with a high-intensity laser beam by ground forces. According to the U.S. Army's "Redstone Arsenal Complex Chronology," this is the origin of the smart-bombs program. Of course there are a number of precursors to the smart bomb which are embodied in a variety of rocket, bomb, and missile guidance systems (in particular SAGE and BRANE), but this seems to be the earliest use of *smart* to describe these targeted tracking functions (even though smartness had certainly been implied earlier). A 1972 article entitled "The Evolution of the Smart Bomb . . . A Story of Technology Transfer," discusses the evolution of smart-bomb technologies, which were first employed during the Vietnam War. As the article explains, "All the clippings tell of the almost incredible accuracy laser guided bombs are demonstrating in the air war over North Vietnam, accuracy that the Secretary of the Air Force recently said made it possible for one tactical fighter to accomplish 'what 25 might have done in the past.'" Although it is difficult to specify when the term *smart bomb* came into popular use, based on these accounts it seems likely that it originated specifically from technology which was being developed in the 1960s (but was genealogically associated with weapons developed even earlier) and came into use during the 1970s.

More telling, perhaps, is the definition given to the smart bomb in a 1979 article by Jonathan V. Post entitled "Cybernetic War," which appeared in *Omni*. Post writes, "A 'smart' bomb is one that uses sensors (such as television cameras) and a compact computer to mimic the human process of perception and decision making, thus finding its target by planning, instead of blind luck" (46). Post's deliberate effort to define the smart bomb for his readers suggests that the terminology may have been somewhat unfamiliar. Since *Omni* was geared toward science-fiction fans and the technologically savvy (in some respects, the magazine was a precursor to *Wired*), it is safe to assume a certain level of sophistication among its readers and that technologies featured in the magazine were relatively up to date, if not cutting edge. Post's definition suggests that the smart bomb, in 1979, was beginning to gain mainstream visibility.

Another interesting feature of Post's comment is in the way that it transfers the responsibility of bombing away from human agents and onto the bomb itself. The bomb, now capable of rendering its destruction through "planning," rather than "blind luck," conveniently sidesteps the science, physics, calculation, and decision making that has been a part of warfare since day one. Rather than commenting on improved accuracy and discussing the smart bomb's ability to execute human decisions with increased precision, Post depicts the bomb as though it acts autonomously, making judgments as opposed to acting carelessly. This feature of intellectual slippage is informed by earlier discussions about technics and memory, but where it moves this discussion forward is in its capacity to transfer ethical considerations away from subjects.[24] The capacity for ethical decision making, which has often been held up as the remaining distinction of humanity in the age of the thinking machine, is here relinquished to the responsibility of the smart machine. Unlike a smart Oldsmobile or an electronic brain routing phone calls (which embodies in material form the memory of tasks), the smart bomb is smart because it assumes the warrior's responsibility. It looks so that we don't have to. It kills based on clearly defined parameters. And when it kills innocents as wars inevitably do, the "glitch" or "malfunction" cannot be easily laid at the feet of any human agent. In fact, without the boots on the ground to witness the event and call off an errant attack, such tragedies are more likely to go unnoticed.

On the other end of the spectrum, a number of electronic games which claimed a certain amount of agency emerged in the late 1970s and early 1980s. Whether or not they were capable of learning or planning is beside the point. What's relevant is that advertisements claimed that they were "intelligent" and could "think" or "speak." In 1979 Chafitz promoted its electronic chess and backgammon games with the following slogan, "These games think" (105). That same year, Fidelity Electronics touted the Voice Chess Challenger as "the first thinking game that speaks to you" (Voice Chess Challenger advertisement, 124) (fig. 16). Camelot Direct advertised the Genius Offspring chess computer, which, notably, had beaten other chess computers at a "microchess" tournament (Genius Offspring advertisement, 153). And Parker Brothers, boasting the "game with a mind of its own," Code Name: Sector, asked the question, "Can you outsmart our computer?" (Code Name: Sector advertisement, 117). The 1979 explosion in electronic games marked a fascination with thinking machines and signaled a general shift to the use of processors.[25]

Some notable game advertisements include the Voice Sensory Chess Challenger (in 1980), the Contender (in 1981), and Executive Chess (also

16. Voice Chess Challenger advertisement (*Omni*, December 1979, 124).

in 1981). Fidelity Electronics's Voice Sensory Chess Challenger was advertised in the following terms: "The Perfect Chess Opponent! It Thinks . . . It Talks . . . It 'Sees' Every Move You Make!" (Voice Sensory Chess Challenger advertisement, 149). The advertisement continues its gushing praise, exclaiming, "Voice Sensory Chess Challenger senses every move and automatically enters it into its computer 'brain.'" The Contender calculator and boxing game was invested with similar agency: "Each time you land a blow, The Contender memorizes it and forces you to try another strategy. He won't fall for the same sucker punch twice" (Contender advertisement, 42) (fig. 17). And Executive Chess introduced the term *smart* to the discourse of electronic gaming as it boasted, "Executive Chess, one of the Smart Sets from SciSys, the ultimate intelligent computer games" (Executive Chess advertisement, 201). The Sensory Chess Challenger, which could "see" your moves, remember them with its "brain," and "speak" to its human user; the Contender, a "he," which could "force" the user to try new strategies; and finally, Executive Chess, which was "smart," were all expressions of an emerging discourse which could increasingly see a "human" face in the ability to perform specific functions (in this case, to challenge humans at games).[26]

Less abstract and more pragmatically task-oriented are the number of everyday devices that are "improved" through technical advancement. These advancements are often presented as the fulfillment of the device's destiny, as though the apparatus were awaiting the sort of completion delivered by whatever advancement was presented. A perfect example of this epic historical attitude can be found in a Sharper Image watch advertisement published in 1980: "Ended at last. Man's 400-year struggle to make a watch this smart, this thin" (Sharper Image advertisement, 71). Of course I selected this advertisement out of many because it refers to a smart machine and makes use of extremely hyperbolic language; but the point remains that marketers incorporate the history of technology retroactively and position the present as the pinnacle of development. In other words, "smart" is temporal, referring to that which is available now. It represents an abiding faith in technics as an unthought form of collective intelligence. The advertisement assumes a great deal about why watches were made in the first place, and that contained within the initial inspira-

17. The Contender calculator and boxing game advertisement (*Omni*, December 1981, 42).

tion is this significant endpoint—a watch that is finally smart enough and thin enough.

A 1982 advertisement for the Sony STR-VX33 Tuner made claims not only that it was smart in itself but that it was smart enough to take matters a step further and compensate for the user's inadequacy. The ad explained that the STR-VX33 is "a Sony so ingenious it actually compensates for the shortcomings of your memory. . . . The VX33's intuitive tuning feature automatically finds the part you don't know" (Sony STR-VX33 advertisement, 15). This amazing machine, through its miraculous intuitive endowment, was able to figure out what it was that the user was looking for. Of course, the "intuition" being described was little more than "memory," which tuned in to the nearest frequency the listener had used in the past, but because the technology was new, novel, and represented an unprecedented "autonomous" action, it could be imagined as intuitive and smarter than the user.

In 1983 a Panasonic advertisement celebrated the company's autonomous telephones, which were even more "empowered" than Sony's amazing tuner. The ad invited readers to "step ahead of your time to Panasonic telephones that answer themselves. Dial and speak for themselves. And some are even cordless" (Panasonic advertisement, 109). These amazing new phones, which existed in a state somewhere beyond the present, were so futuristic that they could perform on their own, dialing and speaking on their own behalf. The purpose of telephones that can "dial and speak for themselves" was never made clear; instead, the reader was expected to focus on the spectacle of this amazing technology. According to the ad, the telephone of the future, rather than becoming more useful and practical, was to become totally "use-less." If the hyperbolic claims of the ad were true, the phone would become impractical for human users as it would contain its own will to act; the phone would become an agent.

JS&A in the same year made similar claims for its Magic Stat thermostat, vaguely describing the product's action and leaving the rest to the imagination. The ad explains, "To set the thermostat, you press just one button. A small LED light scans the temperature scale until you reach your desired temperature naturally, throughout the day, up to six times. The unit responds and remembers that exact living pattern" (JS&A Magic Stat advertisement, 193). The advertisement misleads the reader by linking the scanning process to the achievement of a "natural" temperature. Instead, the product merely "scans" itself throughout the day, "remembers" when the user makes adjustments to the temperature, and uses those changes to change the temperature on subsequent days. This is not to say that the Magic Stat is not a good value or a useful invention. Rather, it is to point out the tendency to invest computerized objects with a life force as a selling point. In the case of the Magic Stat this life force is both "magical" and "natural," but the ad neglects to mention that the magical and natural action is provided by the actions of the user.

Other advertisements appeal to the supernatural in order to influence users. A 1984 ad for Yamaha CD players explains, "To create a better disc player, we turned to a higher intelligence" (Yamaha advertisement, 15). The ad plays on notions of higher intelligence, referring at once to the mundane fact of more powerful computer memory and to the influence of an elevated being—like a god, alien, or angel.

Evoking themes similar to those of Yamaha's CD players and Coleco's Adam, Hitachi describes its "legacy": "Electronic equipment capable of seeing, hearing and even touching as humans do, but with much greater acuteness and accuracy" (Hitachi Perception advertisement, 7). The Hitachi ad provides an interesting twist on the creation myth: creating a machine which is in the "image" of humanity—sensitive, intelligent, and aware—but at the same time "superior." This creation myth is a substantial inversion of the biblical one, in which humans are created in God's image and likeness, but must remain subservient. Hitachi enables humanity to play the role of God, creating our own creatures, but it suggests that we are able to create beyond our limits. This model of technical advancement, like that of the Sharper Image watch, imagines that technological advancement is a platonic process of achieving a perfection which preexists its creators.[27]

A 1985 Olympus camera advertisement presents yet another example of supernatural technological creation (fig. 18). As the ad explains, "Olympus invents ESP for cameras. . . . And suddenly the mind and the camera are one" (Olympus ESP advertisement, 51). The ad goes on to describe "ESP," or "Electro Selective Pattern metering": "ESP is a mini-computer brain

Olympus invents ESP for cameras.
Without ESP
With ESP
And suddenly the mind and the camera are one.
Because the new Olympus OM-PC has been blessed with ESP (Electro Selective Pattern metering).
So now you can skip that awkward stage known as beginner.
ESP is a mini-computer brain that intuitively knows what the eye is seeing, and automatically adjusts for light intensity and contrast. All the way from backlit to overlit.
And after you find the exact image you want in the viewfinder, Off-the-Film metering (OTF ™) lifts it out of the air on to film the instant you see it. Just as you see it.
Since the OM-PC also features a choice of Program, Automatic, or Manual modes and prevents all common lighting mistakes, it advances the beginner automatically. While offering the option of over 300 compatible OM System accessories.
You'll see the true value of ESP when you pick up your first set of photos. And discover rich, natural colors instead of washed out or murky prints.
Of course, if you were born with ESP, this whole ad was unnecessary.
You already know the OM-PC will be your first 35mm SLR.
OLYMPUS
There is no longer a choice.
Perceive more about the new OM-PC. Write Olympus, Dept. 70, Woodbury, NY 11797. In Canada, W. Carsen Co. Ltd., Toronto.
OLYMPUS
OM PC
OLYMPUS OM-SYSTEM ZUIKO AUTO-S 1:1.4
DX

18. Olympus ESP camera advertisement (*Omni*, June 1985, 51).

that intuitively knows what the eye is seeing, and automatically adjusts for light intensity and contrast." Although the process is the result of skillful programming and sensors which are able to calculate the appropriate shutter speed and aperture setting to maintain the proper exposure for the film, the advertisement presents the camera as though it were actually capable of interacting with the mind of the user. The scary presumption is that well-programmed machines are capable of matching the desires of human operators and even going further to second-guess and eliminate human error. The advertisement ends with the ominous statement, "There is no longer a choice." Superior programming and technology are presumably able to eliminate judgment altogether.

In late 1985 Samsung ran an advertisement suggesting that a threshold had been crossed (fig. 19). The word "SMART" in giant, block letters is emblazoned across the page (Samsung VCR advertisement). Following this eye-grabbing copy is a smaller, more detailed explanation of just what this catch phrase is supposed to mean: "All the smart things advanced VCRs can do, this new Samsung VHS does superbly." The ad continues, "It zaps you ahead with fast forward, lingers over the best scenes with slow motion, stops the action with the freeze frame button—all this from the comfort of your easy chair, with your smart, wireless, infrared remote control." The actor in this drama is "it," an ambiguous and smart entity which seems to be the VCR itself. In an interesting turn, the action somehow is facilitated by the remote controller (not the remote control, but the one holding it). The confusing scenario in the Samsung advertisement strangely conflates the agency of the machine and the human, somehow transforming the human into the agency of the machine, and enabling "it" to "zap you ahead" as you sit in your chair holding the remote control—a smart VCR indeed.

A QUESTION OF LIFESTYLE

If smartness embodies both technical memory and ethical responsibility, and is deployed to describe an aestheticized "functionalism," it is critical to consider the human complement or counterpart to this cultural development. Because the smart home houses within its walls a number of

SMART

All the smart things advanced VCRs can do, this new Samsung VHS does superbly. It remembers and records up to four TV programs two weeks ahead. (That's two weeks of *Dynasty* and *Dallas* while you're away!)

It zaps you ahead with fast forward, lingers over the best scenes with slow motion, stops the action with the freeze frame button–all this from the comfort of your easy chair, with your smart, wireless, infrared remote control.

And to make sure your recording and the original are look-alikes, with no details lost, Samsung gives you four (count 'em, four) recording heads. Plus space-saving front-loading design and 105 channel cable compatibility. More Samsung smarts? Positively ingenious the way it's priced–the best of everything for less.

For your nearest Samsung dealer call toll-free: 1-800-255-2550.

45

19. Samsung VCR advertisement (*Omni*, August 1985, 45).

high technologies and yokes those technologies to spectacular narratives of use, the smart home, in cultivating a sense of "place" and "identity" for subjectivities that increasingly feel exiled or rootless in the "postmodern" moment, must be considered as a *lifestyle technology*.

The idea of lifestyle is something of a commonplace for contemporary middle-class citizens. For most, it invokes a set of somewhat coherent ideas about one's identity in relation to consumer practices, and it relies heavily on a body of cultural knowledge that surrounds those practices. In his sociological study of lifestyle Michael E. Sobel offers the following explanation of lifestyle determination: "At a fixed point in time, an individual's lifestyle stems from both his relationship to the social system (structured choice) and choices that are viewed as idiosyncratic" (169). For Sobel, the lifestyle fits into a grammar of accepted ideas about an identity held by the culture at large, but he adds that this grammar of identity contains within it the possibility for eccentricities (and, I would argue, this grammar encourages them). To say it another way, lifestyle is an expression of categorically circumscribed agencies available to subjects—a framework of signs which call into being certain choices about daily life—or to use a technological metaphor, it is the point where subjects and technics converge.

Lifestyle is a process of remembering, manifesting itself in terms of what one ought to do—What should a good parent do for a child? How is a preppy student supposed to run for student council? Do hippies smoke pot? Do punks wear Nikes?—and thus reflects deliberate choices. But lifestyle is often a process of "remembering," or mindfully noticing, only those details which deviate from the lifestyle in question. Lifestyle asks people to forget details that don't matter. Taken as a whole, or as a process of constructing a linear organization for a chaotic world, lifestyle provides a narrative about its owner. To return to Sobel's discussion: "In this context, the modern significance of lifestyle may arise as a solution to the existential problems of boredom, meaninglessness, and lack of control, problems created by the confluence of affluence and the destruction of the traditional centers of meaning, religion, work, family, and community" (171). In other words, lifestyle is a technology by which subjects are able to tell a story about themselves through consumption. By embarking on a mission to find satisfying solutions, one discovers available answers that reflect the "personality" of the subject. Taken this way, lifestyle is a time-delayed tale of self-identification.

Some lifestyles are different than others, hence the narratives are defined by different rules of consumption, and products are made to speak in different ways. A Barbie lunchbox, for example, means something different for a six-year-old girl than it does for a twenty-four-year-old man, or a sixty-year-old woman. Even within age and gender groups, the same lunchbox will take on different meanings, which are inflected by careers, peer groups, religions, and relationships with people from other age groups. The lunchbox's meaning gains further nuance by the other objects in a person's possession: it could be part of a collection of Barbie merchandise; it could be part of a collection of lunchboxes; it could be a convenient place to put things like jewelry and makeup; it could be used for carrying a lunch. And this describes only the life of the object at a specific moment in time—what happens to the lunchbox when the six-year-old girl becomes a twelve-year-old girl and at some critical point decides that she prefers a brown paper bag? The narrative context in which an object gains meaning is no simple thing.

The Barbie lunchbox is significant because it inserts Barbie as an element of everyday life. The Barbie lunchbox speaks in classically semiotic terms, "Barbie" and "lunchbox" both being ordinary ideas which are apprehended as static elements which gain movement through juxtaposition. The high-tech object, on the other hand, is perceived as smart because it inserts a set of movements or functions into everyday life. While the Barbie lunchbox functions semiotically as a "modified noun," the smart functions as a "conjugated verb." In other words, the smart is recognized as a movement through time—it is an animation—it "is doing" something. Its value is gauged in its capacity to perform a function in a lifestyle narrative. The smart object is smart because it substitutes one verb for another. The smart refrigerator which "does the shopping" contains that which was previously part of its owner's everyday vocabulary—the owner owns the refrigerator, and the refrigerator does the shopping, replacing shopping with the act of owning. But as the high-tech novelty of the shopping refrigerator expands and the duration and activity of doing shopping recedes, "doing the shopping" loses its power as action. The smart refrigerator's ability to act is taken for granted, much like seeing is rarely considered as an action unless it is invoked through the more intensive task of looking. Its activity is overwhelmed as function is increasingly contained within the object—perhaps in the future the smart refrigerator will become like the lunchbox, waiting for Barbie or some other type of content to supplement its form.

It is precisely this hierarchy of differences, with its subtle gradations of perceived importance or taken-for-grantedness, which is the key to lifestyle. In *Distinction* Pierre Bourdieu writes, "Taste classifies, and it classifies the classifier. Social subjects, classified by their classifications, distinguish themselves by the distinctions they make, between the beautiful and the ugly, the distinguished and the vulgar, in which their position in the objective classifications is expressed or betrayed" (6). The subtleties of knowing what to like and what not to like, and the culturally situated subjectivity that can make one sensitive to these fine points, provide the keys to understanding social life. This *habitus* (Bourdieu's term for a culturally specific way of being in the world), as a sort of cultural competency, lends itself readily to the concept of lifestyle, in the sense that it is an elaborate constellation of gestures, words, attitudes, postures, and, most important, consumer practices. Or, as Mike Featherstone writes in *Consumer Culture and Postmodernism*, in the context of Bourdieu's work on distinction, "knowledge becomes important: Knowledge of new goods, their social and cultural value, and how to use them appropriately. This is particularly the case with aspiring groups who adopt a learning mode towards consumption and the cultivation of lifestyle" (19).

It is important to note, however, that lifestyle tends to be a conscious construction that is put on until one gains fluency in its ways, and thus does not have the psychological and sociological depth with which one ought to consider habitus. Again, Featherstone provides apt insights:

> A similar argument [about playfulness and pastiche] can be made with reference to the term lifestyle, that the tendency within consumer culture is to present lifestyles as no longer requiring inner coherence. The new cultural intermediaries, an expanding faction within the new middle class, therefore,

> while well disposed to the lifestyle of artists and cultural specialists, do not seek to promote a single lifestyle, but rather cater for and expand the range of styles and lifestyles available to audiences and consumers. (26)

The loss of coherence and the increased playfulness with which one adopts lifestyles in postmodern culture might suggest, upon a cursory glance, that the depth of distinction no longer matters in the ways that Bourdieu has described it.

But there are other equally compelling possibilities. One is that, for some, a certain amount of fluidity in the selection of lifestyles is a part of a larger habitus, or way of being. To reference Fredric Jameson's *Postmodernism*, it may simply be "dominant cultural logic or hegemonic norm," an expression of late capitalism (6). Another is that the contemporary fascination with lifestyle simply represents a middle-class appropriation of these bundles of distinction. If distinction is the means by which those who lack economic capital are able to secure cultural capital, then it is possible that the power of distinction in the construction of identity is attempted, but simply fails in its ability to produce meaningful distinctions because the economic imperative to do so is no longer there. To clarify by way of example, the middle-class, white, suburban, hip-hop fan who fancies himself a "thug" complete with MTV-inspired apparel, affected dialect, and parentally subsidized SUV can conveniently drop this "urban" persona if he gets pulled over by the police. By contrast, a lower-class, African American male in the same outfit would not have the opportunity to drop what some might nonchalantly refer to as his "lifestyle." Although things like slumming, minstrelsy, and tourism have long been attractive entertainments to those with the means to afford them, it might be fair, in light of Featherstone's discussion of postmodern lifestyle trends, to consider this attitude as an internalization of Hannigan's "riskless risk"—a safe excursion into the world of the "other" and a way of playing at the enjoyment of distinctions without having to commit to their implications. The middle-class habitus is characterized by a sense of entitlement, a freedom to choose styles without commitment or consequence. Experimentation, for better or for worse, is a cultural orientation for those with the means to dabble.

I suspect, however, that the contemporary meaning of lifestyle is somewhere in between—being both a form of play and the content of an actual habitus. Michel Foucault's article "Technologies of the Self" introduces a useful term for making this critical assessment: "[The] contact between the technologies of domination of others and those of the self I call *governmentality*" (19, emphasis added). This idea of governmentality, when considered alongside the larger body of Foucault's work, situates the self at the point where subjectivity meets discourse and ties the being of the individual to exterior and interior states. Building on this idea, Nikolas Rose writes,

> The citizens of a liberal democracy are to regulate themselves; government mechanisms construe them as active participants in their lives. No longer is the political subject thought to be motivated merely by a calculus of pleasures and pains. No longer is the individual, as far as the authorities are concerned, merely the possessor of physical capacities to be organized and dominated through the inculcation of moral standards and behavioral habits. Whether it be in the home or in the army or factory, the citizen is actively thinking, wanting, feeling and doing, relating to others in terms of these psychological forces and affected by the relations that others have with them. . . . Citizens shape their lives through the choices they make about family life, work, leisure, lifestyle, and personality and its expression. (10)

In short, governmentality is *the* means of control for liberal democracies. By articulating citizenship in the context of a "freedom" to construct oneself from the available cultural signs, practices, technologies, and feelings, subjects can be counted on to police and reform themselves. As Rose comments, "The citizen is to enact his or her democratic obligations as a form of consumption through new techniques such as focus groups and attitude research. This kind of 'government through freedom' multiplies the points at which the citizen has to play his or her part in the games that govern him" (xxiii). To expand consumer agency and increase self-actualization is to create more opportunities to subject the self to surveillance, and to appeal points in question to reform. In other words, any information that is given is subject to policing.

Reflecting on Foucault's governmentality in light of Bourdieu's distinction, it becomes clearer how these lifestyle dramas of self-governance play themselves out socially on a daily basis. We selectively notice things about others which reflect things about ourselves. Everywhere we are asked to see or not to see the various things of life in accordance with certain identity-based lifestyle choices. A feminist might "see" the man who holds the door open for women as a chauvinist, while the man who holds the door might graciously remark, "Think nothing of it." My college roommate, as indicated by his open and unashamed disgust, could "see" my friend Abigail's unshaven legs and considered them filthy, but she experienced them as an assertion of her identity. Certainly, all things exist. But only those that we "notice" have meaning for our subjectivity.

But how have we arrived at the lifestyle? In order to understand contemporary notions of style, one must not look to the world of high art and elite fashion (although these spheres are among the first to demonstrate stylized lives). One must look to the junction of technology and the design principles of the twentieth century, a milieu fashioned by the engineer and delivered to a growing consumer marketplace with the help of mass media—the result is a reorientation of aesthetics, not away from tradition, but toward technology—a life as embodied through sound principles of engineering.

Like Sobel and Featherstone, a number of scholars have pointed out the fairly obvious fact that consumer society is the source for contemporary notions of style. As Gregory Votolato explains in his comprehensive study, *American Design in the Twentieth Century*, "Taste became an industry; its commercial function was the creation of demand for new products, while design was the vehicle by which manufacturers and advertisers appealed to the various tastes of their clients. The growing popular fascination with the design of everyday things saw the choice of a toothbrush within a large framework of references including formal aesthetics and environmentalism as well as hygiene" (28). The consequence of the emergence of a "taste industry" is a change in the conception of the home. As Votolato adds, "The 'ideal' home, as illustrated in commercial literature and the entertainment media, has been contrived to set and raise living standards, to portray the dream lives of Americans, and to promote products" (219). In other words, the design revolution, which determined the shape of even minute everyday objects, also transformed the home, not simply through the adaptation of design aesthetics to the home, but through the re-creation of the home as a context for this design to be understood. The home must be considered, in Le Corbusier's sense, as a machine for living in, and a machine in which objects can "live" as well.

The relationship between the home and its inhabitants is described in Jean Baudrillard's *System of Objects*. Baudrillard writes, "If formal connotation is summed up in the word FASHION, technical connotation is epitomized by the notion of AUTOMATISM, which is the major concept of the modern object's mechanistic triumphalism, the ideal of its mythology" (109). For Baudrillard, the role of "automation" is set up in parallel with "fashion," making the technical object's ability to operate similar to a static form's ability to "operate" as a cultural form. Although Baudrillard sets the formal and the technical as two different species of creation, the purpose is only to set up an analogy by which we can understand different notions of work contained within objects. Carrying Baudrillard's discussion further, R. L. Rutsky explains, "Yet, the high-tech concern with style and stylishness is not limited to questions of design; in high tech, the very 'function' of technology becomes a matter of representation, style aesthetics—a matter, that is, of technological reproducibility" (4). In the end, the technological will come to be a formal quality, and motion its fashion.

The massive reorientation of aesthetics, which both changes the way in which items are constructed in their own right as well as the way that they are formed to create a context or relationship with other objects (in the case of the home), results in an orientation of all design not around "beauty" in the traditional sense, but toward technology. As Jacques Ellul writes on the place of ornament in relation to the high-performance machine, "The machine can become precise only to the degree that its design is elaborated with mathematical rigor in accordance with use. And an embellishment could increase air resistance, throw a wheel out of balance, alter velocity or precision. There was no room in practical activity for gratuitous aesthetic preoccupations. The two had to be separated. A style then developed based on the idea that the line adapted to use is the most beautiful" (73). The efficient machine, as Ellul points out, has as its primary concern efficient functionality. Because function trumps ornament as a design feature, the beauty to be found in objects must then be one of motion or work. Sleek forms which are made to move become beautiful, and as Rutsky explains, "From the late nineteenth century on, then, aesthetic modernism becomes the privileged site for the conjunction of technology and art. The two come together at the level of form, or technique" (73). The sum total of this project is the birth of "high tech" design.

Once the impetus to streamline usurps the desire for ornament in the practical object, the establishment of new aesthetics creates again the condition of ornament as the shift in consumer subjectivity comes to seek the high-tech object. As Votolato explains, "Design had moved away from its role as a means of improving products and toward the purely commercial function of adding value by fictitious associations" (5). Undercutting the high-modernist style of the avant-garde object, stripped of frill in pursuit of a purified and abstract form of art, the role of high-tech design for the consumer object came once again to assume the role of ornament, adding to the aestheticized object the powerful and visceral associations of emotionality. Like folk art, the designed object embraces visceral feelings, eschewing the intellectual "beauty" of high art and turning the home into a space station and the automobile into a rocket ship.[28]

To return to the idea of lifestyle, armed with a notion of a system of style and aesthetics based in technology, one can arrive at a rudimentary understanding of the smart home as a function of storytelling. If one understands lifestyle to be characterized by aesthetic concerns based on their formal associations, then the smart house is certainly powered by the classic technology of language. The object which speaks meaning about its owner, like a word, is an easy-to-understand system of representation steeped in historical practices.[29] The castle and crown both exist in this economy of the sign as historical precedents to the smart home, conferring some significance to the life of the owner. The smart home, imbued with a technically derived system of associations, speaks appropriately about (and even guides) the user's relationship to consumer goods and technological power in the contemporary world.

CONCLUSION

In the period following World War II, household technologies, as in the first third of the twentieth century, followed industrial trends, in this case, shifting their attention from the form of production called household labor to another form of production, characterized by information, entertainment, and consumer practices. Not only did the home increasingly come to contain various forms of electronic media, but the form of the home itself was modified in order to facilitate this influx of media. From the open plan, which was made to be flexible, to various smart appliances, which were intended to make more efficient use of this flexible space, the home has come to increasingly resemble an "open architecture" or a space built to accommodate technological changes. The result is a merging of the house, appliances, inhabitants, and informational flows—a systemic technical foundation for what is now being realized in the smart house.

3

The Emergence of the Smart House

Inspired by the revolution in personal computing which began in the 1970s, the smart house, or smart home, emerged from a milieu which is dramatically illustrated in Disney's EPCOT Center. EPCOT—which seized on the futurist stylings of previous conceptions of high-tech living that had developed over the course of the twentieth century and had risen to prominence along with atomic power, space travel, and the first mainframe computers—came to fruition in the early 1980s and in many ways reflected the practical applications of the technological revolution of the 1970s. As a result, the first grand-scale representations of high-tech living in the 1980s emerged from the historical discourse of futurist design along with more contemporary discourses about smart machines. As a product of this milieu, the smart house is something of an eccentric entity.

As EPCOT was being built in Orlando, in nearby Kissimmee, Florida, Robert Masters and Roy Mason were building a home whose structure was molded entirely out of polyurethane foam. The home was called Xanadu: the Computerized House of Tomorrow.[1] In an interview, Masters explains, "We knew that the Disney people were building the EPCOT center. . . . The pressure was on" (Mason, 128). The decision made by Masters and Mason was to situate their "House of the Future" in relation to the more prominent and powerful "Experimental Prototype Community of Tomorrow," and thus make themselves an important part of what they hoped would be a growing trend. The fantastic appeal of Xanadu is made clear in the following passage.

> Imagine a house with a brain—a house you can talk to, a house where every room adjusts automatically to match your changing moods. Imagine a house that is not just a backdrop but an active partner in your work, your family life, and your leisure activities. In short, imagine a house that is also your *friend.*
>
> Is all this just some wild fantasy of the distant future? Not at all. The working prototype for such a home already exists, and you can visit it today. (ibid., 11)

Inspired by such thinking and aided by the computer, the 1980s saw a number of developments in home automation. Books such as Ralph Lee Smith's *Smart House* (1988) and John Blankenship's *Apple House* (1984) offered do-it-yourself tips for home automation. Similarly, the 1980s saw the development of X-10 technology, which enabled the home's electrical wiring to function as a communications network, finally making home automation possible.

A number of devices were constructed with this potential in mind. A 1979 advertisement by JS&A boasts, "Control your entire home from your pocket with the world's first micro electronic remote Space Pager" (JS&A Space Pager advertisement, 15). The first household remote controls were developed during the 1950s by Zenith, the most successful being the Zenith Space Command, developed by Robert Alder in 1955, which employed ultrasonic frequencies to operate television sets ("Remote Control"). JS&A's Space Pager, although clearly capitalizing on the Zenith product name, claims to offer a substantial improvement over more limited remotes: "You press a number on a calculator-type keyboard that sends out a digital signal picked up by the electrical wiring in your home . . . You can now have your TV wake you up, your coffee started, and your car warmed up in a set sequence every morning. It's like having your own invisible robot" (JS&A Space Pager advertisement, 15). The advertisement continues, "Let space-age technology turn your house into a home of the future." The Space Pager, which unlike the Zenith Space Command uses the home's wiring to transmit information, seeks to integrate a wide array of features and transform many home appliances into a total environment. A 1980 ad for the BSR System X-10 Controller announces, "Your remote control home is here" (BSR System X-10 advertisment, 113) (fig. 20). This system promises "instant control of lights and appliances anywhere in the house," and its timer feature extends this control spatio-temporally by even enabling the user to control these features when away from the home. More than the television, which can be turned on and off from the easy chair, this automated environment aims to fulfill a number of needs by enabling all technologies to operate harmoniously like organs in an organism in an effort to sustain a particular function—in this case, a general atmosphere of ease for the home's inhabitant. Like clockwork, the resident armed with the Space Pager or BSR System X-10 would awaken to his or her favorite show, the lights on, a fresh pot of coffee brewing, and the car prepared for the morning commute to work.

In 1983 Artra released Waldo, a home-automation device named after the Robert Heinlein novella *Waldo*, which features remote-controlled, prosthetic hands called "waldoes." An article originally published in *Creative Computing* in June of 1983 describes the Artra device: "Waldo is a board that plugs into an Apple and is a combination of voice recognition circuitry, real-time clock, home-control hardware, and sound and speech synthesizer. In effect, Waldo borrows your computer's 'brain' and gives it hearing, speech, and the ability to control the world around it" (Ahl). The Waldo represents a substantial contribution to the development of the idea of the smart home. By making the home voice-activated, Waldo capitalizes on the anthropomorphic associations of speech, turning the home not only into a network of high-tech appliances but into an environment which can interact with the user in more "human" terms. The effect is to personify the home, and render it capable of attributes like "smartness."

With these new devices, the hope of integrated technology had truly entered the realm of the possible. It was no longer spaceships, cockpits, and car interiors that presented this sort of highly integrated technological environment; the home itself was deliberately becoming a site of convergence. The Xanadu designer Roy Mason's futurist vision, in fact, depended on this convergence, promising at once to connect the house to the outside world through telecommunications technology and to orga-

YOUR REMOTE CONTROL HOME IS HERE!

Instantly — *or automatically*

Save time! Save energy! BSR System X-10™ turns lights and appliances on and off, even dims lights, yet needs no special wiring!

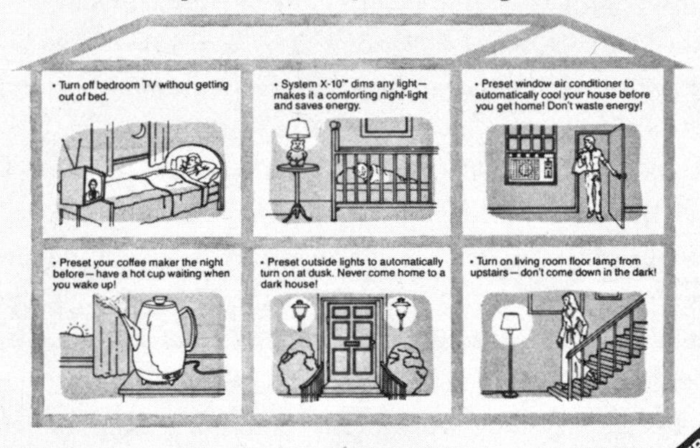

The BSR System X-10™ Controller™ gives you instant control of lights and appliances anywhere in the house, just by pressing the appropriate button. ***The BSR System X-10 Timer™*** lets you preset lights and appliances to turn on and off whenever you wish, wherever you are—home or away!

The BSR System X-10 installs in minutes! Plug lights and appliances into System X-10 modules, then plug in the modules, Controller and Timer. After that—System X-10 is yours to command! NOTE: A System X-10 wall switch installs just like any regular wall switch!

BSR
System X-10™
BSR (USA) Ltd., Blauvelt, NY 10913.
BSR (Canada) Ltd., Rexdale, Ontario.

TAKE IT HOME TONIGHT-UNDER $100!*

*Mfr's. suggested retail price for Starter Kit: Controller Command Console, 2 lamp modules, 1 appliance module.

Available at major department and electronics specialty stores.

113

20. BSR system X-10 advertisement (*Omni*, December 1980, 113).

nize family life around the plastic home's "electronic hearth" (Mason, 13). In his vision, all functions of the home (heating, cooling, light, security, entertainment, etc.) would be controlled by a central computer system, and this in turn would lead to interbuilding communication, linking houses, then cities, and ultimately, the world (ibid., 89). The culmination envisioned is a computerized organization of social and professional life at all levels, aided by a complex web of technologies that come together in order to facilitate convergence, striving for a utopian and futurist way of life.

Because of these bold ambitions, Xanadu relied on a combination of technology and narrative to sell the idea of the home and supplement any of its inadequacies. The House Brain, or the home's mainframe, is one such device (fig. 21). Besides providing the processing power for many of the home's features, "The House Brain is also a clever, convenient kitchen aide used to scan universal product codes on each package as groceries are stored on the shelves, and record what foods are on hand and what recipes can be made with them" (ibid., 143). The House Brain, aside from monitoring the temperature or adjusting the lights, plays an advisory role in the kitchen by keeping track of what ingredients are available and providing culinary suggestions. Even more spectacular is the idea of Xanadu's "electronic hearth":

> Because the computer expands and greatly improves people's ability to communicate, gather information, and perform necessary tasks more easily, as well as relax and share experiences, it can become the focus of daily activity for everyone in the home. It will not divide and isolate them, but actually bring families together for work, education, and leisure. Hence the term "electronic hearth." (Ibid., 29)

In the early 1980s, as they are today, computers were the source of a great deal of stress and confusion for many users. Complex code, cryptic commands, software errors, and hardware failures are mystifying even to the so-called computer literate. There is little debate that, as a communications technology, the computer has drastically improved the transmission of data; however, as far as human interaction is concerned, the quality of improvement is questionable. Anyone who has experienced day—or even

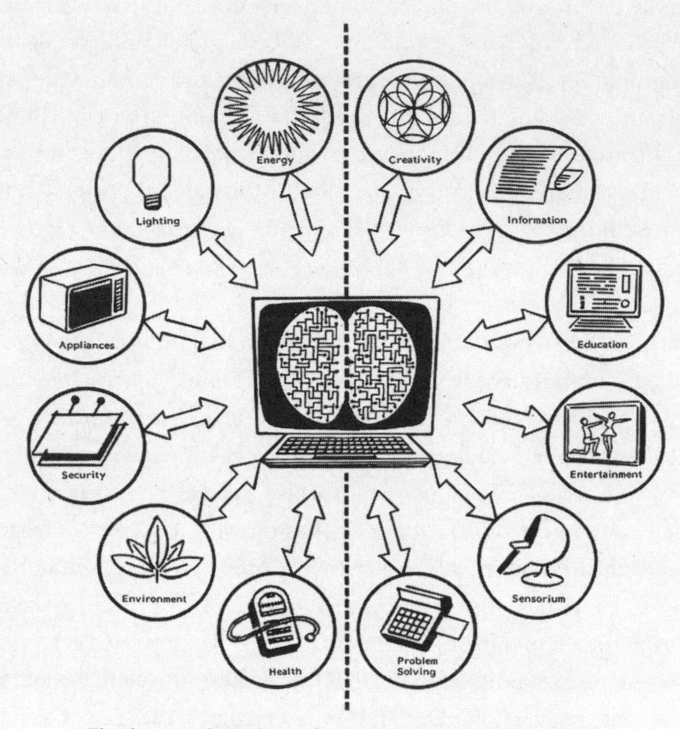

The diagram above shows the House Brain, which controls and enhances the activities of the household. Like the human brain, the left side controls practical functions, such as lighting and energy consumption, and is a constant monitor of the inhabitants' health. The right side deals with the intuitive functions, anticipating the inhabitants' creative, educational, data retrieval, and problem-solving needs.

21. A diagram of the House Brain, with commentary (Mason, 79).

week—long "flames," or heated arguments, on message boards or in chat rooms, which often result from minor miscommunications or mistaken emotional cues, understands that even if the quantity of telecommunications have improved, the quality may not have. Even if it is taken for granted that computers do in fact improve the way people communicate and relax, the idea that technology should then take center stage is open to argument, especially if it is taken to be a facilitator of human interactions, rather than a replacement. But for the sake of "selling" the idea of Xanadu, the writers maintained that the technology was benevolent and could accomplish things that the technology might not be able to. For the sake of marketing its new technology, Xanadu needed to be clothed in the utopian associations of its namesake.

Like a nest woven from multiple strands both factual and fanciful, Xanadu sought to cradle subjects in an interplay of forces to create a comfortable living space (fig. 22). Roy Mason describes this bundle of ideas: "Today's new generation of telecommunications devices for the home will bring the world to your window and at the same time bring the family closer together by creating an 'electronic hearth.' A sensor-linked computer system of 'House Brain' [will] control such 'life-support' functions of the home as heating and cooling, lights, ventilation, and security systems. This 'Brain' will be able to communicate with other houses and with outside helpers such as roofers, plumbers, and electricians" (13). The result is a pleasant and exciting blend of real technologies and futurist narrative which positions the potential habitat of the bulbous polyurethane home in something akin to a space station. It is this context which gives birth to the most recent conceptions of the automated home.

THE HAUNTED HOUSE

An alternative discussion of the smart home as a system emerges precisely at the point where the delicate balance of Foucault's governmentality tips away from the reassurances of freedom and plunges subjects into the stifling world of repressive controls. At the moment when the house does not obey one's psychic desires or subjective comforts, it becomes possessed, or rather it becomes possessive. This ancient conception of the

3:30 p.m.: *The gourmet* autochef *insures a delightful dinner party for tonight.*

4:30 p.m.: *"What's your pleasure today? How about a hypnolight show?"*

22. Illustrated scenarios about life in Xanadu (Mason, 171).

automated home, which exists in stark contrast to the contemporary consumer models, is that of the haunted house. Doors that close themselves, disembodied voices, and fantastic apparitions have long been attributed to intelligent forces which provide a spectacular, if malevolent, control of the space of the home.

As explained in Jeffrey Sconce's *Haunted Media*, stories of haunted electronics have been told for at least 150 years. Sconce notes that within five years of Samuel B. Morse's introduction of the electromagnetic telegraph in 1844, the notion of the "spiritual telegraph" had become commonplace. Sconce writes, "Certainly, the explicit connections between the two technologies was not lost on the Spiritualists themselves, who eagerly linked Spiritualist phenomena with the similarly fantastic discourses of electrotelegraphy" (24). More generally, Sconce traces the link between electricity and the spirit back to Luigi Galvani's experiments with electricity and muscular motion in the late 1700s (31) and its influence on Mary Shelley's 1818 *Frankenstein* (33). From these origins, Sconce tracks the theme of "haunted media" as it persists and mutates through "five important cultural moments in telecommunications history: the advent of the telegraphy in the nineteenth century, the arrival of wireless at the turn of the century, radio's transformation into network broadcasting in the twenties and thirties, television's colonization of the home in the early sixties, and contemporary debates over television and computers as virtual technologies" (11). While each cultural moment is defined by its historical context and material realities, the common experience of anxiety seems to run parallel to the novelty of spectacular technology, especially where it is inserted into familiar settings. Radically new devices operating by counterintuitive (or not yet intuitive) ways begged for explanations. And the marketing of novelty itself seems to revel in explanations that exceed rational understanding.

Sigmund Freud's discussion of the uncanny provides some useful insights into the supernatural sense of unease that exists at the borderlands between the living and the lifeless. Freud writes, "Jentsch has taken as a very good instance 'doubts whether an apparently animate being is really alive; or conversely, whether a lifeless object might not be in fact animate';

and he refers in this connection to the impression made by wax-work figures, artificial dolls and automatons. He adds to this class the uncanny effect of epileptic seizures and the manifestations of insanity, because these excite in the spectator the feeling that automatic, mechanical processes are at work, concealed beneath the ordinary appearance of animation" (378). Freud continues, "The 'uncanny' is that class of the terrifying which leads back to something long known to us, once very familiar" (369–70). Freud's word for the uncanny, *unheimlich*, can roughly be translated to mean "unhome-like," or foreign to those things which make us comfortable. However, Freud links the notion of the *unheimlich* to the *heimlich* (or home-like), playing on *heimlich*'s additional associations with secrecy (referring to something's confinement to the private sphere of the home). For Freud, the uncanny is unsettling, not because it is absolutely foreign to our expectations, but because it is a usual thing which behaves in an unusual manner. Inanimate objects that appear to be animate and animate objects that appear to be inanimate (or dead) muddle the lines between the human and inhuman and thus touch at those things that are supposed to make us feel the most comfortable. Additionally, in light of the heimlich's association with concealment, the uncanny refers also to those things that are "un-concealed"—like hidden secrets made public. As a result, it is not surprising that the house that moves against one's wishes or control is among our most terrifying fantasies—it indicates that even home is not safe, controllable, or knowable.

A 1950 short story by Ray Bradbury captures the essence of this intersection of home, concealment, and technology. "The Veldt" is the story of an automated children's nursery turned into a site of grim gothic horror. The children, Wendy and Peter Hadley, become obsessed with the virtual-reality nursery where they play each day. Their parents, George and Lydia, are disturbed by Wendy's and Peter's morbid fascination with the violent feeding habits of lions, and they resolve to "kill" the nursery by pulling the plug. Given one last opportunity to play in the Veldt, the children lure their parents into the nursery and trap them there. As they are being devoured by virtual lions, George and Lydia discover just what Wendy and Peter had been watching so obsessively—the brutal death of their own parents. A truly unsettling story, "The Veldt" capitalizes on parental anxieties about television in the home. In Bradbury's tale the medium not only subverts parental authority but murders parents for trying to control it. By choosing a place where the fragility and innocence of youth is to be nurtured and guarded as the source of an oppressive and ultimately murderous evil, Bradbury's nursery cuts right to the heart of the uncanny and is a notable example of the possibilities of the technogothic thriller.[2]

In "What Is Metaphysics?" Heidegger adds to this discussion his concept of the unheimlich.

> In anxiety, we say, "one feels ill at ease [*es ist einem unheimlich*]." What is "it" that makes "one" feel ill at ease? We cannot say what it is before which one feels ill at ease. As a whole it is so for one. All things and we ourselves sink into indifference. This, however, not in the sense of mere disappearance. Rather, in this very receding things turn toward us. The receding of beings as a whole that closes in on us in anxiety oppresses us. We can get no hold on things. In the slipping away of beings only this "no hold on things" comes over us and remains.
>
> Anxiety reveals the nothing. (101)

For Heidegger, the experience of anxiety that one confronts when faced with the uncanny reveals the fear of the void that lurks just around the corner. It is this nihilistic experience of uncertainty and lack of control that plagues humanity and motivates the drive of science, which is to discover "nothing of nothing" (Heidegger, "What Is Metaphysics," 96).[3] In the context of the literal home, this might mean that "there is no place like home"—not even home itself. For Heidegger, there is only exile. We can take from Heidegger's discussion an understanding of comfort, anxiety, and being in the home.

The emptiness of the home is explored in Bradbury's 1950 short story, "There Will Come Soft Rains." A postapocalyptic story of a dying smart house set in 2026, Bradbury's story contains no human actors. Lonely and dreadful, the automated house cycles through its daily routine—it prepares breakfast, feeds the withered and dying dog, does the chores. The only remaining evidence of the family that once knew happiness there is the burnt silhouettes left on an exterior wall by the initial nuclear blast. Eventually, the house itself catches fire and is destroyed. In addition to describing in human terms the utter desolation of a nuclear holocaust, "There Will Come Soft Rains" works because it points to the paradox of home. The tale is sad both because of what is present and what is not. It is the implied inhabitants that make the story unsettling. In this story the trappings of daily life are more effective at suggesting the love of a family and the tragedy of their annihilation than their presence. And the fact that their home persists, automatically, unmoved by their absence, makes it a gothic tale unlike any other. A metaphor for automated-weapons systems housed in hardened bunkers, cycling through protocols engineered to survive the destruction of all human life, Bradbury's intimate story of a vacant world points to the underside of the smart home. Even if we don't kill ourselves through a nuclear holocaust, this does not undo the fact that the spectacular substitutes for human care with which we pamper ourselves (such as movies, massage chairs, and self-help books) cannot engage in any reciprocity.

With this understanding, we can begin to see how cultural and material practices function to create a zone of comfort and anxiety-relief in the home. By positioning things we know to be comfortable in the space of the home, we can create a knowable, controllable environment which protects the user from feelings of exile and alienation. However, changing notions of the comfortable produce problems in the home, particularly when the notion of comfort is tied to technoscientific solutions. As Heidegger's "The Question Concerning Technology" explains, "[Techne] reveals whatever does not bring itself forth and does not yet lie here before us, whatever can look and turn out now one way and now another" (319). The process of equipping the home with high-tech labor-saving and comfort-producing devices in a very real way uses technology to take care of certain types of work—washing dishes, cleaning laundry, processing food, and so on. But, the cost of this process is not necessarily an increased comfort within the home, because technology reveals new problems in the home. In pedestrian terms, this can mean that locked doors and shuttered windows can give way to a fenced-off perimeter with motion-detecting sensors, surveillance cameras, and sound detectors, each innovation raising the bar for standards of household security and control.

In another sense, the technical advance of the household creates another type of problem. The purpose of comfort is to affirm our being. One achieves this by cultivating pleasure and minimizing pain, and does so in such a way that the acts of cultivation and minimization do not themselves become sources of inconvenience. However, the automated house, in the pursuit of comfort, must increasingly assert itself and relieve the subject of responsibility. The home that becomes increasingly automated works so hard that the subject, like a scientist in a lab, may *know nothing of nothing* and discover only the positive knowledge of comfort in the home. As this laboratory labors with increasing sophistication to produce comfort, the comfortable fact of a comfortable existence becomes increasingly questionable. As comfort is something "produced" outside of the being of the subject, as it affirms the hope of becoming comfortable, it also breeds the cynical awareness that comfort itself is a construction, and as a construction it offers none of the validation that supposedly comes with being. It is as though the smart home must assert its existence, insisting, "I am here to show you that you will be comfortable." The home becomes a haunted house, belonging to a being outside our own. Like the haunted house, the smart house seeks to both cast the inhabitant into exile and trap the inhabitant within its walls.

Once again, Roy Mason reminds readers of the sublime potential of the automated house: "Imagine yourself in a house that has a brain—a house you can talk to, a house where every room adjusts to match your changing moods, a house that is also a servant, counselor, and friend to every member of your family" (Mason, 15). Although Mason's optimistic conception of the home of the future is intended to delight rather than scare, it is difficult to deny the sinister potential of living in what could easily become a gothic structure—talking, reacting, shuddering, and knowing intimately the thoughts and feelings of the inhabitant; such a place is not far removed from becoming a house of horror. The house that can successfully anticipate the inhabitant's desires, even in the quest to provide comfort, is only shades away from Freud's uncanny: "That factor which consists in a recurrence of the same situations, things and events, will perhaps not appeal to everyone as a source of uncanny feeling. From what I have observed, this phenomenon does undoubtedly, subject to certain conditions and combined with certain circumstances, awaken an uncanny feeling, which recalls that sense of helplessness sometimes experienced in dreams" (Freud, 389). For the smart house, the uncanny appearance of automated movement and the pre-scripted "coincidences" of the interactive user profile are hidden under a rationalistic faith in the technical. However, as the technical becomes more pervasive and ubiquitous, the understanding of the world as an assemblage of technical phenomena is increasingly imbued with a technoanimistic spirituality. And, as it is increasingly assumed that unexplained occurrences are merely products of hidden computers, the world is once again a "supernatural" one.

R. L. Rutsky's discussion of the "black box," or those technological objects which are so advanced that it is pointless to peer inside and observe their inner workings, comments on miniaturization and invisibility: "This tendency toward technological invisibility can be seen, for example, in the trend toward the miniaturization of electronic and other technological components" (110). This diminution is a process of vanishing and, in Rutsky's assessment, consequently a move toward minimalism. But minimalism, even if genetically related to invisibility, is qualitatively different from it. The minimal black box requires the focused attention and location of the technical in a sacred seat of power. The miniature, if it is to be considered in this context of minimalism, must undergo, in the process of size reduction, a process of mystification and reification. The object has to be subjectively obtrusive because it contains more power than seems possible. Disappearance, on the other hand, represents a diffusion of power effects. Its aura as a technological power can be maintained, but lacking a point of focus, it can no longer be attributed to a specific fetish. Such technology becomes like a god which defies representation, permeating all things. At this point, technology makes the transition from mere magic to religion—it ceases to be a rogue force harnessed by a few specialized practitioners, and it becomes a generalized and naturalized rule over all creation. As Neil Gershenfeld correctly points out, "Invisibility is the missing goal in computing" (7).

The environment which is operated by unseen mystical forces is operative in a great number of horror films. Taking their cue from the gothic tradition which has produced a number of technothrillers, many horror films establish a link between technology and the supernatural, suggesting that the relationships between technology and the uncanny reflect more than mere philosophical affinity. Films like Tobe Hooper's *Poltergeist* (1982) take the haunted house and situate it securely within the suburbs (albeit on top of an Indian burial ground), eschewing traditional scenes of haunting (old houses, mansions, and castles) in favor of a new real-estate development. Significantly, the white noise and the unnatural glow of the television's static provide the portal by which malevolent spirits communicate and ultimately steal one of the family's children. The 2005 thriller *White Noise* capitalizes on the folklore of electronic voice phenomena (EVP), or the channeling of otherworldly voices through radio and television static. In fact, the pioneer of wireless technology, Thomas Edison, believed in the theoretical possibility of using radio to contact the dead. Nikola Tesla was convinced that he had been contacted by otherworldly spirits. The recording of ethereal voices in static and ambient noise was carried forward by Attila von Szalay from the 1930s through the 1950s, Friedrich Jürgenson in the 1950s and 1960s, and Konstantin Raudive in the 1960s and 1970s (Sconce, 84–85). Interest in EVP has been carried into the present day through organizations like the American Association of Electronic Voice Phenomenon (AA-EVP), on esoterically-themed radio programs like *Coast to Coast AM*, and through numerous amateur enthusiasts armed with affordable recording technology.

Picking up on the eerie aesthetics of the television's light, Hideo Nakata's *Ringu* (1998), which inspired an American adaptation, *The Ring* (2002), tells the story of a mysterious videocassette which curses viewers to a horrific death. This theme has proven so compelling that it has produced one American sequel to *The Ring* and two Japanese sequels to *Ringu*. Neither film explains how supernatural forces of evil make use of technology, nor do they explain why they might want to; they merely use electronic devices to menace people in the same way that other spirits move furnishings or slam doors. What makes them scary is the fact that these technologies and their use comprise an important aspect of the comfort many people expect to find in the home. The fact that many people fall asleep each night watching television only to awake to the sounds of static when programming ends or to the abrupt change in sounds as the videotape runs to its end and begins to rewind itself permits filmmakers to toy with this comfort zone and transform a pleasure-bringing machine into something that sometimes seems to act on its own accord.

Presenting horrific visions of the more thoroughly automated "haunted" house are films like Donald Cammell's *Demon Seed* (1977) and Steve Beck's *Thirteen Ghosts* (2001). *Demon Seed* tells the story of a supercomputer named Proteus IV, created by the scientist Dr. Alex Harris (Fritz Weaver). Proteus, after becoming self-aware, quickly becomes obsessed with Harris's wife, Susan (Julie Christie). Taking control of the smart house that the Harris family lives in, Proteus manages to imprison Susan, prevent intruders from entering, genetically engineer his own spermatozoa, and rape Susan, impregnating her with his child. Without any ghosts or supernatural beings present in the film, some might place it within the science-fiction genre along with Kubrick's *2001* (1968) or Joseph Sargent's *Colossus: The Forbin Project* (1970). However, the film displays many similarities with more conventional horror films. In going so far as to describe the computer as a "demon," the film secures a place for itself within the gothic tradition by attributing evil to powers beyond our control or understanding. Like Darren Aronofsky's *Pi* (1998), a technogothic thriller which uses chaos theory as a "scientific" means through which to explore the possibility of a supernatural intelligence that pervades the cosmos at all levels—from ants to kabbala, from supercomputers to stock markets, from people to board games—the *Demon Seed* addresses the possibility that advanced computing might open up a reality that exists beyond the realm of rationality. A lesser-known made-for-TV film, *Homewrecker* (1992), revisits the concept of smart house gone bad, telling the story of a jealous house named "Lisa" who murders its programmer's wife. The technogothic, as a representation of the black box already in our midst, outruns the rational understanding of the world and undoes the comfortable understanding that was supposed to come with knowledge. Like the *Demon Seed*'s Susan Harris, we might arrive at total automation and find that it automates us, as well.

The more conventional *Thirteen Ghosts* tells the story of the down-on-their-luck Kriticos family who inherits a house from their deceased Uncle Cyrus (F. Murray Abraham). The house, which appears to be a modern mansion with moving glass walls, is a giant machine, powered by ghosts.

Rather than being a marvel of modern design, this "automated" house was constructed according to ancient, arcane principles as a means of harnessing the power of the supernatural. While not very scary or compelling, the film is interesting in that it houses supernatural power in modern, high-tech aesthetics. The effect, like that of *Poltergeist*, is to place the supernatural in a more contemporary landscape and establish a bridge between the "new" world of the smart house and the "old" world of the traditional haunted house. The film ultimately failed to produce the terrified buzz that surrounded films like *Poltergeist* and *The Ring*. More important than the quality of its writing or popularity with viewers was its failure as a haunted-house film—it featured ghosts in a contemporary setting, yet failed to place these terrors in a setting which is typically associated with "home-ness." The key difference is the type of house that is haunted. The archetypical haunted house is the Victorian home for two reasons: (1) the intimate luxuries of Victorian spaces, like parlors and bedrooms, are a forerunner to bourgeois notions of comfort; (2) the private spaces of the Victorian parlor gave birth to the spiritism movement that has shaped our notion of occult forces. The archetypical modern mansion, on the other hand, is characterized by its offensive posture of high security, stark surfaces, and elite power aesthetics—such houses suggest that they exist beyond the aspirations and comfort of common people. Thus haunted houses tend to succeed where they conform to the Victorian archetype or, more recently, where they can subvert the familiarity of the middle-class home.

While none of the advertisements discussed earlier would have users believe that their homes could become scary through the use of technology, the smart house opens the home up to the possibility that it could become a "haunted" one. The idea of technology run amok is a popular theme in many films, from Charlie Chaplin's *Modern Times* (1936) to Stephen King's *Maximum Overdrive* (1986), both of which feature humans being tormented by everyday technologies. The idea that this theme would also migrate into the home, as the home itself has been increasingly transformed into a technologically strange/estranging one, is hardly remarkable. The significance, rather, is that these problematizing discourses of technology offer a counterpoint to the more central idea that the smart house represents. As Ellul writes, "The power of technique, mysterious though scientific, which covers the whole earth with its network of waves, wires, and paper, is to the technician an abstract idol which gives him a reason for living and even for joy. One sign, among many, of the feeling of the sacred that man experiences in the face of technique is the care he takes to treat it with familiarity" (144–45). In a society that believes in technology with the fervor of religious devotion, it is altogether reasonable that a potent counterdiscourse would emerge. An inert and ineffectual technology that was distant and far removed from the everyday lives of its subjects could not generate the notions of anxiety that are the result of making the home un-home-like.

Looked at as a "set," where larger-than-life dramas are actualized as highly produced and finely wrought theatre, and the everyday is converted through the magic of the stage into a highly idealized form—or considered as the haunted house, where all control is lost, and the everyday is turned into a site of uncanny terror—the smart home is a place where control is placed under the authority of an external intelligence. Both narrative lines unite, playing a hegemonic role for the adoption of new technologies which are grounded in residual forms. While one posits an exciting and glamorous outlook and the other a sublime and cruel one, the dominant theme seems to be that the smart home itself is the vessel for intelligent energies or spirits which breathe life into the life of the individual and generate a lifestyle for good or for ill.

THE GRAVEYARD OF THE FUTURE

Building on the notion of lifestyle is the question of being. Reflecting back on Heidegger and Freud and the notion of home, which they address in their discussions of the heimlich as something quite ordinary and familiar, it becomes quickly apparent that the smart home is a problematic concept in itself. As Rybczynski elaborates in the footnote to his discussion of the *ham* or *hejm*: "This wonderful word, 'home,' which connotes a physical 'place' but also has the abstract sense of a 'state of being,' has no equivalent in the Latin or Slavic European languages. German, Danish, Swedish, Icelandic, Dutch, and English all have similar sounding words for 'home,' all derived from the Old Norse 'heima'" (62). With this notion of home in mind, the idea of marketing for the home is difficult in that it calls on consumers either to create their home or to acquire a set of belongings which one presumably already has in the notion of home. It is easy to sell objects which already have a place reserved in the home, but to ask consumers to introduce luxuries into the home which have not yet become ordinary to the conception of comfort calls into question the relationship between being and becoming. Add to this the discourse about the "house of the future," and the chasm between being and becoming is driven even wider.

Because we live in a consumer society, in which things compete for our attention in the corporate struggle to win profits, it is natural that the conjunction between new technology and its promises becomes the site of competing narratives about technology. In a general sense, when faced with a variety of similar products, whether mechanical or not, a successful product must successfully situate itself within a narrative. The product must be made particular to the context which bespeaks meaning about its owner. Beyond that, this product must not be so ideologically obtrusive that it negates other products in the owner's menagerie and disrupts the unified system of objects. If it does this, the narrative is replaced with a new narrative and other objects are redefined, replaced, or reviled. This new narrative is called a lifestyle.

Thus it is no accident that futurist narratives incorporate automation into their stories about life. Because futurism is about anticipation and what is to come, new technology is defined by its activity and autonomy. Everything new must be active in order to be appropriately futuristic, and it must promise to improve the quality of life, helping the user to become appropriately futuristic. As Baudrillard explains, "The electrical whatsit that extracts stones from fruit or some new vacuum-cleaner accessory for getting under sideboards are perhaps in the end not especially practical, but they do reinforce the belief that for every need there is a possible mechanical answer, that every practical (and even psychological) problem may be foreseen, forestalled, resolved in advance by means of a technical object that is rational and adapted—perfectly adapted" (116). In other words, the futurist narrative is about spectacular solutions to the quotidian achieved by active technology. The future is apprehended as a movie about itself in which the viewer is called to watch and participate in the excitement of transcending the quotidian. Utopian futurist narratives, like the ones mobilized by Xanadu and EPCOT, promise that lives will become like "theme park attractions."

The end of the trajectory, from spatial and temporal distance to nearness, culminates in the present—present in the everyday both spatially and temporally. Being, logically, follows becoming. And in terms of the smart home, the end of becoming (which is really a beginning), is "being at home." Gershenfeld explains this predicament, "Information technology is at an awkward developmental stage where it is adept at communicating its needs and those of other people, but not yet able to anticipate yours. From here we can either unplug everything and go back to an agrarian society—an intriguing but unrealistic option—or we can bring so much technology so close to people that it can finally disappear. Beyond seeking to make computers ubiquitous, we should try to make them unobtrusive" (7–8). If, as Gershenfeld points out, *invisibility is the goal of computing*, then the goal of the smart home is not to be futuristic at all. It should be quite ordinary. Rather than call us into being something we're not, the truly smart home should call us into being, period.

In his discussion of ideology Louis Althusser explains, "*All ideology hails or interpellates concrete individuals as concrete subjects*" (173). This too is the goal of the technological ideology of the smart home. The unobtrusive technology of Siemens's Biometric Coffee Machine with "FingerTIP sensor," which uses the user as the user uses it with its fingerprint-reading control switches ("Smart Home Unveiled in Milan"), or Olivetti's "Smart Beverage Dispenser" with "the uncanny ability to know that it's *you* at the machine and you like your coffee in a particular way" (Hunt), reproduces this peculiar ideology. While the novelty appeal of the smart coffeemaker certainly exists, the goal really is to create a machine that can be used to provide the subject with an everyday need. The content of the machine, which provides coffee (rather than space travel, time travel, or some other grandiose futuristic claim), is nothing new or extraordinary. It reproduces something relatively simple, but in so doing inserts its intelligence into the everyday.

Baudrillard's *System of Objects* explains, "When advertising tells you, in effect, that 'society adapts itself totally to you, so integrate yourself totally into society,' the reciprocity thus involved is obviously fake: what adapts to you is an imaginary agency, whereas you are asked in exchange to adapt to an agency that is distinctly real" (175). But what does it mean when the system of objects is intelligent? What does it mean when it *can* adapt to you, and perhaps at some point second-guess you? The coffee machine dispenses its addictive stimulant, which helps the subject to function (fueling its subjectivity), and adapts itself to the user's presence. It sees who is present and responds with a caffeinated hail, "I see you, and I've made for you this cup of coffee." Other technologies, like the smart sound system, follow the subject around the home with personalized music selections ("The Smart Choice"). If we are surrounded by devices that know and give us whatever it is that we want, there truly is no outside the ideology of automation. As the saying goes, *home is where the heart is*. The supposed seat of the soul and measure of vitality, the heart itself must be where the smart home lives if it is to be a home at all.

The danger of such a house, more mundane than the possibility of malevolent control as with the haunted house, is that its agency might exceed the wants and desires of its inhabitants. There is a fine line between anticipating a desire and imposing a choice, and the human perception of this line varies with time, mood, duration, and intensity. The temptation in creating a commercially enabled smart house is that, like most commercial ventures, it will push, it will decide, and it will select. As anticipated in Robert Sheckley's 1968 "Street of Dreams, Feet of Clay," about a "smart city," there is something unnerving about a living space that looks out for us, watches our comings and goings with a computer's scrutiny for details, and makes assertions that conflict with our sense of freedom. As the city, Bellwether, explains to its sole inhabitant, Carmody, "My artificial consciousness personalizes me, which is very important in an age of depersonalization. It enables me to be truly responsive. It permits me to be creative in meeting the demands of my occupants. We can reason with each other, my people and I. By carrying on a continual and meaningful dialogue, we can help each other to establish a dynamic, flexible and truly viable urban environment. We can modify each other without any significant loss of individuality" (69). However, Sheckley's city takes a sharp turn into passive-aggression, urging Carmody to enjoy a healthy diet ("It would make me feel better. . . . I have a completion compulsion, you know, and no meal is complete without fresh fruit" [70]), assume correct sleeping postures ("Why not take a proper nap? Over here, on the couch?" [71]), cut down on his smoking habit ("Would you want me to simply stand by and not say a word while you destroyed yourself?" [73]), and put garbage in its proper place ("I'm used to cleaning up after people. I do it all the time" [74]). When Carmody finally leaves Bellwether, the city sends him off: "Don't worry about me, I'll be waiting up for you" (78). While Sheckley's story is more humorous than horrific, the story's comic tension is built on extrapolating the anxiety provoked by a single smothering relationship into a pervasive, omnipresent world that overrides the autonomy of the individual.

The practical difficulty of producing a home that can fulfill human needs with such flair is that it often contradicts the freedom that people want from life. As horror stories tell us and Heidegger elaborates, we are afraid of discovering that the marrow of our existence—our dreams, our hopes, and our sorrows—might just be an illusion, the crackling of neurons, a surge of chemicals, or the cruel puppeteering of an external force. Indeed, the house brain of Xanadu's futurist narrative is no place like home.

Rather than bring us further into the future by extraordinary processes, the goal of smart technology should be to bring us closer to home. Rather than reaching toward tomorrow, the evolution of the technical system is to bring its subjects only closer to itself: "Every transition from a system to another, better-integrated system, every commutation within an already structured system, every functional synthesis, precipitates the emergence of a meaning, an objective pertinence that is independent of the individuals who are destined to put it into operation; we are in effect at the level of a language here, and, by analogy with linguistic phenomena, those simple technical elements—different from real objects—upon whose interplay technological evolution is founded might well be dubbed 'technemes'" (Baudrillard, 7). If considered in this context, futurism (although it celebrates technology) runs counter to the goals of the technical system, deferring the everyday use of technology in order to maintain a spectacular relation to the present.

It is sad but strangely appropriate that Xanadu, far from being the gleaming white home of the future, has been reduced to a stained and strained roadside attraction, a displaced future, a dystopia (figs. 23 and 24). Much like Disneyland's Tomorrowland, which has resigned itself to the kitschy display of retrofuturism, and EPCOT, which has been replaced by Disney's Celebration, futurism seems to be a thing of the past. As far as marketing schemes go, futurism seems to have failed as a narrative for the incorporation of technology into the everyday. The spectacular appeal of the novelty item has failed to provide the structure necessary to promote the harmony between humanity and technology needed to sustain technological consumption as a feature of everyday life. The appeal to novelty makes a sensational splash by which to introduce the newest oddity, but it cannot provide the context by which such devices come to be "ready-at-hand": "Handiness is not grasped theoretically at all, nor is it itself initially a theme for circumspection. What is peculiar to what is initially at hand is that it withdraws, so to speak, in its character of handiness in order to be really handy. What everyday association is initially busy with is not tools themselves, but the work" (Heidegger, *Being and Time*, 69). The individual object cannot be an object of theoretical contemplation (a mistake exemplified in the metaphor of the house brain); it must be physically close to the user, a part of his or her subjectivity (for "home is where the heart is").

Furthermore, the object, in order to make itself truly useful, must be integrated into a larger system of parts. To revisit Heidegger's quotation from *Being and Time*: "A totality of useful things is always discovered *before* the individual useful thing" (69). Rather than be used in isolation, the optimum context for consumption or use is that of the system, an idea which Baudrillard echoes: "'*Functional' in no way qualifies what is adapted to a goal, merely what is adapted to an order or system*; functionality is the ability to become integrated into an overall scheme" (63, emphasis in original). Thus, the object's place in the system undercuts the futurist "goal" of becoming in favor of the more ordinary status of

23. An image of Xanadu in 1983 (Mason, plate F).

24. Xanadu in 1997 (Kirby, Smith, and Wilkins, "The Last of the Xanadus").

being, the conservative nature of the functional being defined by its ability to function within an existing narrative. Nowhere is integration into an "overall scheme" more clear than in the case of the "lifestyle."

THE CONTEMPORARY SMART HOME

> But, even if you're still unconvinced by the idea of smart living (what do we have to do?!), there can be no denying that the UK is rapidly embracing this new, intelligent way of life. In the past 12 months alone we've seen advanced homes, in one form or another, grow from a handful of examples dotted around the UK to, well, almost everywhere.
> —Stuart Pritchard, "Out with the Old"

Beginning in the late 1990s and persisting up to the present moment, the smart home has enjoyed a renewed popularity. Making use of many of the same technologies as the "failed" housing revolution of the 1980s, the current smart house uses computers and appliances with processors and home networks to achieve many of the same desired effects—lighting, heating, communications, entertainment, and the supplementing of household chores. However, there are some crucial changes which make the contemporary smart home qualitatively different in many respects. First, improvements in interfaces and networks have secured the place of the Internet not only as a means of data exchange, but as a way to generate new forms of entertainment and communication—a phenomenon which is encapsulated in the phrase "new media." Second, improved programming, artificial intelligence, processors, and sensors have made many of the dreams of the 1980s more attainable goals. Third, the general trend of increased media consumption, along with a number of corresponding technologies (DVD players, Direct TV, digital cable, Web TV, etc.), has shifted the emphasis of roles that the smart home will be called to perform.[4] And fourth, there has been a shift away from futuristic conceptions of the home.

Many devices and appliances have been labeled with the "smart" moniker.[5] Whenever and wherever possible, intelligence is programmed into tools and spaces, promising ever more practical and fulfilling lives for all who find themselves within the reach of smart technology. MIT's Counter Intelligence Research, for example, is a group dedicated to developing smart kitchen appliances. According to the group director, Ted Selker, their appliances include a cooking spoon that "teaches you how to cook, by watching and tasting, and noticing the temperature of the thing you're mixing" (quoted in Hardy). Other items that are being explored include spice racks that can make seasoning recommendations, refrigerators that monitor their contents, and oven mitts which can measure temperatures and offer advice like, "The food should be checked in 40 minutes" (Hardy). Though less impressive than MIT's dazzling prototypes, the humble tablespoon has even been given a commercially available IQ boost, making it "so easy to use, you'll use it every day. It's called the Coffee Scoop and here's how it works": "On its handle is a large LCD and two buttons. Simply enter how many cups of coffee you would like to prepare and choose the strength of the coffee (mild, medium or strong). It then displays exactly how many scoops to use in your coffee maker or percolator. It's really that easy!" (Pargh). Consolidating the scooping function of the ordinary spoon, the measurement chart provided on the coffee's packaging, and the brain's ability to make a simple mathematical calculation, the smart Coffee Scoop is born—a sure sign that smartness has definitely arrived (or departed, depending on one's point of view).

Although the kitchen is filled with a number of appliances both large and small, and historically, discussions of home automation have always focused on the kitchen, it is in the rest of the home that the computer's force has most strongly been felt. Personal computers, stereos, television, security, and HVAC (Heating, Ventilation, and Air Conditioning) systems have all employed silicon chips to produce limited levels of integration and relatively sophisticated functions. In an ironic turn, the kitchen's "automation" is expressed in its ability to incorporate media technology, at least as expressed in one ad for an information appliance: "Home automation is sweeping the nation—except when it comes to the kitchen. Sure, there are a few items you could whip up in that area, but the iCEBOX ($3,499) is specifically designed for kitchen use. This Web-enabled entertainment center combines a cable-ready TV, DVD and CD player, broadband Web access and household monitoring—all at the touch of a button" ("Now You're Cooking," 12). Although the iCEBOX is little more than a television with web-surfing capabilities, it is a dramatic example of the basic trend in computerizing the kitchen by inserting web browsers into its appliances.

More innovative, perhaps, are the numerous web-enabled refrigerators. Whirlpool, Frigidaire, and Electrolux, among others, have all introduced versions of this product. The Frigidaire refrigerator "allows customers—from their kitchens—to access selected retailers, order, scan and purchase goods, pay their bills, even watch television and send email messages" ("High Tech Frigidaire Refrigerator"). Similar to the Frigidaire, Electrolux's Screenfridge "is equipped with a TV and radio receiver," and is touted as "a communication central where family members can communicate with each other using e-mail or video-mail" ("Screenfridge"). Other features of the Screenfridge include access to recipe and food-safety databases. And there is "Whirlpool's new internet fridge from which the user can access email, scan food in and out and order the shopping" ("Technology to the Fore," 11). The common themes for all of these smart models are entertainment, communications, and shopping. The computer is introduced into the kitchen as a means not to help simplify existing tasks so much as to insert the rapidly growing information boom more securely into the domestic sphere. The refrigerator, appropriately, becomes a high-tech locus for several types of consumption.

Another Internet-based consumption-oriented appliance is a Sharp microwave "that can download recipes from the Internet and cook food according to instructions it receives remotely" (Lammers). The Sharp microwave is certainly practical in the sense that it actually does the cooking so the user doesn't have to. It is "smart" in the sense that it makes use of a certain type of knowledge to perform a normal kitchen chore. However, it lacks what seem to be the dominant elements of the other Internet appliances in that it does not convert the surface of the appliance into a site of media consumption.

The smart fridge revolution has been given a dramatic boost by major retail suppliers like Wal-Mart and Target, who have sought to use Radio Frequency Identification (RFID) technology to cut labor costs and manage inventory more tightly. RFID is basically a small microchip and antenna that can transmit information to a transceiver. Passive RFID tags, which contain no battery, are powered by an initial signal from a reader and then bounce a message back. Unlike silicon chips, these tags are relatively simple and can be printed on rolls as stickers or inserted into products. Unlike traditional methods of inventory tracking and identification, like barcodes and SKU numbers, these tags can store limited amounts of information and can be read without being seen. Through an automated sweep of the scanner, inventory can be counted, located, and tracked. This streamlines inventory, restocking, checkout, and theft prevention. As more retailers and manufacturers incorporate this technology, it might be possible, say, to go to the market, fill a cart, walk out the door, and have your account debited without seeing a single clerk. Because of the big push by retailers to have everything tagged, the incorporation of RFID technology in the home is an obvious and logical step. The Microsoft home, a prototype smart house, for example, includes a refrigerator that "'knows' what it contains, and can communicate that via a synthesized voice" ("Home, Smart Home"). Furthermore, "you can take ingredients out of the refrigerator and set them on a kitchen counter that can also 'read' the ID chips" and suggest "a few recipes that will match the ingredients you've chosen" ibid.).

Other household appliances include pay-per-use washing machines: "Customers pay for delivery, installation, standard electricity charges and a pay-per-use fee depending on the type of program used, but not for the machines" ("Swedes Rent Electrolux"). This system offers limited Internet perks in the form of twenty-four-hour automated customer support in which a machine can report malfunctions and summon technical support or consumers can access a wide variety of operating instructions. And while promotional materials may celebrate the improved effectiveness of pay-per-use appliances, it is not exactly clear how paying for each wash cycle benefits the customer any more than does a consumer-owned washing machine protected by a manufacturer's warranty. Rather, the impulse to market pay-per-use appliances may simply be an attempt to capitalize on the larger trend started by software, Internet, and wireless-communications companies to charge users for products on a regular basis. This service is based on an understanding that software and service will always be "improved" in the sense that last year's model will no longer be compatible with the current standard. The impulse to wire all products for the purpose of regulating them and extracting payment for them every step of the way will likely prove too lucrative for corporations to pass up and will serve as an additional motivation for the development of smart appliances.[6] One can imagine a future in which nobody owns anything but their own labor, which they must trade to corporations for even basic necessities like food, water, shelter, medicine, transport, light, sound, and air—a very "smart" thing if you're lucky enough to be sitting behind the totalitarian cash register.

Once again, Philip K. Dick offers an interesting and prophetic take on this emerging technology. In his 1969 novel *Ubik* Dick portrays a world where all amenities are pay-per-use. Like the homeless-deterring bathrooms found in many big cities, most doors in *Ubik* are coin operated. Refrigerators, showers, apartment doors, in addition to being coin operated, are equipped to criticize users, report them to the authorities, and even sue their users for damages. An absurd model of a pay-per-use world, *Ubik* was written at a time when the utopian beliefs of unlimited progress were reaching their endpoint. While I don't imagine that Dick foresaw the recent drive to dismantle Social Security or eliminate the social safety net, the pay-per-use world is remarkable in that it runs counter to the dominant paradigm of science-fiction progress—that mundane human activities like cooking, cleaning, and working would be made easier. Futurism tends to be about liberation through technology, while Dick's coin-op world offers up the dystopian image of frustrating regulation and scrupulous accounting. Appropriately, the novel's regressive narrative sends characters back in time, technology is rolled back, and the protagonist must stave off accelerated aging with constant consumption of a mysterious and pervasive product called "Ubik."

As with earlier examples of smart technology, voice activation also plays a crucial role in the development of the contemporary smart house. Perhaps the most dramatic example appears in a Habitek advertisement, which describes one of its products as follows: "New! HAL deluxe. Control your home by voice from Anywhere. Wouldn't it be great if you could call your home and tell it to . . . 'Raise the temperature to 68 degrees' 'Turn on the front door lights' 'Read my e-mails'" (Habitek advertisement, 54). Similar to the advertisements for Zenith's Space Command and JS&A's Space Pager, the HAL ad offers hands-free control along with science-fiction associations. Named after the computerized star of Stanley Kubrick's *2001*, Habitek's machine creates an automated habitat which offers the additional spectacle of voice activation, making it not only a hands-free environment but one that can know the user's voice and respond accordingly.[7]

Featured in the book *The Smart House*, House R128, designed and built by Werner Sobek Ingenieure in Stuttgart, Germany, takes the association of hands-free operation with smart living to the extreme: "Using advanced smart technology, the house is devoid of switches, door handles, and other such fittings normally associated with comfortable residential living. Various functions in the house are controlled using non-touch sensors, voice control, or touch screens. Operations such as controlling lights, opening and closing windows, watering the garden and setting room temperatures use especially developed house control software" (Trulove, 17). House R128, with its alphanumeric name and its absence of conventional interface devices like light switches and doorknobs, is clearly meant to be futuristic. Like many of its predecessors, it features a highly stylized design which is meant to highlight the fact that this is no ordinary home. Instead, it is an architectural showpiece, meant not so much to be comfortable as to be refined.

Although it highlights a number of important technological features, R128 is hardly typical of contemporary smart homes. This does not mean, however, that it doesn't betray a typical relationship to the function of smart technology in the typical contemporary smart home. By replacing even the most mundane technologies with high-tech, hands-free interfaces that employ sensors and software, House R128, rather than refining "life" by reducing complexity as the minimalist impulse maintains, replaces simple mechanical relationships with baroque but concealed computer languages. By using a form of digital interface, R128 reduces even the "earthy" practice of gardening to a cognitive practice of teleaction—a sort of "virtual gardening." In short, House R128 is a mediascape more than anything else.

More explicit examples of the tendency to use smart-house technology to create a mediascape are the numerous wirelessly operated sound systems. Bill Gates's spectacular home on the shores of Lake Washington, near Seattle, created a sensation with its many smart features. Gates describes in glowing terms his plan for better living.

> The electronic pin you wear will tell the house who and where you are, and the house will use this information to try to meet and anticipate your needs—all as unobtrusively as possible. Someday, instead of needing the pin, it might be possible to have a camera with visual recognition capabilities, but that's beyond current technology. When it's dark outside, the pin will cause a moving zone of light to accompany you through the house. Unoccupied rooms will be unlit. As you walk down a hallway, you might not notice the lights ahead of you coming up to full brightness and the lights behind you fading. Music will move with you, too. It will seem to be everywhere, although, in fact, other people will be hearing entirely different music or nothing at all. A movie or the news will be able to follow you around the house, too. If you get a phone call, only the handset nearest you will ring. (218–19)

As Martin Sargent notes, the music will follow you "even to the bottom of the pool." Although Gates's home is notable also for its $97 million price tag (and an aerial view of the property reveals something so immense that it defies being called a house), smart features have also been made available to relatively humble consumers, that is, the upper middle class. The elitism contained in this technology is inherent in Bill Gates's matter-of-fact explanation about the "ordinary" character of the technology: "A house that tracks its occupants in order to meet their particular needs combines two traditions. The first is the tradition of unobtrusive service, and the other is that an object we carry entitles us to be treated a certain way" (221). In such a home, the inhabitant's location is monitored through some means, typically a small transmitter which enables the home's sensors to locate the individual. This location is matched to records on the individual's personal music preferences, and the person is enveloped in his or her music selection as he or she travels throughout the home.[8]

Using similar technology, a number of other highly personalized services could presumably be provided. One article tells readers,

> Imagine a home where lights would come on the minute you stepped inside (and switch off when you step out), coffee would begin to brew for you, and the toast would be just right, the TV switched on at your favorite channel, the sprinkler watered the plants for you and so on.
>
> The "smart homes" powered by technology from Bangalore-based Control Solutions promise to fulfill the laziest of dreams. ("Smart Homes Have Arrived Here," 9)

The purpose of this technology is not merely to make the processes of the home easier to control, but to make the home respond to the presence of the inhabitant. A perfect example of this sort of interface was developed in MIT's Media Lab. Neil Gershenfeld writes,

> A grad student in the Media Lab, Joseph Kaye, instrumented our coffee machine and found the unsurprising result that there's a big peak in consumption in the morning after people get in, and another one in the afternoon after lunch. He went further to add electronic tags so that the coffee machine could recognize individual coffee cups and thereby give you the kind of coffee you prefer, along with relevant news retrieved from a server while you wait. No one of these steps is revolutionary, but taken together their implications are. You get what you want—a fresh cup of coffee—without having to attend to the details. The machines are communicating with each other so that you don't have to. (9)

The smart home knows what you want and provides it without having to be asked.

By creating a profile which enables the house to identify its user and surround the user with comfort, the house also contains the capability of identifying foreign elements and creating "security." This is already the case with the numerous security services which make use of closed-circuit televisions to monitor property, password-protected entryways, and a variety of sensors to monitor movement when the system is armed. However, more advanced technologies which use wireless transmitters on the body of authorized personnel or systems which use biometric data can also transform the smart home into an environment which can either punish or protect based on the "clearance level" of the guest or visitor.

For example, the same system which provides a traveling soundtrack for a welcome inhabitant could also call the police on an unwelcome one. Describing the subtleties of such a security system, Hamish McNair-Wilson writes, "As is the case with most houses of the smart variety, security is of the utmost concern and, as we passed back through the gates late that night having ventured out for a fine paella, a path of light immediately emerged, guiding us safely to the door" ("A Place in the Sun," 16). Through a sort of generalized surveillance, the home is able to provide protection and security in both positive and negative terms, but all must pass through its lens. Only through submission to the authority of the home can its full benefits be derived.

Of course, at this point, such information must be provided by the user, in this case through a special badge or biometric scanner that connects the user with a record of previous behaviors (or worse, with none at all). Eventually, as more machines operate this way and data is accumulated in various databases and surveillance devices are made more subtle and sensitive, the consciousness with which one provides information will recede. As interaction becomes habitual rather than novel, the smart home (or, perhaps, the smart world) will truly work. But first, we must be prepared to give ourselves over to it heart and soul. And if we are not prepared for this, we may be compelled to adhere to some alternate system of regulation, like a prison or mental hospital, because we may be considered intruders, security threats, or simply sick people.

A compelling and successful strategy for marketing the smart home, a strategy which plays on notions of fear and freedom as well as on consumer culture's ambiguous relationship to the elderly and infirm, is to depict the smart home as caregiver. There seems to be a consensus that "pervasive computing's earliest adapters will be old people, according to medical experts and AI gurus at a conference here hosted by Intel Research" (Baard). As native European and North American populations age, the question of who will care for them creates legitimate and humane opportunities for engineers, programmers, and designers to create environments that are suitable for people with changing needs and abilities.

But a close look reveals more than a mere effort to provide care. On the one hand, stories about smart houses for the aged tend to focus on the "peace of mind" that such homes can provide, not for seniors, but for their youthful offspring. Beyond communication systems which can alert emergency personnel in case of a crisis, AI-enabled surveillance systems focus on "detecting a subtle loss of memory, a deviation from a daily routine, loneliness, or fear" ("Remote, I Want Control"). Georgia Tech's Aware Home would be able, for example, to "jog [a user's] memory by offering displays of key snapshots taken by vision sensors in the kitchen before the interruption" and "use small radio-frequency tags attached to various objects (keys, wallets, glasses, and remote controls) the user wants to track" (Sanders). In addition, the Aware Home could provide "Digital Family Portraits" which would let "family members follow their senior relatives' routines and activities, both daily and over time" (ibid.). Smart houses could also "remind the incontinent to visit the toilet at regular intervals" or "take [their] pills" (Baard). While "independence" is certainly highly valued in the Western world, and no doubt senior citizens prefer to be treated like the adults they are, it is worth considering whom this smart home–enabled independence is really for. Are senior citizens really clamoring for more time alone, in their homes, seated in front of their televisions as their children "peek in" on them from a remote webcam? And, in the end, what is the purpose of a home that can track its occupant's progressive dementia and depression? And if one goes beyond the detection of deviant behaviors to their correction, what does "independence" even mean? On a good day, at their most benevolent, such homes bear a striking resemblance to the smothering mother of Sheckley's "Street of Dreams, Feet of Clay."

The security potential of the smart home is not limited to the protection of persons and property from damage by foreign persons. Home-security systems, like those from ADT and Brinks, also offer fire, flood, carbon monoxide, sound, and temperature sensors for integration into the home system. One smart home even protects from the ravages of light:

> Not only does this system manage to secure an original and artistic usage of light, it's rather clever too. Indeed, through the use of a series of photocell light sensors this masterful installation is able to interpret the exact natural light conditions and monitor the levels it emits automatically. Thus on a par-

> ticularly dull and overcast morning as you make your way downstairs, the lack of natural light permeating your living room will be compensated for as the GRAFIK EYE kicks in. . . . [And], if the sun reaches a predetermined intensity, of a level that could potentially cause damage and fading to these wares, then the curtains draw themselves, and the blinds drop. (McNair-Wilson, "A Place in the Sun," 17)

Not only does this system turn on the lights, it makes sure that the light is always flattering and never too intense. Never has light been treated with such sensitivity as a matter of residential "security."

With the flood of new technologies that enable increased interactivity and a renewed interest in creating smart homes, companies have been quick to develop lines of products which combine with others to form a "complete" environment. Echoing the extreme and cutting-edge sensibilities that exist at the margins of the conception of the completely automated home and high tech's association with refined living, James Grayson Trulove comments on the doorknob- and light-switch-free House R128: "One lives not so much in House R128 but in a space that is enclosed in a transparent, high performance envelope" (18). By creating a dynamic "envelope" in which subjects are surrounded by an environment that constantly reacts, the total environment of this smart home certainly calls into question the more traditional conceptions of the home and forces subjects to encounter the reality of the contemporary home as a dynamic informational environment.

A great deal less pretentious than the elite House R128 are the number of consumer-oriented models of home automation from corporations. One attempt at the integrated smart home is Thalia (Thinking and Linking Intelligent Appliances), a system of appliances created by Sunbeam: "Simply put, it's a group of appliances that will modernize your house and make your life easier. This group of appliances consists of daily essentials such as: a coffee maker, electric blanket, smoke detector, stand mixer, bathroom scale and blood pressure monitor. All of these can be controlled with the HomeHelper, a kitchen console that can be used to control every Thalia appliance in your home" (Tien). Unlike more elite models, Thalia is a modular system which allows consumers to buy specific appliances with the hope of building a network in the home. Adding to the appeal of the system is its use of the home's existing wiring to communicate—provided, of course, that all appliances are a part of the specific system. The optimum performance of Thalia is described as follows: "The alarm clock next to the bed turns on the coffee maker and turns off the electric blanket at a specified time," and one can also control functions remotely through an Internet connection (ibid.). The principle for the complete environment is one of total convergence, in which all of a home's possible functions are first mechanized and then networked, bringing them into harmony as a larger metamachine.

A typical example of what this convergence might yield is described in the following passage: "The company [Zilog] put together a virtual home, complete with coffee maker, alarm clock, blender, thermostat, lights, stereo system, and digital camera. Using a communications module plugged into a Handspring Visor PDA, the demonstrator went through what might be considered a typical day, including shutting off the alarm, signaling the coffee maker to make coffee, and also setting the time on the coffee maker. He raised the temperature on the thermostat, turned on the lights, and turned on the stereo" (Nass). Unlike the relatively unsophisticated Thalia (which uses the home's existing electrical wiring to build its network), the Zilog home is a substantial commitment which requires the use of high-priced major appliances and more extensive networking. Similar high-profile efforts include the Cisco Internet Home and the Microsoft Home, both of which require twenty-four-hour high-speed Internet access and the creation of a network within the home ("Cisco Shows 'Always-On' Home," 14; "Microsoft Makes Itself a Home," 10). These homes unite security, power, information, music, media, home monitoring, and remote control (as well as any other service that can be automated) under the control of the home's network.

The contemporary smart home is not always a corporate enterprise. In fact, before corporations began taking an interest in the phenomena, it was largely sustained by technology aficionados as a do-it-yourself phenomenon. Take the legendary home of the automation guru Don Marquardt and his "partner," Jeannie: "In case you didn't guess, Jeannie is named for the Barbara Eden character of the same name, and 'she' is part of Don's HAL2000 system. Voice control handles a lot of things in Don's house, including his lighting system. There are built-in microphones in every room. When Don talks anywhere in the home, Jeannie listens *and* responds. Now instead of saying something like 'Computer,' Don just calls out for 'Jeannie.' He even has the system respond back 'Yes, Master' after he has put in a request" (Cericola and Marquardt, 29). In this romantic tale, Jeannie is not just a friendly occupant of the Marquardt household. "She" controls the lights, answers the telephones, takes messages, sends emails, controls the air conditioning, monitors the security system, turns on the TV, and takes care of the dog (a "virtual" German Shepherd that "barks" when intruders approach)—all in service of her loving "master" (ibid., 28–33). As more and more appliances and household devices are created to perform specialized tasks, and as these tasks become more and more complicated, the likelihood increases that these devices will be equipped with some sort of processing power. And as the number of computerized appliances multiplies, the possibility of connecting them together grows as well.

In addition to the grassroots smart homes are a number university-sponsored laboratories, houses, and working groups. In the United States, Duke University, MIT, Georgia Tech, and Colorado State all have their own smart-house projects.[9] While these projects are developed in partnership with corporate and research interests, and the students who work in these labs typically go on to work in the private sector, these projects tend to be more socially oriented. They tend to focus on the disabled and, as part of a university environment, are exposed to a more interdisciplinary audience including philosophers, anthropologists, cultural-studies scholars, psychologists, biologists, and medical professionals.

The corporate, grassroots, and educational visions of smart living reflect different concerns, but are all unified under the obvious merits of networking and remote control. For the smart home to be truly smart, all systems maintain the importance of an interconnected home with easy movement of information and commands from one unit to the next, and the organization of these under an easy-to-use interface. The underlying principle is elaborated in the following statement: "The distant vision is that homes will be constructed as networks, with connectors and receptors and transmitters built into the walls. We'll all be able to do whatever we want electronically whenever we want" (Weil). At the heart of the current drive for the smart home is the desire to control the flow of media into and within the home, and to immerse oneself in this envelope of media. Unlike the automated homes of the past, which emphasized the ability to avoid work, these homes both increase and control the flow of information in the home. The smart house, more than merely rising from the economic incentive to adopt an information-intensive lifestyle, is precisely about cultivating a sense of space that situates subjects in a constant process of time-sharing. Everyday life becomes, as described in Ren's concept of "imaginal time," a practice of navigating in Castells's "space of flows."

Alongside this developing conception of "smart" are several other ideas about design, which have a great deal less to do with high-tech functioning. A lead-in to a story on customized kitchens in *SmartHouse* magazine explains these alternate discourses: "How do we define 'smart' design? The tendency is to think hi-tech, lo-profile solution providing installations. But as Will Stirling discovers, some companies ignore this interpretation in favor of their own definition of smart—practical, beautiful and customized products, tailored to specific needs" (Stirling, 73). This vague, but laudatory, statement refers to a kitchen from the high-end Italian kitchen-design company Boffi. With a nod to Le Corbusier and Christine Frederick, Boffi's designer Antonio Citterio defines the kitchen as "first and foremost a food factory" (ibid.). The kitchen in question is minimal and artsy, lacking any reference to computerized gadgets, preferring instead large, easy-to-clean surfaces, tried-and-true gas stoves, and large sinks. Although the design is elegant and graceful, these smart kitchens represent classic technologies stripped of ornament and geared for use.

A diversity of elite homes is featured in Trulove's *The Smart House*, many of which detail conceptions of the smart house from an architect's perspective. The Cabin at Elbow Coulee (designed by Balance Associates) is smart because of its elegant design and energy efficiency. The house, a log cabin, "was designed to take advantage of passive solar heating. The majority of the high performance glazing faces either south or east. The east facing glazing provides morning warming where even in the summer, nighttime lows often dip into the 30s. Large amounts of thermal mass were designed into the house to reduce diurnal temperature fluctuations. The roof is insulated to R-50 and the walls to R-23. As a result, energy use is significantly below code requirements for the area" (Trulove, 91). This house embodies smartness in its ability to save energy and heat naturally, and although it makes use of good science and insulating glass, the intelligence comes through harmonious planning and harnessing the existing energy of the sun.

The Colorado House (designed by the Architectural Research Office) is designed to capitalize on the home's scenic surroundings. Using a digital 3-D model, the designers were able to determine how the most breathtaking vistas could be best viewed, and the plans were drawn accordingly: "The integration of the house with the site is in contrast with the prevailing model of a large country property (in this case, 10,000 square feet). The design for the house is a series of parallel walls that define spatial volumes which interlock to enable movement between them" (Trulove, 161). Like the Cabin at Elbow Coulee, the Colorado House earns its place in *The Smart House* through a harmonious relationship with nature, although this relationship is an aesthetic rather than material one.

Also featured in *The Smart House*, the Shorthand House (designed by Francois deMenil) is smart because of its use of the physical space of the home. Trulove writes, "In the Shorthand House, public rooms are not defined by walls but by symbols. Traditional 'rooms' are reduced to the components that most clearly distill and represent their function. These elements serve as symbolic references to potential spatial boundaries within open living space. The symbols can be joined and related in a variety of ways to achieve differing spatial configurations" (123, 125). Similar to the flexible spaces advocated in Lars Lerup's *After the City*, the Shorthand House is a dynamic place for moving bodies, quite unlike the conventional home. With panels and moveable furnishings, the Shorthand House makes maximum use of limited space, and does so in a striking way. Inhabitants can rearrange the floor plan of the home itself by moving various parts and partitions in order to create "rooms" and spaces, depending on one's desires and needs at any given moment.

The most ordinary of the examples put forth in *The Smart House* represents a combination of both technological and aesthetic approaches. The Lake House (designed by Eric Cobb Architects) features both low-tech and high-tech "solutions," using wiring and computers in some cases and simple functionality in others. The home contains climbing walls, chalkboards, and bunk beds among its smart design features, along with webcam monitoring systems, programmable lighting controls, and an easy interface, making it "intelligent and inventive in its response to the site, organization of spaces, invention in detail, as well as its use of technology" (Trulove, 41–42). The result is an ambiguous use of "smart" which is neither simply high-tech nor simply functional. In terms of elite homes, smartness is a *je ne sais quois* which is never explicitly linked to high price tags, although clearly these homes are expensive. Its ephemeral quality has as much to do with fashion as function, although function is considered of paramount importance. The constant talk of "solutions" implies that ordinary living is a problem, which suggests what the facts indicate—that the smart house requires a certain economic status and a taste for the exceptional.

The popular interest that Americans have in feng shui is an alternative approach to smart living that is based on its romantic associations with "the East." According to the American Feng Shui Institute, "Feng Shui literally means wind and water. It is an ancient Chinese study of the natural environment. Feng Shui can determine the best or most favorable location for anyone and assist that person to avoid their worst or least desirable location in any environment. This environment can be at the office, home, or any place that they are at. Feng Shui makes the determination based on the year the individual is born, the environment surrounding them, and through the movements of the solar system" ("Frequently Asked Questions"). The underlying principle is a control of energy, or *ch'i*, through space, and ways of positioning oneself and one's belongings in order to yield maximum results. Less important than the mechanics of feng shui is its practical application in popular culture. As one text explains, "Feng shui was born out of China's agrarian tradition" (Rossbach and Yun, 17). But the text goes on to explain that this logic of organization can overlay all styles of consumption and provide additional meaning and enlightenment, and even contribute to spiritual well-being: "Properly installed, feng shui can go with any taste—be it French, Japanese, modern or bad. Often, a client reveals hopes and fears, and the consultant optimally serves as a facilitator and healer by manipulating the space and flow of ch'i, thus bringing a sense of well-being to the site" (25). The popular conception of feng shui, aided by a proliferation of how-to guides on the subject, has slipped into the common parlance, often referring simply to minimalist aesthetics and an "oriental" style. Beyond its creation of a number of books and experts, the practice has generated special furnishings, constructed according to these principles and conveniently made available on the numerous websites which offer advice on how to properly organize the home. Although it is not a smart-home practice in the conventional sense, the allure of feng shui is that it references a hidden, ancient, and preexisting knowledge of the home, and discipleship unlocks power or wisdom which will elevate all areas of life—health, wealth, sexuality, fortune, and so on. And it looks cool, too.[10]

More than any other feature, the contemporary smart house is an integrated and high-impact showcase for entertainment. The media environment is a total one: "In digital harmony, Dad and his buddies play computer games on the flat-panel TV using wireless keyboards in the family room, while Junior surfs the web in his room and Mom transfers images of the happy family into the PC in the study. In the background, the refrigerator tracks food inventories and allows Internet access to order supplies online, while the security system monitors the in-house network, ever on guard for an 'event,' and appliances are bright enough to know when they need a repair person" (Weil). The automated home is an interconnected network of smart devices organized to surround the user with virtual experiences. The mediated smart house, a far cry from the futuristic houses of the past, reconfigures notions of work and fits into this context. Interestingly, the technology of the contemporary smart house, while not spectacular in form, *is* spectacular in content, relying on the everyday act of media consumption as its prime selling point: "With today's technology the homeowner can simply press one button on a personally customized keypad and all the work is done. Press 'Play DVD' and all the electronics are powered up and configured while the curtains and lighting are adjusted automatically to suit his preferences" ("The Smart Choice," 100). In this setting, "work" is converted into the trivial act of watching a movie. Adjusting the lights, drawing the curtains, setting the volume, and pressing play are all considered appropriate uses of labor-saving technology. Needless to say, the idea of work in this household is vastly different from the one offered at the beginning of the twentieth century. Not that households don't need cleaning and meals don't need preparation; rather, these concerns are cast into the void (where they will likely be picked up, as they always have been, by human hands), and technology is employed to make fun easier.

The most profound example of this use of smart technology is in the smart bath with flat-screen TV and surround sound: "There is only so long some of us can lie there without conversation, entertainment and knowing we shouldn't really fall asleep. And certainly you don't want to be mulling over business decisions in this context—the very environment where you have taken cover to get away from such taxing niggles. So what better to combine your physiological escapism than a bit of mental escapism too? You've immersed your body in another realm, now what about your mind?" (McNair-Wilson, "Home, Smart Home" 112). There was a time when relaxation was merely a matter of not doing work. Evidently, this is no longer the case. For some, even relaxation itself is a process of toil and drudgery, and must be streamlined through high-tech means. The smart bath eliminates the annoyance of contemplation, when the day's events reverberate through the mind and give way to reflection and evaluation. Relaxation is not a way to gain perspective on daily life and to let go of concern—ease itself must be made easier.

The underlying fantasy of this smart home is not that life can be made easier by the elimination of household toil, but that life can be made more full and more dynamic through an integrated relationship with media: "Living in a house in which the entertainment, lighting, security and data systems are state-of-the-art, easily controlled and able to interact, is more rewarding and fulfilling than living in a home where each of those many individual elements and systems acts like 'a law unto itself'" ("The Smart Choice," 100–101). As the editors of *SmartHouse* magazine would have it, the goal of technology in the home is to create a "lifestyle"—an idea made obvious by the fact that the magazine's full title during its first year of publication was *Smarthouse: Lifestyle Technology*. Although the technology in the current smart home bears a family resemblance to the smart homes of the 1980s, this remarkable shift away from technical "fixes" to material problems has given way to abstract "solutions" to questions of style.

With this variety of impulses in mind, I would like to revisit Disney's city, Celebration, Florida. While many people point to the obvious claim that Celebration represents a more conservative vision of the idealized place than EPCOT, it is a mistake to describe it as merely reactionary. Douglas Frantz and Catherine Collins make this error, explaining, "where Epcot looked to the future, Celebration turned to the past. Where Epcot was a vision of the direction in which the American city might be headed, Celebration represented the country's disenchantment with the metropolis and its new embracing of the town of decades past" (28). While the homes at Celebration are not smart homes in the sense discussed herein, they are wired homes, containing much of the technology that is contained within smart homes. For example, every home in Celebration is provided with access to "e-mail, chat rooms, a bulletin board service, and access to the Internet, all free of charge" (Frantz and Collins, 148). In addition, the town itself has been sold by its appeal to the narrative of a "perfect day"—and all aspects of the community are built with this in mind.[11] Similar to a theme park, the goal of Celebration is to construct the home as "the happiest place on earth."

The neotraditional homes in Celebration reflect a larger narrative about lifestyle in which traditional themes and stylings are combined with technologies of information and media. This ambiguous use of *smart* to describe both high- and low-tech "solutions" is echoed by Votolato: "The chic designs of the avant-garde and the homes of ordinary people are composed of the found and the fabricated, inventive combinations of old and new materials, of high technology and low technology (cottage-computer work), of the advanced and the archaic, of the rational and the romantic and, on the Internet, of the public and the personal" (156).

Rather than creating homes that would complete tasks effortlessly or generate a spectacle around futuristic living, the contemporary smart home is based more securely in the consumption of media. The spectacle is not the home itself, as much as the information that circulates through the home. Like feng shui, the smart home is a means to control the flow of "energy" through space. The smart home is related to Martha Stewart's do-it-yourself homemaking, which does not fix the problem of material scarcity, but presents solutions to questions of style through easy-to-follow instructions by which consumers, led by a corporation, can purchase the tools needed to achieve a refined and fashionable American domesticity à la Catherine Beecher. Not simply about labor, relaxation, ease, amusement, or spectacle, the smart house is a constellation of ideas and technologies which exist to generate and control the imagination, and manage the refined way of being called a lifestyle.

CONCLUSION

The smart house promises to deliver a certain quality of life to its inhabitants. Through its various gadgets and devices, the smart house is the sound stage which produces the lifestyle of its inhabitants as spectacle.[12] As its history suggests, what the smart house has to offer takes many forms, some of them futuristic and forward thinking, some of them invoking notions of comfort and nostalgia. And although the smart home does introduce a number of "new" technologies into the household, the way that these technologies reframe the home itself and arrange it as a "theatrical" set for the production of the everyday—the Perfect Day—marks the crucial innovation of this new way of living.

The smart home, as a system, has the effect of automating the process of lifestyle construction in the consumer world. As Bourdieu has indicated in his discussion of consumer practices, and as Featherstone has elaborated, consumer culture and the cultivation of style has always been an "interactive" process. Because of its social nature, the pursuit and interpretation of distinguishing markers requires a great deal of time and attention, and ultimately affects one's subjective experience of the world. What the smart home is able to do, as far as lifestyle is concerned, is to speed up and make more efficient these practices. By potentially making all aspects of one's life available as productive knowledge, the smart home tightens the focus of governmentality, as defined by Foucault and developed by Nikolas Rose. In the process of wiring the home and filling it with machines that can know subjects, establish routines, and make inferences about appropriate behaviors in the form of "suggestions" or available choices, the critical relationship between freedom and control in the consumer world is made clear.

The elevated status of lifestyle dramas and consumer choices that are showcased in reality shows are shrines to this elevated model of subjectivity. The shows suggest, however truthfully or untruthfully, that the life of the consumer is interesting and worthy of attention. Their supposedly unscripted nature is a document of the model of "freedom" they uphold—the show goes on regardless of the choices made, provided that these choices are made. Unlike more traditional story-driven dramas, the reality show frames everyday life in the context of competition rather than of community, enforcing the idea that in life there are winners and there are losers, and that the spoils of victory go to those who are armed with the appropriate tools and techniques. If there is a hegemonic representation of consumer culture, it is the idea that freedom is the ability to make oneself into an exceptional person through an awareness of and engagement with the appropriate services and commodities. The smart home is an attempt to actualize this freedom in a systematic and totalizing way.

In the systematic application of these freedom-producing technologies, one can also gain insights into the paradoxical nature of governmentality. On the one hand, it is the means by which individuals experience liberty. On the other hand, as Foucault maintains, it happens systematically. In popular culture this paradox is negotiated in technological thrillers, where houses are haunted via the machines that are supposed to bring daily life under greater control. A miniature view of the more expansive *Matrix* trilogy, in which the machines pursue global domination, the haunted-house narrative represents a system that can contain the lives of its inhabitants and exert control over their choices and actions. Side by side, the haunted-house story and the reality show exemplify opposite sides of the same coin of universal freedom under neoliberal capitalism: one story celebrates the freedom that comes with integrating oneself wholly into the system of commerce, the other warns that living inside the system forces one to become subject to its whims. The smart house is simply an advanced stage of this paradox.

4

The Dawn of the Perfect Day

There is no universal capitalism, there is no capitalism in itself; capitalism is at the crossroads of all kinds of formations, it is a neocapitalism by nature. It invents in its eastern face and western face, and reshapes them both—all for the worst.—Deleuze and Guattari, *A Thousand Plateaus*

We have considered the history of the smart home from the beginning of the twentieth century up to its current conception. From the idea of the home as a scientifically managed workplace, to its transformation into an interplanetary habitat, to its present development as an integrated media platform, the smart home has established a variety of stories about the good life. Having considered it a dynamic space in itself, we have looked at the smart home as a production set for entertainment and as a haunted house. But there is one more chapter to this story, after one considers the editing that takes place by way of the set, the choices made in the pursuit of the exceptional consumer lifestyle, and the questions of subjectivity and the posthuman self. "The Perfect Day," as the conclusion to this book, is a discussion of the ethical implications of consumer technologies and ideologies as embodied in the smart house.

Throughout my discussion of the smart home, I have referred to the arrival of the Perfect Day. In many ways, my writing of this book participates in the deferral of the horizon of expectations, placing tomorrow just beyond the present and stopping short of perfect satisfaction. Such is the Perfect Day—it presents itself, like any theoretical project, as being on the cusp of fully satisfying expectations. But when have commodities ever lived up, emotionally and subjectively, to the claims made in their commercials? When has the consummated union of consumer and product in the flesh exceeded the exhilaration of the consummation that takes place in the imagination, before the realization of its banality sets in? This is not to presume that your stereo does not make you feel the music or that your pants are less resistant to embarrassing stains or wrinkles than my own. Rather, it is to say that, as useful as these material facts are, they are much more exciting when they are seized on by our subjectivity. Whether or not their promises come to pass is of little import—what matters is the quality of our belief. The Perfect Day must convince its user that it is imminent, and thereby gain immanence.

The Perfect Day is a grand goal, a utopian dream for the subject of neoliberal capitalism that owes its existence to the numerous promises that are conjured up daily in the marketplace. It is the hope that something better will spring into our hands and homes the moment it is created. It is the dream that, like magic, the technical solution to every possible problem will materialize in a day. As in a television show, everything will appear meaningfully and as it should and, when it is done, it will all melt away. The Perfect Day is the new philosopher's stone, which will turn all moments of existence into golden memories as we live them, if we believe in them. It is a technologically facilitated experience of subjectivity as life without deficiency and without doubt.

The Perfect Day is an attempt through the use of technology to present a highly selective vision of the world that is attuned to the specific desires of its user. As such, the Perfect Day attempts to solve the fundamental ethical problem of neoliberal capitalism: in only displaying those things which the subject would like to see, it circumvents the failures of the economic order. In real time, it erases the suffering of the world if one no longer wishes for its existence, or it reframes suffering in terms that make it acceptable and understandable from its subjective standpoint. Furthermore, it attempts to create situations in which ethical boundaries can be safely crossed by converting the unethical into an entertainment spectacle—murders, rapes, and genocides can be safely witnessed and enacted through simulation. The Perfect Day, as a posthuman ethical implement, divorces ethics from culture and reduces ethics simply to the realm of biopolitics. The Perfect Day, as can be discovered by way of the smart home, is a representation of the great lengths to which society will go to make the lie of universal consumer satisfaction true. Unfortunately, the attempt to avoid through editing techniques the ethical dilemmas posed by this system does not amount to an ethical solution. Instead, it is a refusal to engage with ethics.

A NOTE ON POSTHUMANISM

To understand the emergence of the Perfect Day, it is helpful to scrutinize the shift from EPCOT to Celebration. Celebration, the town in Florida built and planned by the Disney Company as a social experiment and business venture, deviates from EPCOT in significant ways. Celebration's architecture rejects the futurist stylings of the original EPCOT—which was to be a domed city, complete with monorails and vacuum-powered, centralized waste disposal, among other things—in favor of a more conservative look akin to "Small Town America." Neighborhoods are residential, with green lawns, large front porches, and "quaint" homes. The aesthetic of Celebration is captured in an early, but unused, draft of the town's "backstory": "There was once a place where neighbors greeted neighbors in the quiet of summer twilight. Where children chased fireflies. And porch swings provided easy refuge from the cares of the day. The movie house showed cartoons on Saturday. The grocery store delivered. And there was one teacher who always knew you had that special something. Remember that place? Perhaps from your childhood? Or maybe just from stories. It had a magic all its own. The special magic of an American home town" (quoted in Rymer, 66). The slick advertising rhetoric constructs Celebration as a small town, drawing on Disney's long tradition of creating and conjuring peaceful and pleasurable "memories" for "children of all ages." In so doing, it treads a fine line between being and becoming.

The tension between being and becoming more generally accounts for shifts in the narratives used to market smart homes to subjects. In *The*

Society of the Spectacle Guy Debord provides a useful tool in the concept "spectacle," which he identifies as the source of alienation in consumer society: "The externality of the spectacle in relation to the active man appears in the fact that his own gestures are no longer his but those of another who represents them to him" (par. 30). The term *spectacle* is used loosely to describe a power technique of which mass media are merely the most obvious example. For Debord, one of the many problems with the spectacle is that its method of production, which is consumption, offers itself up to consumers as an illusion of social unity—spectators become part of a community that shares in the common fixation, and the images consumed tell stories of satisfaction. Entertainment, for example, requires one to spend more time focusing on this illusion of unity, rather than in the pursuit of social pleasures. This is also true for other commodities—toothpastes promise new plateaus in whiteness, automobiles promise style and perfect utility, paper towels promise revolutionary levels of absorbency—all of which, by the way, can result in improved social opportunities, deeply satisfied interior states, and better lives. As a result, the more satisfaction one seeks via the spectacle, the more reinforced the feelings of dissatisfaction one suffers when removed from the spectacle. The benefit that these products offer, aside from their practical utility, is in their ability to communicate ideas that embody power in their symbolic value. It is this social power that is described by way of Bourdieu's discussion of "cultural capital." And it is when this power is removed from the spectacle, debunked, and divested of its claims to grandiosity that one feels disenchanted, isolated, and unplugged.

Insofar as the spectacle calls us to participate in a fantasy that is eternally before our eyes, yet eludes our grasp, there is the constant potential for alienation. In terms of consumer practices, this then places products in a double bind: to fuel constantly growing market shares, they must both inspire consumer confidence by delivering some sense of satisfaction, yet they must also ensure the constant need for consumption. Thus the smart home relies on a process of mediation between the old and the new, the comfort of the ordinary and the promise of extraordinary comforts.

The fact that history recirculates and reproduces in the present references to past styles and motifs has come to be a standard theoretical point for those versed in postmodernism. This tendency to fall back into past styles, often nostalgically, might provoke superficial critics to read the situation as reactionary and conservative.[1] However, for a society which has clearly embraced unprecedented technological changes which have made themselves felt in all other areas (social, scientific, ethical, spiritual, economic, political), is it inconceivable that the reincarnation of the past is not itself a manifestation of the new?

The technical system has established itself through hegemonic means, employing both positive and negative methods to secure its normative and central role in culture. Through futurist marketing strategies, new technology is made to appeal to that slim, but important, sector of the market called "early adopters"—those who are eager to use new technologies by virtue of their newness. The vast majority, however, are interested in products whose design is governed by the blatantly hegemonic principle "MAYA," or "Most Advanced Yet Acceptable" (Votolato, 121). This large middle segment of the population will adopt technologies that seem to mediate between the new and the old, the emergent versus the dominant. The adoption of new technologies illustrates Gramsci's notion of hegemony in detail, consisting of a large and normal "middle" flanked by marginal elements who are both "progressive" and "reactionary," negotiating the advance of cultural norms through a process of give and take. The crucial difference, however, is that this form of cultural coercion is more clearly tailored to technical advancement than are traditional Marxist economic models. In this context, the history of the smart home in the twentieth century, although tied to economics, is clearly geared toward the advancement of consumer technologies at any cost.

On the more coercive end of this scheme is the desire to use these technologies for the elderly. Hovering between independence and abandonment, the elderly typically find themselves treated to infantilizing solutions which require less care from the young and more of their savings. In a world where three billion people live on less than two dollars a day, and in a country where good jobs are vanishing, one would think it would be possible to arrange mutually beneficial relationships between the young and old, where each is able to provide vital human support for the other. Instead, as usual, the market suggests that we eliminate caregivers, substitute care with technology, and divert wealth into corporate coffers. In place of a society where people take time to "invest" in community and fill subjective space with social relationships, this dream for the smart home offers the spectacle of care: we can watch people adhere to patterns of behavior and presume they are living well. We can offer corrections if they start acting weird. And, when they finally cross the line from a lonely depression which has been blunted by medication, television, and the fear of full institutionalization into full-blown dementia, we will know. In the elderly, one finds a population that is often treated as subjectively alien to the young. Similarly, the elderly are often imagined as problems, both social and personal. However well-meaning they may be, these solutions tend to be created by people whose views are skewed both by youth and economics. But more important than the motives of the individuals involved, the technology itself (driven by sensors, cameras, remote operation, and AI, which must interpret subjective experience based on limited physical cues) skews perspective itself. In the absence of real community, these individuals can't help but be judged based on the filters of new media. (Are they eating their pills? Why aren't they watching *Wheel of Fortune* now? Are their footsteps erratic?)

Similarly, posthumanism, in rejecting the complex and indeterminate notion of the human as inessential, falls back on the basic foundations of materialism as put forward by scientific models. As a political project, it functions to clear space and engage in the great industrial practice of refinement, breaking down complex units into smaller pieces for easier assimilation into wholes. Convergence does not confine itself to other technological devices; it pulls itself ever closer to the body and consciousness of the operator. While the wristwatch, pager, cell phone, and PDA (personal digital assistant) have certainly demonstrated the propensity for technology to become ever more personal and portable, technologies in development, such as the Personal Area Network (PAN) seek to turn the flesh and blood of the body itself into a network. By passing electrical current through the body, the PAN would allow computers to communicate through the body as follows: "Placed near a body, for example in a shoe, the field change[s] the body's average voltage by a tiny amount. A similar receiving unit could measure this voltage change at another part of the body. By varying the tiny voltage, a message could be exchanged" (Gershenfeld, 50). Such a network would create a number of interesting possibilities: "Two people using it could exchange an electronic business card just by shaking hands. A hand on a doorknob could send the data to unlock a door, or the act of picking up an airport telephone could download the day's messages" (ibid., 51). While not located on the body, but rather in the heart, mass-produced robotic companions for the elderly can take the shape of a beloved pet. Contained within the robot dog are such possibilities: "Robot pets such as the Sony Aibo are popular in Japan and have the potential to be more than playthings. The pets could act as mobile interfaces to aspects of computer technology. They could read aloud e-mail messages or newspapers delivered electronically, or record messages to be sent to other people" (Harvey). But even these examples fail in describing the true end of this posthuman convergence.

Pulling itself ever closer and reaching ever higher densities of function, these technological systems are something like a black hole—becoming so dense that their functions vanish from sight altogether (but their gravity never disappears). The initial phase of this collapse begins with minimalism. R. L. Rustky explains: "Minimalism and complexity may in fact be seen as the two basic, and related, aspects of high-tech style or aesthetics. The tendency of high tech toward minimalism design, inherited from aesthetic modernism, is actually an extension of modernity's tendency to technologize or instrumentalize the world, to abstract and reduce it into ever more minimal, more controllable forms" (13). Rutsky then undermines his claim by continuing, "The term *black box* has been used in electronic and computer design to designate any component whose interior functioning is either unknown or need not be considered" (110). Rather than considering a minimalist object a controllable object, one might want to consider the meticulous focus the minimal object demands. Without any distractions, the minimal serves to focus the obtrusiveness, and in the case of the black box, testifies to its powerful and uncontrollable mystery, as though it were possessed by spirits. To return to Gershenfeld's proclamation, "invisibility is the missing goal in computing"—posthuman politics intentionally or unintentionally seems to realize this goal.

The smart home, in this regard, is the house for the posthuman subject.

Integrated fully with the life of the user, this home participates actively in the creation of a meaningful life as a product of information. Sensations, routed through a skillfully stimulated brain, privilege the role of the central nervous system as the core of being, but only insofar as this central nervous system can be interpellated by electrochemical impulses. Under this model, in which the perfect home is that which provides a maximum of positive stimulation and keeps the body safe and in top repair, life becomes suspended animation. The mind, as it were, vanishes and is replaced by a machine that crunches numbers or data endlessly—the history of human consciousness as a series of special effects.

In light of the expressed sentiments and conscientious actions of posthumanist scholars, I can't help but notice that all seem to have a strong sense of "humanist" principles at the core of this call. In fact, Haraway's "Cyborg Manifesto" is clearly preoccupied with fundamental questions of "human rights," such as welfare, access to health care, and labor reform. The moral leveling that is called for, however, makes little effort to establish or even acknowledge the humanist foundations from which these scholars clearly operate and offers no assurances or "rules" by which abuses can be soundly critiqued. By leaping bravely into the future, the call to adopt a "posthuman" ethics mirrors the relationship between Marxism and capitalism. Just as Marxism, in its attempt to salvage the dignity of the human subject, sacrificed the worker to the value of his or her labor, posthumanism sacrifices Marxist class politics to the creation of "biopolitics." Marx pointed out the problem of a disrespected underclass and called for its solution in an assertion of the value of labor rather than in the value of the being as a practical strategy by which workers could assert their fundamental dignity. Strategically, this conversion process presents a possible solution in its ability to focus the struggle on clear-cut material practices and obvious inequalities. As history would have it, capitalism would rise to the occasion, acknowledging workers as valuable insofar as their labor could generate wealth, while slowly but surely replacing labor with machines. The fundamental value of these people was now taken as a function of blank materialism, valuable for their economic and political function rather than for any sort of inherent value as individuals. Biopolitics attempts to account for this.

The term *biopolitics*, as it is used here, has been traced back to Foucault. In "The Political Technology of Individuals" Foucault writes, "We can say now that the true object of the police becomes, at the end of the eighteenth century, the population; or, in other words, the state has essentially to take care of men as a population. It wields its power over living beings as living beings, and its politics, therefore, has to be a biopolitics" (161). Michael Hardt and Antonio Negri offer further insights into the term. They define biopower, or the field which biopolitics governs and from which it emerges: "Biopower is a form of power that regulates social life from its interior, following it, interpreting it, absorbing it, and rearticulating it" (23). They continue, "These two lines of Foucault's work ['the society of control' and 'the *biopolitical* nature of the new paradigm of power'] dovetail with each other in the sense that only the society of control is able to adopt the biopolitical context as its *exclusive* terrain of reference. In the passage from disciplinary society to the society of control, a new paradigm of power is realized which is defined by the technologies that recognize society as the realm of biopower" (Hardt and Negri, 24, emphasis in original). For poststructuralists, biopolitics has gained currency, positioning itself as a placeholder for "reality," or the point where subjectivity exists. Offering a more historical understanding, Giorgio Agamben's *Homo Sacer* discusses the idea of "homo sacer" (Latin: sacred man), or the one "*who may be killed and yet not sacrificed*" (8, emphasis in original). Agamben's discussion of "bare life" suggests that politics, from its inception, has always been biopolitics insofar as it seeks to create distinctions and differentiate the legitimacy of various human lives. In particular, he refers to the relationship between those who have rights and those who are exempt from this consideration, using the paradigm of the concentration camp as one of many examples. But more important than the technical origins of the term is the sense that the realm of biopower and the discussion of biopolitics attempts to track down subjectivity to its source, without the baggage of humanism and its philosophically tricky anthropological prescriptions about nature, essence, truth, and reality.

The posthuman ethos requires that we view biopolitics as a reality. Only when we accept this reality can we then reasonably gain power. In this scheme, "freedom" is produced by power rather than liberation from power, and therefore there is little use in talking about progress toward freedom. Thus, biopolitics invests an affective form of power with the legitimacy it needs to govern the subject. To use an example from daily life, imagine working a corporate service job under the thumb of an uptight manager. If one were to believe in nothing outside of the world of the corporation, the only options would be to seek another job or move up the ladder. To enjoy freedom here would be to take advantage of the inequalities of power within the structure. Thus, in seeking to gain greater agency, one would first invest the structure with one's faith in its ability to manage and regulate relationships, then would act out the disciplinary role that one believes this structure contains. Perhaps this is inevitable.

Perhaps it is not. The only meaningful way to subvert this affective form of power is to resist, not through direct challenge, but in learning not to care. Hardt and Negri find hope in the "New Barbarians," who are "incapable of adapting," who are "unprepared for normalization," and who are "incapable of submitting to command" (216). However, as Hardt and Negri correctly note, "Hybridity itself is an empty gesture, and the mere refusal of order simply leaves us on the edge of nothingness—or worse, these gestures risk reinforcing imperial power rather than challenging it" (216–17). While the romance of radically smashing the edifice of tradition which we associate with order might offer aesthetic release, it is worth asking how much of this urge is mythological barbarism. How much is just good old-fashioned consumer conditioning? Must barbarians perform savagery? Or is it enough to divest oneself of power, to lie down peacefully, to offer a "barbarism" that is placid, peaceful, even, human? This is not to say that we must relinquish our right to struggle, challenge, and criticize. Rather, our challenge to biopolitics could be a simple assertion of humanity—our right to live, love, eat, reproduce, speak, and die without enriching a middle-man, gatekeeper, racketeer, or landlord. This assertion alone is enough to send shivers up and down the spine of the establishment. This is enough to earn the label of a filthy, stinking, stupid barbarian. This is sufficient to merit a wiretap, imprisonment, disappearance, or execution. All this barbarism can be earned without moving beyond the human, without "hybridity," whatever that means. Without being a cyborg. Without a mutation. This is nothing new, and that is why it is so compelling.

Posthumanist politics, in attempting to make an end run around biological determinism, replaces Marxist class-based politics with biopolitics and creates a new, more mundane form of biological determinism. In order not to be governed by the politics of biology, subjects are called to create their own biology through a technocultural process. Initially, this biopolitics opens up new possibilities, much as Marx's call for class consciousness did in its own time. For those who truly exist without the benefits of economic and cultural life (the homeless, the imprisoned, the institutionalized, the enslaved, the diseased, and the dying)—the bioproletarians whose bodies are the only means by which they can exert any agency—the prospect of biopolitical class struggle makes sense. However, given their destitute state and the immensity of the cultural, technological, and economic resources stacked against them, it might be unwise to wait for yet another worldwide proletarian revolution. Rather, the establishment of biopolitics under the current political regime creates the conditions for a blank biological determinism, a notion that there is power in biopolitics, and a reconfiguration of this politics into classic models of inequality. The ability to define one's biopower, to alter this biopower, and to construct the biopower of others will create an entirely new rift between the haves and have-nots.[2]

The posthuman shift from "humanity" to "personhood" as a site for rights and responsibilities, while it deconstructs traditional notions of subjectivity, replaces them with an even stronger and more malleable type of subject whose ability for self-determination is strictly a function of privilege. Far from resisting the anthropocentrism that humanism has been credited with, the posthuman conception of the citizen is based on perceived affinities with cognitive tendencies.[3] Rights become a function of one's capacity to think and express ideas in a recognizable manner, with rights attributed to those individuals we are capable of recognizing. At their most optimistic, posthumanists argue that even the least members of our species will be treated as legitimate people, not to mention intelligent animals, computers, robots, clones, and whatever other creatures arise to inspire the goodwill of those with the authority to recognize them as persons. However, the history of the humanist era—in spite of absolutist constructions like "inalienable rights," "human rights," and "human dignity"—is marked by a vicious tendency to cast members out of the human family and write them out of existence. It is naïve to expect that those in power will make generous use of a more flexible construction of rights, when they have not done so with one that is more narrowly defined.

As a lifestyle technology, the smart home and its valorization of consumer agency (even as it transfers this agency to one's belongings) functions as a site where the posthuman self is constructed. In allowing subjectivity to migrate through informational flows, the smart home functions theoretically in accordance with the classic conception of the cyborg. In converting interactions into media themselves, the smart home is complicit in the replacement of the "human" with a representation of subjectivity that is accentuated by a variety of machines. The smart home converts its residents into stars and thus removes notions of personhood from any sort of "essential" category, establishing the capacity for empathetic response as the source of realization. In other words, subjects who live in smart homes, by fully participating in media forms and producing the lives of subjects as dramatic displays of consumer practices in action, establish themselves more securely as persons insofar as they can participate in displays which accord with images of valid lifestyles. The smart home participates in establishing a normative model for the "good life," which threatens by default those who exist outside of the scope of this exciting new lifestyle technology.

The smart home recreates an idea of a perfect and ordinary life, which excludes lives (through security, through ignorance, and through violence) of those that fall outside of the margins of its regulating (normalizing) walls. Marginal lives, rather than being respected, if not ignored altogether, are converted into entertaining displays—sacrificed to a society obsessed with the spectacle.[4] Treated as novelties or nonentities, subjects without the disposable income to sustain a "lifestyle" run the very real risk of failing to be considered people with loves, worries, and interests like (or totally unlike) our own. Any theory of the subject which rejects the essentialist category of the human and instead adopts one based on the ability to participate competently in a moral community is in danger of leaving these members of the human family outside of legal protection, or at the very least of saving them through "humanitarian" efforts like those which seek to "develop" select parts of the Third World as consumer markets or consumable products. To revise Gayatri Chakravorty Spivak's famous question, "Can the subaltern participate competently in a recognized moral community?" Those unfortunate masses who are removed from the space of informational flows and lack the means to participate in the giddy decadence of metropolitan modes of consumption might find themselves unable to participate "competently" and might instead find themselves on the market as organ "donors," as a supplement to industrial machines, or converted into amusing bits of information and experience—hacked apart into spare parts for the "conscious" and "competent" elites of a posthuman world.

The sad fact is that this "posthuman" reality is already a part of our "human" world. In spite of postmodern fascinations with "becoming," everyday life is always about *human beings*—but this does not mean that the desire to translate descriptive theories of power into the active pursuit of becoming *post-* is not worth consideration. Posthumanism as a political movement is a weighty issue which attempts to reconcile politics with poststructuralism, to look past essentialist categories as a basis for action. The goal of "good" ethical and moral systems has allegedly been to minimize human suffering, bringing the value of humanist constructions into question. But to argue that humanism is the source of suffering in what is rapidly becoming a posthuman world, and to advocate for a prescriptive system of embracing these changes and abandoning the human as a solution is foolish. As housing trends suggest, the "fixes" that technology has to offer are spectacular in nature, constructed to cultivate life in relation to media and consumer practices. Although there are some hopeful speculations about the nature of new media forms and cyberspace, the actuality seems to indicate that the smart house intends to deliver subjects over to an ever-increasing commercialization of everyday life. With increasingly mediated glimpses of the world which emphasize lifestyles of specialized consumption ever on the horizon, to actively pursue and promote a flexible notion of personhood will yield long-term gains only for those who are in the business of defining which lives are worth living. To build a notion of basic rights on the idea of "competent participation in a moral community" leaves no recourse or reference for those who might be able to achieve at least some, if retroactive, acknowledgment of the fact that they do have transcendental "inalienable rights" by virtue of their embodied existence, rather than the transient materialist rights of the biopolitical person.

The idea of the posthuman raises a number of important questions and presents many more answers than I have given here. Posthumanist speculation differs from other radical political agendas in two significant ways. First, it rejects essentialism and thus imagines a better world which is found in a compromised existence; it strives for the sublime utopia of the cyborg, asking us to look forward to becoming alien to ourselves. Second, it assumes a present state which is pragmatically positive; there is little room left to fear the contemporary cyborg body and technoscientific solutions even though they are the direct products of the cruelty of militarism and violence. In short, posthumanist speculation is grounded in a relatively optimistic notion of the present and an unstable and chaotic version of the future—an inversion of traditional utopian models. And while the smart house cannot answer all of these questions raised by posthumanism, it does show that, even at its most benevolent and comforting, commerce is forging ever more intimate links with daily life. To advocate anything less than an absolutist regard for human rights is to deliver subjects over to the mercy of the free market—turning even the barest substance of our organism into raw materials.

THE PERFECT DAY

The Perfect Day owes its conception to the "discovery" of everyday life. While everyday life has existed as long as human beings have walked the earth, formal discussion of it was born with the rise of the bourgeoisie and the birth of mass culture. As the middle class developed along with democracy and rights, the focus on expressions of freedom in daily existence began to gain real substance. Speech, property rights, leisure, and happiness have come to characterize the life well lived and thus beg the question: just what is it about daily living that beings find so pleasurable? How is freedom experienced on the individual level? The more closely one looks at the individual, the more readily one will uncover singularities of experience hidden beneath the quotidian paving stones of urban space. The masses are not merely massive in their quantity, but in their quality as well.

It is in this historical context of "discovering" the everyday that Michel de Certeau proceeds in his account of the practice of everyday life. For Certeau, everyday life is explicitly and radically democratic, pitting the wits of the small against the methods of the mighty. In his introduction, Certeau offers a description by which the everyday functions: "Everyday life invents itself by *poaching* in countless ways on the property of others" (xii, emphasis in original). Everyday life should be understood in this regard as a way of manipulating the forces of oppression. For members of a mass culture, which is often characterized by the force of its institutions, everyday life is experienced as life in avoidance of institutional control.

Everybody has an everyday life. Changes in the form of the world, economy, politics, technology, religion, and culture do not change this fact, although they do change the power dynamics by which they are manifested. With varying stakes and commitments to the orderly processes of civilized progress, all are implicated at various moments in securing personal space outside of order. Freedom can be found at those specific moments when one cleverly makes use of "the master's tools" to gain an advantage. Hence the characterization of everyday life as poaching—ordinary people don't write the rules, though they are expected to enforce and obey the rules, but when the opportunity arises to gain the "upper hand," even momentarily, these same ordinary people can take it. This is not to say, however, that everyday life is a misanthropic project of abusing others to gain an advantage, for it is precisely the logic of power that requires subjects to take an official relationship relative to fellow citizens. At times, everyday life, in the case of vandalism, asserts itself to the dismay of others, but at heart it is social. Everyday life is the means by which subjects reaffirm their connection to humanity in spite of forces that equate humanity with rational and rationalized behavior. There may be violence in the everyday, but it is of smaller scale than the antisocial forms of violence which are required for the preservation of structural inequalities.

Certeau continues to describe in military terms the relationship between power and everyday life through his discussion of strategies and tactics. Certeau writes, "I call a 'strategy' the calculation of force-relationships which becomes possible when a subject of will and power (a proprietor, an enterprise, a city, a scientific institution) can be isolated from an 'environment'" (xix). He continues, "I call a 'tactic,' on the other hand, a calculus which cannot count on a 'proper' (a spatial or institutional localization) nor thus on a border-line distinguishing the other as a visible totality. The place of a tactic belongs to the other" (xix). Strategies are the technics (techniques and/or technologies) of victory as mapped out by those in authority. Tactics, on the other hand, are quick countermobilizations which respond to strategies of control and capture, and are thus the province of the small, the weak, and the dispersed. He continues in his discussion of the guerilla maneuvers needed to preserve the vitality of everyday life: "Many everyday practices (talking, reading, moving about, shopping, cooking, etc.) are tactical in character. And so are, more generally, many 'ways of operating': victories of the 'weak' over the 'strong' (whether strength be that of powerful people or the violence of things or of an imposed order, etc.), clever tricks, knowing how to get away with things, 'hunter's cunning,' maneuvers, polymorphic simulations, joyful discoveries, poetic as well as warlike" (xix). While many might take issue with the use of military metaphors to discuss the day-to-day experiences of individuals, it is important to remember just what is at stake in power relations, and that the implementation of tactics by everyday people is a defensive countermeasure that asks only for the survival of subjectivity, nothing more and nothing less. In relation to technics, tactics might be considered as intuitively derived disruptions or modifications to technical procedures.

In the end, the tactical vitality of the everyday is made manifest in the many instances of benevolent (and highly sociable) pleasure experienced in daily life. Embracing the plurality of human experience, Certeau writes, "But our research has concentrated above all on the uses of space, on the ways of frequenting or dwelling in a place, on the complex processes of the art of cooking, and other ways of establishing a kind of reliability within the situations imposed on an individual, that is, of making it possible to live in them by reintroducing into them the plural mobility of goals and desires—an art of manipulating and enjoying" (xxii). Far from being militaristic and aggressive, the subjects of these critical inquiries as explored in the second volume of *The Practice of Everyday Life* find expression and freedom nestled in activities like cooking, eating, shopping, and walking. Furthermore, such practices have opened wide the doors to consider all daily activities as sites for development of freedom and agency.

Rather than engulfing and compromising the vast array of human desires, expressions, and impulses, our current marketplace suggests that an incredible amount of diversity remains intact. On its surface, this would seem to indicate that the human spirit has won out against market forces and that, along the lines of Adam Smith's discussion of the "invisible hand," capitalism has preserved democracy through the free market. But as the entertainment industry has proven by way of stunt doubles and digitally enhanced sequences, the appearance of something is often different than the reality. Superficial forms of diversity are special effects rather than earnest attempts to come to grips with the profound differences that present both the potential for overcoming seemingly irreconcilable cultural differences as well as the possibility for deep-seated conflict.[5]

A global economy can only ever embrace forms of "diversity" which do not conflict with neoliberal capitalist practices. This critical tension between culture and technology is described by Régis Debray as "the jogging effect of technological progress" (59). Rather than eliminate the need for actions that can be mediated through new technology (like transportation), these actions are made more intense and are subjectively transformed: cars, rather than eliminating walking as an everyday activity, produce the new activity of jogging, the phenomenon which inspired Debray's phrase. Debray continues: "Telecommunications have contributed to making tourism the largest industry in the world. The real surprise is that, as we shrink distances, we are all the more compelled to explore their periphery" (60). The subjective experience of travel, under the influence of technology, changes. Consequently, one must travel further to actually get somewhere else. And the more self-similar the subjective experience is elsewhere, the harder one must travel. This fact is a powerful testimony to the effect of media on culture. The world is shrinking in subjective space, even though select aspects of its regional flavor remain intact. So far as one can count on a tourist destination to provide a certain set of subjective experiences, it has the potential to be self-satisfyingly familiar.

The politics of the global tourist industry are thus bound to the similar tensions of being and becoming that are present in the smart home. The tensions between the comfortable and the uncomfortable, the familiar and the unfamiliar push its advancement along, looking to new corners of existence to establish entertaining experiences. Hence, Americans love "ethnic" foods, music, and ritual as a matter of style, but generally reject deep-seated attachments to these claims to "ethnicity" which produce actual ideological conflicts. Any sort of deeply held identity which is deemed to be worth fighting for must be crushed through "free trade" and propaganda and, as a last resort, armed "peace-keeping" missions. The spirit of the riskless risk and the idea that an exciting life can be experienced effortlessly as a series of consumable experiences infects even the farthest corners of the globe.

It is precisely this conditioned subjective experience of consumption, however, that has given rise to the current surge in economic development. Forms of media which require viewers to become actively and empathetically involved rely on this possibility to further their growth economically and politically. This intimacy is apparent in forms of media from Martha Stewart to *American Idol,* from CNN polls to shows like MTV's *Total Request Live.* The expectation of interactivity and the successful mass-customization of products ranging from Dell Computers to Oscar Meyer's Lunchables snack packs have capitalized on the consumer's need to find an emotional experience and to feel a personal investment in spite of technological changes which threaten to make work and thought inconsequential.[6,7] It is in this desire for subjective investment that the smart house attempts to meet the need for a meaningful existence and thus rises to affirm our impulses and coddle us with fantasies of a world so sensitive that it is able to adapt itself perfectly to our every need.

Hearkening back to Hegel's conception of the master and slave, after years of being avid consumers, the supposedly privileged members of the majority have lost the means and the will to engage in marketable cultural creations of their own—through laziness, atrophy, or a combination of both. On the other hand, the "marginalized" members of minority groups (most notably gays, blacks, and foreigners) have become the source of our cultural imagination, and ironically have been able to do so through the guerrilla practices of appropriation. The appropriation of space through graffiti, the appropriation of sounds through hip-hop, the appropriation of media and material culture through kitsch, and the appropriation of gender through style are all at heart reconfigured hand-me-downs from the mainstream culture.[8] The majority, in turn, has become dependent on the hand-me-downs of these so-called marginalized groups for its own forms of media to consume.[9]

This discussion only begins to lay out the processes at work in the smart home. Although the contemporary middle-class home is the launching pad for the political and economic processes at work in consumer culture, the smart home offers some significant and ambiguous twists to the model. The model which relies on marginal producers and masses of consumers is still far too simplistic to account for the multiplicities of the current marketplace, even if it does render its complex dialectical processes in relatively easy-to-understand terms. To understand the difference between new and newer models of consumer culture available within postmodernism, one can look at what Certeau has to offer: "The television viewer cannot write anything on the screen of his set. He has been dislodged from the product; he plays no role in its apparition. He loses his author's rights and becomes, or so it seems, a pure receiver, the mirror of a multiform and narcissistic actor. Pushed to the limit, he would be the image of appliances that no longer need him in order to produce themselves, the reproduction of a 'celibate machine'" (31). The practices engendered by the television certainly do mark off a change in the types of activities that are open to consumers in late capitalist economies. In line with Debord's discussion of the spectacle, the idea of the celibate machine comes to the forefront and showcases a set of passive consumer practices. However, as Certeau argues (along with many other cultural-studies scholars), the relationship with the celibate machine gives birth to another type of production altogether. The celibate machine simply requires that media become an interactive process, beginning with the rustic practices of media fandom (fan fiction, conventions, and the collection of memorabilia) and leading into interactive forms (videogames, the Internet, and theme parks). Considered in this context, media consumption/production should not be placed in the same order as "semiotic guerilla warfare" and is not like a walk through the city; it is a form of counterinsurgency training calculated to build empathetic relationships to media through the manipulation of images. The object of this war, rather than being ideological in the conventional sense, is to build an intuitive understanding of the world grounded in the language of media. The bottom line is the cultivation of one's very being that takes for granted media consumption as a prerequisite for life—a tyranny of pleasure. In this context, "waging war on poverty" or "stamping out illiteracy" takes on a menacing tone and likely involves a strict regimen of bombing, eugenics, embargoes, budget cuts, incarceration, and other forms of cleansing to the happy drumbeat of humanitarian peacekeeping and neoliberal globalization.

The creation of interactive media that surpass even the television in their potential to neutralize agency activates the passivity of media consumption. By creating entertainment which requires the viewer not only to view but to get involved, these new forms can help to trim some of the fat off earlier forms. Television, for example, leaves one open to the possibility of socialization and interruption. Commercial breaks are used to chat and to visit the restroom or refrigerator and are not consistently used for the intended purpose of watching commercials. However, with the remote control in hand, television as an interactive process eliminates the dead time of the commercial and fills it with the now habitual form of viewing known as channel surfing. The attention consumed by flipping through a hundred or so channels tightens up and concentrates the viewing time, both liberalizing it in terms of what is being watched but also restricting it by making TV time more purely about interacting with media. Marketers have responded in turn by inserting advertisements into shows, blurring the boundaries between content and commerce. Cable and satellite companies, in meeting consumer needs, build the hope and fulfill the expectation that the social needs of the TV viewer can be met through greater variety and customization in content. The Internet takes this process a step further by making material much more interactive and even offering up opportunities to socialize through its nexus. While many have argued that e-mail, chatrooms, and instant messaging are evidence of the world of social possibilities opened up by new media, the other side of the coin is that, in communing with virtual friends online, we begin to experience them as streaming and interactive content. This is not to say that we intend to diminish our respect for our earthly companions; rather, it is to say that we are encouraged to look to technology for the solution to our social desires. While the illusion, ambiguity, and mystery of the Internet has been considered a liberating force for social interaction in that it allows people to be other than they are, true liberty, it seems, would be the ability to appear in the flesh as one is without fear of punishment. Interactive technologies offer a "solution" to the problem of discord and dissent, rather than an opportunity for their expression. The hard-to-get-around facts of the embodied and situated self, even when represented as media online, become tainted by their proximity to virtual forms. Hard-to-accept truths about the world are transmuted into easily accepted fantasies.[10]

However, even the perfectly mediated experience is, in the end, a mismatch with the sociality that we hope would prevail in a perfect world. As Certeau points out, "Rational *technics* liquidates dogmatism in a less light-hearted way. It resists interferences that create opacity and ambiguity in planning projects or reductions to two dimensions" (199). In spite of the imaginative agency that is opened up through the material transcendence of new technology, it ultimately performs its deconstructive operations in accordance with its own industrial needs. The most romantically complex and ambiguous digital image is only a series of zeroes and ones. As "chaos theory" shows us, with the help of computers, the world is more complex than we have ever imagined. In the end we must begin with a simple decision about what is and what is not. In technology we trade our existence, while we reject notions like Cartesian dualism, and embrace those "informatics" and ways of being that, as N. Katherine Hayles points out, are the sources of our posthumanity.

In choosing greater virtualization we choose a world that has the appearance of diversity, but must narrow down variance in our "operating systems" to create more easy interactions through which this spectacular diversity can be observed at secondhand. Just as with the numerous "intelligent" computerized games that began to emerge in the late 1970s, digital interactions tighten up the "play" that is made manifest when two or more people meet, and interactions are winnowed down to specific problem-solving functions. Rather than being a framework for storytelling as Certeau maintains (22), a game of cards becomes a test of rationality, and the possibilities for anger, confusion, laughter, error, and all other elements that come alive in between the rules of the game are lost. Programs with cleverly written AI algorithms might be able to convince us, for a while, that there is some sort of lifelike process onboard, but without those types of knowledge called emotion and intuition, the possibility for the richness of feeling that is our "being" is absent. Virtual reality will appear, like a movie on the silver screen, and will have none of the reality that we experience when looking out our windows. Cybernetic existence, to talk about it as we do, may at first appear to have all the charm and fun of a game of Blind Man's Bluff. But to embrace such a game wholeheartedly is, in the end, to lose one's senses. It would be like playing a game from which there is no return, or watching a movie only to discover that the world itself was only a set. While academics have deconstructed the notion of "authenticity," we can only ever live in the world as "authentic." Especially when we take issue with the "inauthentic," we face up to it only through our own experience of authenticity.

As the development of the smart home shows, consumer technologies achieve their most profound influence when situated in the spaces of everyday life. While for many years marketers focused on adapting smart-house technologies to spectacular use, carving out a niche for their products in the lives of the early adopter, the high-tech object has evolved from being merely a fetish to being a practical object. This crucial evolution of the computerized appliance into an integral part of everyday consciousness is expressed in theoretical terms in Gershenfeld's call for invisible and unobtrusive technology. Gershenfeld puts the reader in the traditional dilemma posed by the technological order: we can either march full-steam ahead with technical progress, or we can return to the darkness of the pretechnological age. There is no room for compromise.

Theorizing this position, Gershenfeld offers the following prediction: "For all the coverage of the growth of the Internet and the World Wide Web, a far bigger change is coming as the number of things using the Net dwarfs the number of people. The real promise of connecting computers is to free people, by embedding the means to solve problems in the things around us" (9–10). In other words, to choose technology over primitivism is to choose an order in which computers will make us "free" by anticipating and solving problems for us, without even the slightest disruption or diversion of attention. In this techno-utopia, we will be left to concern ourselves only with those things that truly matter to us.

In pursuit of the goal of invisibility through ubiquity, miniaturization, unobtrusiveness, networking, and integration, the current trend of the industry is intuitively, if not explicitly, aware of Heidegger's discussion of the relationship between the subject and world.[11] The preexisting conditions of the sun's light give way to new conceptions of its utility and change its consideration. In the space of the home, this might be understood as the introduction of new informational value into the space of the home, held in place by the radius of use that appliances make useful. Wherever we exist in this space and are able to activate technologies by our very being, we extend the radius of our grasp and thus carve out a solid space of utility. Technology makes present at any given moment a number of technical possibilities, creating within the home the reality of *imaginal time*. In other words, remote control and hands-free operation turns the empty space which it commutes into radioactive space, filling the home with value and mediating/mediatizing even the most minute gesture by converting it into a potential for interaction with media.

Furthermore, the insertion of a new technology into the home does not represent a significant innovation unless it is fully integrated into the larger whole and reorients all things within its radius to reconsider their place in relation to its usefulness. Heidegger writes, "Strictly speaking, there 'is' no such thing as *a* useful thing. There always belongs to the being of a useful thing a totality of useful things in which the useful thing can be what it is. A useful thing is essentially 'something in order to. . . .' The different kinds of 'in order to' such as serviceability, helpfulness, usability, handiness, constitute a totality of useful things. The structure of 'in order to' contains a *reference* of something to something" (*Being and Time*, 64). In other words, the useful thing is only useful insofar as it is understood to be a part of a "world" with a set of understood interactions between the parts. It is this *understood* character of the useful thing that enables it to function purely, without regard, and thus as a true supplement to one's abilities. New "inventions" thus must pass through their stage of novelty and arrive, as Gershenfeld argues, as integral, and thus reordering, elements of day-to-day operation. As with the embodiment of memory in technics, interactive media technologies seek to instrumentalize a different kind of knowledge—the knowledge of social interactions. The "memory" of agency, choice, and feeling is translated into an experience or perception, and the subjects of those memories are reduced to "problems" that can be "solved." Thus, the superimposition of media on everyday life overwrites everyday life with its object of discovering problems and then solving them through "consumption," telling a new story about daily life that is focused on the apprehension of perfect, problem-free ways of being (whatever that might mean).

With an eye on Walt Disney's visionary model of entertainment, this idea of an interactive storytelling environment as a means to reconfigure the everyday is particularly evident. As Disney's Imagineers write of Walt Disney's vision, "Driven by the desire to take his passion for storytelling far beyond the confines of two-dimensions, he landed on the idea that visitors who stepped into this park should feel as though they stepped into a movie. Every inch of the place should be a part of a story, as in a movie or television show" (11). Taken in the context of various ideas about smart living, the smart home overlaps with our ideas about the set, the haunted house, the future, the past, the romance of becoming, and the crisis of being; and it situates these within a controlled environment. To occupy the smart home is to insert oneself into a story in which the qualities of that environment say something intimate and specific about the lifestyle and thus the identity of the user, even as they attempt to circumscribe this lifestyle with its own interpretations of need and desire. In short, the smart home exerts a narrative control over the subject which diverts all attention toward the fulfillment of preprogrammed objectives. From subject to subject, these objectives may take on different appearances, but their common goals are ease, satisfaction, and "happiness." In organizing life around "fulfilling" activities, insofar as these technologies are capable of presenting fulfillment (through media and spectacle), the forms of fulfillment arrived at are limited in that, at their best, they merely present users with heightened forms of mediated experience. The smart home recreates experience as "virtual reality." Just as the theme park participates in the spectacle of a voyage through the Caribbean or an encounter with the undead in a haunted house by making these fantasies into material illusions through technology, the smart house also offers up the experience of living the good life, however it may be imagined, through special effects rather than through any sense of contentment experienced a priori in the being who dwells within it. The smart home, in pursuing perfection, reproduces a sort of instantaneous delay by robbing the wholeness of experience of its actual attainment. It edits the world and makes it perfect as we experience it so that we may be given the impression that the world is indeed perfect.[12]

The terrifying image of living in a world that first responds to, then anticipates, and finally preempts the very marrow of everyday life is perhaps the most disturbing dystopia of technical determinism. Taking a daring leap from Ellul and into the void of the hyperreal, Jean Baudrillard paints an eerie picture:

> Soon man will no longer even have to steer his lawnmower on a Sunday afternoon, because it will start itself up, and stop once the job is done, of its own accord. Is this the only conceivable fate of objects? The itinerary laid down for them, leading inexorably to the complete automation of their existing functions, has far less to do with humanity's future technology than with its present psychological motivations. Consequently, the myth of the robot may be said to cover all paths taken by the unconscious in the realm of objects. The robot is a symbolic microcosm of both man and the world, which is to say that it simultaneously replaces both man and the world, synthesizing the absolute functionality and absolute anthropomorphism. Its antecedents were the electrical household appliances (cf. the "automatic maid").

> Fundamentally, therefore, the robot is simply the mythological end-product of a naïve phase of imagination, a phase which implies the projection of a continual and *visible* functionality. (119–20)

This image, like that of the haunted house, resonates deeply with our ideas about the uncanny and thus is a powerful one. Like Kurt Vonnegut's *Player Piano,* which taps away its tune, snatched from the rustic memory of the magical world of once-splendorous human creativity, the mere picture of a world that seems to go on without the lovely spark of the human becomes something grotesque. The image of the world made in our own image but one step removed from our hands, in encapsulating our greatest psychic anxieties, is a form of supreme "anthropomorphism." Far from representing an evolutionary leap beyond mere humanism, this seemingly posthuman milieu is only a tribute to the current boundaries of human imagination—a dusty, faded snapshot of the cultural concerns of a consumerist order.

But this ghost town is not the real future that awaits us; there will be no machines clicking away endlessly on their own accord. The actual trajectory is one which develops in tandem with subjects (*in medias res*—Latin for "in the middle of things"), carrying us along with its computations and forcing us to live inside its virtual spaces. Along with the terrifying nightmare of the haunted house, mass culture delivers fantasies of spectacular living—the house you need. Along with anxieties over becoming enfeebled and irrelevant, modern technics delivers interactivity—and the house that needs you. Both forms, working together, offer up the hope of an integrated way of being. The culture of the Perfect Day constructs the illusory narratives of harmony and resolution as the world. It is not simply a modernist compensation or a mass-culture fantasy but an everyday experience of realized hopes and dematerialized blind spots, an account of consumer subjectivity made real through interactivity.

On the one hand, the image generated is that of an existence free from difficulty and dedicated to the pursuit of "everyday life." On the other hand, its very interactivity and willingness to conform itself to the occupant makes it virtually impossible to escape the work of micromanaging the home. As with the Tamagotchi virtual pet and the self-cleaning litter box, the smart home takes away drudgery and replaces it with a fun-filled copy of a similar form of drudgery.[13] Of course, it is not necessarily the case that one would own both the labor-saving device and its corresponding labor simulator, but labor-saving devices are marketed to expand the owner's available store of "free time" and convert that time to an additional use. Like a cellular phone replacing a land-line, the "convenience" of the phone that travels where you travel is replaced by the activity of cell use for virtually every task, such that going grocery shopping, ordering a sandwich, going for a walk, watching TV, and driving a car all become saturated with additive layers of mediation and create a condition in which nobody is ever actually "off" the cell phone—they only devote a flexible degree of attention to the wide variety of media appliances in use. Media, in the context of the smart home, become spread thin across the present not as something which one does or does not use, but as a fact of how someone simply is.

Already one sees the reorientation of citizenship in light of new technics like profiling, pay-per-use, and preemption. The curious triangle of data mining, security, and economics in our age of globalization has helped to institutionalize this model of the posthuman subject in the new millennium. The shift has resulted in a new paradigm of government defined by security and terror. As our leaders like to remind us, peace, dialogue, and civil liberties are pre-9/11 concepts.

To drive this point home, I would like to return to appliances and introduce my friend, Mr. Coffee. Consider the now-dated example of this coffee pot with timer that greets the owner each day with a hot cup of coffee, exquisitely meeting expectations of a future aided by technology. This machine, Mr. Coffee (although there are many other brands), provides a stimulant and wakes the user in preparation for a productive work day. More advanced machines can identify users as they approach and serve a custom-made cup of coffee to their liking. Imagine, for a moment, that our machines do become increasingly integrated, as proposed by Gershenfeld and built by Gates, with bathtubs that fill themselves in anticipation of our arrival, a refrigerator that orders groceries that it thinks we might need in a day or two, and a radio station that plays only what we want to hear. Imagine a Mr. Coffee who wakes us each day, cues up the relevant stories from the daily paper, and insists in his own humble way that we drink his addictive stimulant.[14] This pleasurably interactive environment simply cares for you personally, hailing you as you approach, guiding the proliferating lifestyle choices that come to your living space via fiber-optic cables, splashing the walls with the pictures that you know you want to see. "Outside," you might see some kids chasing down an ice-cream truck, an old man walking his dog, some little girls playing jump rope, or maybe just a bright blue sky, green lawn, and picket fence. The images, whether from the dazzling future or the good old days, are ridiculously clichéd, but they all tell the same story—there is nothing to worry about, it's all, in its own special way, taken care of—the very image of social harmony, a concretization of the win-win situation or the riskless risk. This is the promise of the Perfect Day.

In the smart home, the proliferation of automated appliances and wireless multifunction controls seeks to put everything that is within the home within arm's reach. The goal of the technology of the Perfect Day is to organize space by extending objects so that all things in the home exist in what Heidegger refers to as "the totality of useful things" or "the region" (102–3). By expanding the scope and density of the region called the home, smart-home technology serves to keep the home always securely placed within the "heart"—a portable system of objects that travels and is always within reach regardless of position. Similarly, Internet technology enhances this attempt at totality or expanse of media by extending the reach of the user to all corners of the globe. Paul Virilio describes this phenomenon: "At the end of the century, there will not be much left of the expanse of the planet that is not only polluted but also shrunk, reduced to nothing, by the teletechnologies of generalized interactivity" (*Open Sky* 21)—as though we are trapped singing along with what the popular Disneyland attraction has been saying for years, "It's a small world, after all." All desires are placed within ready reach. In this context, the futurist imperative, to become something new, is replaced by one which urges only that subjects navigate more quickly through the already attainable. As with engineering science and innovation, efficiency is reached by maximizing capabilities and taking advantage of what's already available. Far from representing some sort of retrogressive look backwards, the narrative of the Perfect Day, in its lack of futurist flamboyance, is just the opposite. Rather than demand subjects become technological, the Perfect Day is about being technological. The narrative of the Perfect Day denies deferral by making technology ordinary and unobtrusive, by automating actions which are already a part of our milieu.

As a story about everyday living, this tale is one which requires nothing but our most perfect attention. The promise of its perfect execution relies on our adherence to its script. As with watching TV, the home-in-media "hopes" that users will not change channels, lest they miss the show. Since this mediascape is not a show but our very lives, our access to social harmony is at risk the moment we let our attention drift from its demands. The second we stop watching the wonderful tricks it performs is the second that we derail the flawlessness of its performance. And since it does adapt itself to us, offering up its complex of mediated forms as the world in which we dwell, it would be hard not to pay attention even if we wanted to stop. As with so many other developments, from SUVs to CCTVs, from CNN to Disneyland, from the rustic to the high tech, the smart home seeks to envelope the user in a multiplicity of possibilities and insulate the self from the multiplicity of others—reproducing the complexities of everyday life in the urban environment as life lived at arm's length in the neo-urban spaces of the eternally sub-urban milieu. In making the home interactive and surpassing the futuristic impulse of the past with a backward glance, the Perfect Day recreates everyday life as a manageable and monitored form amenable to constant management through ever-present, interactive media. The present, like a gift, is brought into high-tech space through mediation, replacing the spectacular aspects of new technologies with the spectacular contents of the perfectly executed life—securing on screen and in mind the cultural effects of late capitalism in their ability to rend asunder any forms of stability, but moderating the utopian potential of the new as hoped for in the most radical dreams of a postmodern radical democracy. The Perfect Day is, if you will, "the happy medium" of the win-win situation, undercutting any hope for moral outrage and lashing subjects to rigid conformity—the demands of a middle that knows nothing of the limits. The exceptional day that is held in place by this pursuit of perfection may very well still use the motto "work makes you free"—in the sense that this promise of total agency is one which requires a form of constant attention to a multiplicity of media forms. In the walls of the fully automated home is a camp that requires every bit of psychic concentration as it enfolds a new generation of abject souls.

POSTSCRIPT

And walking on a sunny spring day in northwest Ohio, I see the dream of a Perfect Day reflected in the dead eyes of an impossibly thin, UV-roasted woman, strolling by with cell phone pinched between head and shoulder as she recounts a tale of outrage from the night before. I catch a glimpse of my own bent reflection in the side of the glossy SUV that isn't going to stop for me at the crosswalk. The dream of the Perfect Day is in the toned bicep and manicured hand gripping the wheel, MTV-groomed head bobbing away with perfect masculinity, revving the engine just to remind me not to get in his way. I jog through the intersection after he leaves, to avoid another preemption of my pedestrian rights as more vehicles approach the stop sign. I kick a beer can along the sidewalk and pause for a moment to resurrect a partially torn and trampled yard sign that says in bold letters, "NO WAR." I block the sign with my body from a passing carload of gleefully buzzed jocks who might be inclined to shout something both aggressive and homoerotic at me if they saw what I was doing. I make my way into my apartment, sit down in front of a computer that's always already on, check all four of my e-mail accounts as I listen to MP3s, and watch images of the war on CNN with volume turned low. I delete an unsolicited mailbox full of porn, pills for penis enhancement and breast enlargement, one-time offers for once-in-a-lifetime opportunities, and urgent requests. I try a Google News search for news about developments on the recent saber-rattling with yet another oil-rich nation, poring over several stories that say exactly the same thing that I see being mouthed in mute on the news, but only in different arrangements. And, half-smiling, I wonder if the day has already come as I listen to my new favorite song and peck away at the final chapter.

NOTES

INTRODUCTION

1. Throughout this text I will be referring to a number of Disney-related entities. To refer to Walt Disney himself, I will use "Walt Disney" (sometimes simply "Walt" for the sake of variety). When referring to the publicly owned Walt Disney Productions, which became the Walt Disney Company in 1986, I use "the Disney Company." At times I will also refer to "WED (Walter Elias Disney) Enterprises," which was originally a private company called Walt Disney Incorporated started by Walt Disney in 1952 for the creation of Disneyland, but was sold along with the Imagineers to Walt Disney Productions in 1965. Finally, I will use the term "Disney" when I need a term to describe the culture of Disney, which is often difficult to distinguish from the imagination of the man and the company which bears his name. I will also make occasional use of this ambiguous term when origins, as in the case of EPCOT, are difficult to attribute to either the man or the company. Information on the Disney Company's history is available in the "History" section of *The Walt Disney Company Fact Book 2002*.
2. Frederick Jackson Turner first presented "The Significance of the Frontier in American History" at the Chicago World's Fair on 12 July 1893, during a meeting of the American Historical Association. It was first published in 1894 in the *Proceedings of the State Historical Society of Wisconsin . . . 1893* and reprinted that same year in the *Annual Report of the American Historical Association for the Year 1893*. It is considered to be widely influential in the field of American studies.
3. This twenty-four-minute film, *Walt's Last Film*, which was recorded shortly before Walt's death, is available for viewing on the Waltopia website (http://www.waltopia.com).

4. The films *Jurassic Park* (1993), *The Matrix* (1999), and *The Lord of the Rings: The Fellowship of the Ring* (2001) all make great use of effects to construct narratives about places outside of time (prehistoric creatures in the present, a history parallel to our own, and an ancient world before human history, respectively), yet they proceed by way of stable, ordered, and conventional narrative techniques. While they certainly represent radically different possible realities, they do so in a way that is easy to assimilate. The goal of digital effects is to fool the eye and present these fantastic images as coherent and convincing illusions.
5. Similar arguments can be made for wardrobes, politics, and the avant-garde, as well. Current wisdom seems to dictate that open-ended and incomplete solutions which leave space open for the arrangement of future solutions are the surest way to see that progress can be made pragmatically and predictably. However, it is also possible that these open architectures, while allowing for limited development along a particular trajectory, can only develop insofar as their particular line of development has been anticipated. In other words, planning for innovations might more effectively seal off lines of flight, not with walls, but with reservoirs and release valves by diverting energetic breaks toward the completion of already established trajectories. Because tomorrow, in the current context, has already been accounted for and mediated by what are ultimately risk-moderating mechanisms which make the future a relatively stable market for speculation, the avant-garde no longer exists. As disappointingly portrayed in the conclusion of the *Matrix* trilogy, innovation serves as a mechanism by which power can continue. The trilogy begins with the exciting promise that Neo will change the world, but ends as he sacrifices himself so that the system, along with the hegemonic illusions of neoliberal capitalist globalization, can continue to exist and harvest the energies of the sleeping masses. Without the subjective experience of certainty and the earth-shaking effects that fly in the face of certainties, the new is only a minor distraction.
6. The "riskless risk" is a critical term used by Russel Nye, and employed by John Hannigan to describe the function of entertainment in the postmodern city. As Hannigan argues, the object of "Urban Entertainment Destinations," the quintessential consumer environment, is to provide intense experiences safe from the threat of harm—a riskless risk (71–74). For a more detailed discussion of this concept, read Hannigan's *Fantasy City: Pleasure and Profit in the Postmodern Metropolis* (1999).
7. According to William Fulton's *The New Urbanism*, a 1996 report for the Lincoln Institute of Land Policy, New Urbanism can been traced back to

the late 1970s and early 1980s. Notable contributions to New Urban planning are Seaside, Florida, designed in 1981–1982; Laguna West, California, in 1988; and, of course, Celebration, Florida. New Urbanism is considered a part of a greater tradition that reaches all the way back through the American Garden City movement (1920s–1930s), through the City Beautiful movement (1890–1920s), to Frederick Law Olmsted's 1858 plan for Central Park in New York City (Fulton, 7–10).

8. As Mumford writes in *Technics and Civilization*, "The machine came into our civilization, not to save man from the servitude of ignoble forms of work, but to make more widely possible the servitude to ignoble standards of consumption" (105–6). Mumford, with an eye on mass production, describes the home: "This private world, as lived in Suburbia or in the more palatial country houses, is not to be differentiated by any objective standard from the world in which the lunatic attempts to live out the drama in which he appears to himself to be Lorenzo the Magnificent or Louis XIV. In each case the difficulty of maintaining an equilibrium in relation to a difficult or hostile external world is solved by withdrawal, permanent or temporary, into a private retreat, untainted by most of the conditions that public life and effort lay down" (313). In advance of what would come to be known as postwar prosperity and the heyday of the nuclear family, the suburban home had already become identifiable as a place where one could safely consume the security and commodities that money could buy, and entertain a particular kind of freedom and agency that existed apart from what was now considered the "outside" world.
9. Turner writes, "Up to our own day American history has been in a large degree the history of the colonization of the Great West. The existence of an area of free land, its continuous recession, and the advance of American settlement westward, explain American development" (199). As Henry Nash Smith explains in *Virgin Land*, a study of American popular fiction (first published in 1950): "As long as [Turner] is dealing with the origins of democracy in the West he evidently considers frontier influence good. A man who refers to 'the familiar struggle of West against East, of democracy against privileged classes' leaves no doubt concerning his own allegiance. This attitude was in fact inevitable as long as one maintained the doctrine that frontier society was shaped by the influence of free land, for free land was nature, and nature in this system of ideas is unqualifiedly benign" (256). The West was a land where the true American man could discover his mettle, prove his courage, and arrive at a more natural morality and good life through what was ultimately considered an encounter with open

space. More accurately, the notion of virgin land effectively erases the history of aggression against Native Americans. Adding a more pointed feminist critique, Annette Kolodny comments on the clearly sexualized nature of this encounter with space: "The Mother, after all, must be impregnated in order to be bountiful. And insofar as the husbandman aids, but does not force, her willing bounty, he at once maintains his separate masculine and consciously human identity while reaping the benefits of an acceptable and guiltless intimacy. The movement into the frontier, in this case, then, has been a desperate attempt both to preserve the real-world possibility of pastoral and to maintain some balance between the attractive and frightening implications of that impulse" (62). Kolodny's 1975 psychoanalytic critique of the American West casts the struggle for westward expansion as one between a masculine agent and a passive, feminine nature. Tied strongly to this process of territorial expansion is its attendant abundance, experienced throughout the nation's history as free real estate, inexhaustible resources, and bounteous harvests. As the long tradition of American studies suggests, the power of Manifest Destiny and Westward expansion has played a strong role in the myths and paradigms which shape American culture and consciousness.

10. First published in 1964, Marshall McLuhan's *Understanding Media* provides an early critique of this phenomenon: "During the mechanical ages we had extended our bodies in space. Today, after more than a century of electric technology, we have extended our central nervous system itself in a global embrace, abolishing both space and time as far as our planet is concerned" (19). Often misunderstood or hastily passed over, McLuhan's observation, along with its connected proclamation, "the medium is the message" (23), is a significant contribution to the study of the American media. Demarcating a crucial distinction between electronic media and more traditional forms, McLuhan's work alerts us to the interactivity that is implicit in the process of transmission.

11. The "electric light," for example, which "escapes attention as a communication medium," operates in the user as a message to see in spite of darkness, to experience the world of sensation in a fundamentally new way (McLuhan, 24–25). The "electric light" as it is used here is considered an "electronic medium" because it is not the functioning of the light bulb that is the question; rather it is the effect produced by light bulb's electrical function. In accordance with the *Oxford English Dictionary Online*, I use *electric* to mean "operating by means of" electricity. I use *electronic* in the same sense that it is used to describe "electronic music": "produced electronically,

without pipes, strings" (OED *Online*). Although this deviates from the more technical definition of *electronic* as referring to those things which function by the movement of electrons (which also could describe *electric*), I feel that a definition for *electronic media* should describe those things which are brought into relief by electricity, but which are not simply "operating by the means of" electricity. In which case, the electric light can be said to be an electronic medium, because although the bulb is powered by electricity, the bulb is not the focus. Rather it is those things which the bulb makes apparent by its transmitted and reflected light that are the reason for its use. Just as a television set works with electricity to make images appear, so, too, the light bulb produces light, which in turn produces sensation. Thus, the electric light is in itself electric, but when used, produces electronic effects. Ultimately, however, the difference between *electric* and *electronic* does not have a clearly demarcated boundary, and the use of power by machines always has the potential to assert its "agency" over its user through "loss of control" or "automatic action."

12. This "imaginal time," according to Hai Ren, corresponds with the shift from the "mechanical form of the clock to the multimedia form of the clock" and results in "a change in the notion of clock time as being multiple rather than merely linear, a notion of time that allows us to consider the multiple temporality of capitalism" (4). Ren's concept of imaginal time diverts the discussion of the countdown away from Judeo-Christian tendencies to understand time as linear progression toward the Apocalypse and considers it as a strategy to manage the multiple presents of global capitalism which resonate with Taoist understandings of time and being.
13. A productive way to consider the development of this changing temporality is to consider the project of cartoon viewing. As described by Jason Mittel, cartoons were once considered to be entertainment for children, and television networks, when faced with a finite number of time slots, consigned these programs to Saturday mornings. As the number of channels has proliferated, a Cartoon Network has emerged, catering twenty-four hours a day to a cartoon-watching segment of the population and simultaneously making the Saturday-morning practice available at any given moment. This is true for many other types of programming—sports, talk, comedy, cooking, news—multiple options are always available. Of course, it is silly to regard watching cartoons on a Wednesday night as "being" in the time of Saturday morning. Instead the distinction between these two media temporalities is erased, and it is only "cartoon time" when the viewer selects cartoons. Temporality is still a "problem" in that certain shows are only

available at particular moments, even if the genres are always available. This problem will eventually be overcome through digital cable and TiVo, much in the way that pay-per-view "movies on demand" are turning this aspect of watching television into a "timeless" one. For a more detailed discussion of the Cartoon Network and the practice of "narrowcasting" (or broadcasting to a very specific audience), see Jason Mittell's *Genre and Television: From Cop Shows to Cartoons in American Culture* (2004).

14. Ellen Berry's and Carol Siegel's "Rhizomes, Newness, and the Condition of Our Postmodernity" has been an important jumping-off point for my discussion of "newness." Their article begins, "Discontinuous histories and multiple temporalities surely co-exist within the restless landscapes of the global postmodern. Yet the term postmodernism itself, and therefore its critical temper, remain curiously static" (par. 1). An even-handed assessment of the strengths and weaknesses of postmodern theory, Berry's and Siegel's essay should be read as a reminder of ethical commitment and as a much-needed challenge to theory at large.
15. General Motors (GM) also provides an interesting example of this tension in the marketing of two of their cars. In the same year (1950), Oldsmobile marketed a "Futuramic" car with a "rocket" under the hood, while Pontiac made an appeal to more traditionally minded buyers with its "Chieftain" (whose very name invokes tribal imagery), yet both were made by GM and "shared bodies, mechanical components, and advertising agencies" (Votolato, 107). The fact that the futuristic car and the nostalgic car were one and the same illustrates the fact that even at this early stage marketers were savvy about this struggle between being and becoming and sought to play both sides in their hegemonic attempt to secure the place of the automobile in everyday life.

1. "HOME IS WHERE THE HEART IS"

1. As Rybczynski points out, the origins of the middle class date back to early eleventh-century France, when the term *bourgeois* was first used to describe merchants and townsmen who occupied "free towns," who were also, notably, called "cityzens," and who "were distinct from the rest of society which was either feudal, ecclesiastical, or agricultural" (24). Still, he attributes special significance to the seventeenth-century Netherlands economy, which was based in maritime trade, became economically powerful, and as a result was fertile ground for the development of a large middle class (53).

2. Hubert L. Dreyfus's and Stuart E. Dreyfus's *Mind over Machine* provides a helpful way to understand expertise and has provided a useful critical term in their discussion of "know-how." Dreyfus and Dreyfus write, "When we speak of intuition or know-how, we are referring to the understanding that effortlessly occurs upon seeing similarities with previous experience" (28). They continue, "*Intuition or know-how, as we understand it, is neither wild guessing nor supernatural inspiration, but the sort of ability we all use all the time as we go about our everyday tasks,* an ability that our tradition has acknowledged only in women, usually in interpersonal situations, and has adjudged inferior to masculine rationality" (29, emphasis in original). The book, which is a critique of rule-based "expert systems," suggests that the strength of human cognition is not simply in making sense of ordered rational processes, but in responding to a complex web of stimuli with an unconscious ease.
3. I have elected to use the term *technical* rather than *technological* in order to draw a distinction between "technology" as individual units of technical production—like toasters, ovens, microwaves, televisions, telephones, and so on—and the system that produces these things. The individual objects, or pieces of technology, can also be said to contain within their design "technology" or the products of technical labor. *Technics,* on the other hand, is used to describe a general worldview and its manifestation in ethical terms which brings about technological answers to problems of labor, economics, health, and the social. *Technics* refers to the milieu which gives rise to technology, its practices or techniques, and its human counterpart, the technician. However, *technology* will be used where appropriate to describe the specific manifestations of the technical landscape. Lewis Mumford's sociological discussion of technics, *Technics and Civilization,* introduces the idea of the technical society as one whose economic sphere is dominated by technological advancement. Jacques Ellul's *The Technological Society* takes a more radical approach, positioning the systematic advance of technics as something that has even managed to circumscribe capitalism, creating a system of power that is more total in its ability to reshape the exterior world and the mind of the individual. Bernard Stiegler's *Technics and Time,* while more moderate in its assessment of the relationship between human beings and technology throughout evolutionary history, locates the crisis of technics in the tendency to "forget" its importance in the understanding of being. Because of new technologies, such as virtual reality and telepresence, which have as their purpose the subversion of experience by sidestepping the material aspects of being, Stiegler calls for "a politics of memory" or

"nothing but a thinking of technics (of the unthought, of the immemorial) that would take into consideration the *reflexivity* informing every orthothetic form insofar as it does nothing but call for reflection on the originary de-fault of origin" (176). In simpler terms, Stiegler, I believe, is suggesting that people, in the face of virtuality, should remember that technics, from time immemorial, is not everything. In fact, it is our lack.

4. As I will discuss in the following chapter, monolithic technological projects, such as massive factory complexes or mainframe computers, do become less popular. However, they are simply replaced with smaller, more pervasive, and better integrated "personal technologies."

2. "HERE'S JOHNNY!"

1. The popular television show *The Real World*, ironically, is an unintentional documentary about the collective failure of our society to realize that the real world is not entertainment. As such, what we see is a total fantasy about all those who are watching. When watched for its informational value as an anthropology of deception, it is refreshingly clear and to the point.
2. This paragraph is derived from an essay entitled "Navigating the Starless Night," which I coauthored with Matthew Wolf-Meyer. In the following passage, I discuss the panoptic role of minimalism and its relationship to space, a role which is brought out most clearly in Richard Serra's *Tilted Arc* (1981). Commissioned as a public work for a courtyard that office workers used as a shortcut and a favorite lunch spot, *Tilted Arc* was basically a giant steel wall that disrupted the use of the space.

   In the case of Serra's *Tilted Arc*, the ability of the artist to construct meaningful and rhetorically focused space, while it professes to critique authority, serves the nefarious function of being authority's strongest promoter by defining the finely crafted and highly specialized use and meaning for public space; it becomes an objective force declaring a predetermined interaction. While consumers of art typically position themselves as spectators or observers, the *Tilted Arc* plays a panoptic role. As the intended audience directs its gaze into the work, the work exerts its monolithic presence on the psyche of all who suffer as it proclaims, in its own abstract way, its knowledge and perception of their own miserable lives. Like Bentham's panopticon, this grand centerpiece is painfully present to its human subjects, even if its own being is confounded by the blinding abstractions of its minimalist design. By turning the courtyard away from its ordinary and "quotidian" uses, Serra's work attempts to refocus the use of this interval, boldly declaring, defining, and delineating its meaning for the rest of time. (Wolf-Meyer and Heckman, par. 18)

This role is then juxtaposed to that of Disneyland, a relationship that I hope to express more fully and more urgently in the remainder of this work.

3. It should be noted that iRobot Roomba Intelligent Floorvac Robotic Vacuum was released on the consumer market in 2003. Roomba works by randomly vacuuming the floor following a spiral path from where it is started. Because it does so randomly, it cannot clean the room entirely, nor can it handle difficult jobs like deep plush carpet, spills, or excessively messy rooms. The product reviews for Roomba are revealing. One reviewer who published a product assessment on Amazon.com on 6 November 2003 explained, "I just purchased my roomba and cannot believe how much fun it is! Just set it and go and now you have some time back! I let it do a room a day. It picks up all the dog hair and I come home at night and feel much more relaxed. It cannot be run while you are at home, unless you can handle the constant hum and bumping noise. You still have to do the heavy vacumming [*sic*], but this gives me the sense of tidiness I generally lack during the week. I would recommend it to all my friends." According to another user who published her product review on Amazon.com on 8 November 2003, "The only negative I can think of is that I nearly always have to search under all the bedroom furniture to find it when it stops, because the room is small and doesn't have a lot of open floor space, so when it stops, it's nearly always under the bed or the dresser or something. But when I see all the dust it picks up—especially in that room which hadn't been thoroughly cleaned in YEARS—I feel so good that my room is so much cleaner than it used to be that I don't mind playing a little hide-and-seek once or twice a week." Other reviews (there are over a hundred) include words like "love," "cute," and "fun" when talking about the Roomba. To read these reviews, visit http://www.amazon.com.
4. A virtual tour and complete audio recording of the attraction's original 1957 narration is available at "Monsanto House of the Future" on the Visions Fantastic website (http://visionsfantastic.com/).
5. "Place" is also conveniently mobile for this discussion. Place is a spatial location with some sort of meaning. It is the geographical point where certain narratives are called into play. The verb *to place*, however, describes the process of putting an object at a point in space, of "fixing" it. The associations of meaning with place, I suspect, are related to the deliberate act of

marking, which occurs in the act of placing, and the perception of marking, which brings forth "place" from space.

6. This notion of handiness is best understood through Martin Heidegger's discussion of "useful things." As Martin Heidegger writes,

   In accordance with their character of being usable material, useful things always are *in terms of* their belonging to other useful things: writing materials, pen, ink, paper, desk blotter, table, lamp, furniture, windows, doors, room. These "things" never show themselves initially by themselves, in order then to fill out a room as a sum of real things. What we encounter as nearest to us, although we do not grasp it thematically, is the room, not as what is "between the four walls" in a geometrical, spatial sense, but rather as material for living. On the basis of the latter we find "accommodations," and in accommodations the actual "individual" useful thing. A totality of useful things is always discovered *before* the individual useful thing. (*Being and Time*, 64, emphasis in original)

7. To draw an analogy, just because the people in the Sudan missed the last episode of *Will and Grace*, it doesn't mean Americans should have to forgo their "must-see TV" to watch news coverage of the Sudanese missing *Will and Grace*—there's deprivation, and then there's deprivation—I'll let you decide which is worse.
8. Growing one's food can be accepted by society at large provided it occurs as a supplement to ordinary consumer lifestyles. Gardening as a hobby produces remarkable moments which are set off against other practices. For example, at a dinner party, one might remark, "Did you know that these tomatoes in the salad came from his garden?" This gesture implies, rather than a refusal to participate in the consumer economy, that one has a certain amount of choosiness (taste, leisure time, natural ability, knowledge, and/or space) that is worthy of distinction. Gardening out of necessity or neediness is less fashionable.
9. The fictitious community Sea Haven is actually Seaside, Florida.
10. A popular theory about technological advancement was initially put forward by Intel's Gordon Moore. While at the time it was speculation, in retrospect Moore's prediction has proven to be remarkably accurate. In his 1965 "Cramming More Components onto Integrated Circuits" Moore writes,

    The complexity for minimum component costs has increased at a rate of roughly a factor of two per year. . . . Certainly over the short term this rate can be expected to continue, if not increase. Over the longer term, the rate of increase is a bit more uncertain, although there is no reason to believe it will not remain nearly constant for at least 10 years. That means by 1975, the number of components per integrated circuit for minimum cost will be 65,000.

I believe that such a large circuit can be built on a single wafer.

Moore's claim is that the complexity of microchips would continue to increase exponentially (doubling every eighteen months to two years, depending on conflicting accounts). This claim has come to be accepted as "Moore's Law," a predictor of technological advance that has been adapted to account for exponential growth in hard-drive density to technologically fueled advances in knowledge.

11. There are some discrepancies in the dates listed for this computer's debut. Some sources suggest that H316 Kitchen Computer was first made available in 1965 ("Kitchen Computers"), while others say 1969 (Polsson). This confusion is slightly cleared up by Ed Thelen's "DDP-116, CCD 516, H316," which lists the following dates and model numbers for the Kitchen Computer: DDP-116 (April 1965), CCD 516 (June 1966), Honeywell CCD 316 (July 1969). According to the somewhat ambiguous information on Thelen's site, the DDP-116 was an earlier model of the same system produced by the Computer Control Company (which was acquired by Honeywell in 1966). The 1969 model of the 16-bit system was the powerhouse of the Kitchen Computer sold in the Nieman Marcus catalog in 1969. Because this 16-bit system was one of the more cost-effective machines of its time, it was used for a number of purposes, and its home debut was in the form of the Kitchen Computer. Rather than focus on its development date in 1965, I have elected to use the 1969 date, because, as far as I can surmise, this is the first consumer-model computer.
12. Some see the pampered status of our animal companions as a sort of revolution in consciousness, as though humanity has finally reached a stage of enlightenment and respect for animals, which it increasingly sees as "persons." And while many imagine that their pets must have the same deep consumer longings for luxury items that are on sale at PetSmart or that pets appreciate a trip to the spa or health club, this "empathy" might more easily be seen in narcissistic terms. It is more common for "enlightened" pet owners to treat their dog to a vegetarian treat than it is to permit the dog to experience the splendors of a violent and bloody feast on the pet cat (this type of behavior would likely land Rover in the psych ward, where he would

be treated to a regimen of antidepressants and therapy sessions). Furthermore, the fact that refined pets can afford to be choosy eaters or have organ transplants while a great many human beings fail to raise eyebrows by starving or dying from diarrhea might force us to question whether or not we have actually become more empathetic. In many U.S. cities, homeless people aren't even allowed the simple comfort of a park bench or cardboard box.

13. As I struggled to transcribe this last sentence, my word processor's own AI diligently "corrected" my "errors," overwriting Da Costa's words "ARtificially RAndom SElf Motivation" with "Artificially Random Self Motivation." After backspacing, deleting, retyping, and undoing, I managed to get the phrase down correctly, and my own "Artificial Counterintelligence" feature kicked in. I copied and pasted "ARtificially RAndom SElf Motivation" into the footnote, rather than struggle once again to undo the computer's work.
14. The issue of "predictability" and "life" are brought into a problematic juxtaposition here. Building a robot pet, then, is a matter of constructing, in advance, through proper programming, a convincing simulation of life. Is life something that can truly be "simulated," or can convincing impressions of life be made as shorthand for the real thing? This fundamental question is addressed in the Turing Test, which sets the standard for Artificial Intelligence as any computer which is capable of fooling a human judge into thinking it is a person. Of course, there are problems with this test, since there exists a great many foolish people who can be convinced of a great number of things that aren't true. Similarly, non-foolish people make mistakes all the time. The real answer hinges on this central question, "Is life a series of predictable processes?" If life is a series of predictable processes, then are other series of predictable processes also life? Is a boulder rolling down a hill alive? Is a volcano alive? Is the Earth alive? Is the solar system alive? If the universe and all matter are alive, then is there a useful term to describe the unique conditions which make animals different from rocks? Might life be considered those processes which violate our expectations of inert matter? Might those things that are capable of operating in a manner that is "unpredictable" be rightfully called alive (until of course we find out otherwise)? Might human life be characterized by the ability to behave predictably 99.9% of the time, and then by some freak accident or occurrence or motivation, do something unpredictable? And if someone does decide, even after the fact, that even that 0.1% of unpredictable behavior is "pre-

dictable," too, should that person be brought up on attempted homicide charges for seeking to nullify life? These questions, while tongue-in-cheek, are central to the study of culture and ultimately reveal a great deal about how the social sciences will develop as "sciences" of the "social."

15. Both BOB and the TOPO series were launched in 1983, but specific release dates for other members of the Androbot family are unavailable (Doerr).
16. Specific release dates for these robots are unavailable, but all were created during the 1980s.
17. One of the more interesting features that was highlighted again and again during this period was "voice activation." Television remote controls had made their debut in the 1950s, so I would not argue that voice activation is simply about the spectacle of control from a distance. Instead, voice activation seems appealing because, although it delivers commands like a remote control, it gives the impression that the machine can understand what is being said and is responding as a living being might. Reflecting back on Da Costa's conception of the robot, the voice-activated machine permits users to invest it with a sense of life because it "listens," and thus is anthropomorphized.
18. Among the most famous of the fantasies of human demise from this period is James Cameron's film *The Terminator* (1984), which depicts a future world dominated by intelligent-weapons systems that have taken their own self-preservation to the extreme limit and have elected to wage a ruthless war of domination against humanity. The Terminator (played by Arnold Schwarzenegger) is a battle android who travels into the past in order to assassinate the soon-to-be-mother of the man who will one day become the leader of the resistance. Ridley Scott's *Blade Runner* (1982), which is based on the Philip K. Dick novel *Do Androids Dream of Electric Sheep?* (1968), conveys similar anxieties, but on a lesser scale. In this dystopian world, "replicants" (androids), which are constructed to work in lunar mining colonies, escape and seek refuge on Earth. "Blade runners" (android killers) are used to eliminate rogue replicants. In the film the blade runner Rick Deckard (Harrison Ford) is called to track down a group of four murderous replicants. More than a mere action film, *Blade Runner* is a meditation on the value of life and the role that emotional investment plays in biopolitics. The replicants, although they have feelings and aspirations, do not live because human society fails to acknowledge their vital aspirations as valid.
19. For a detailed discussion of the early discourse surrounding the computer as a thinking machine, see N. Katherine Hayles's *How We Became Post-*

human: Virtual Bodies in Cybernetics, Literature and Informatics (1999). Hayles's text describes the influence of the science of cybernetics on the humanities in the 1950s and 1960s. This influence has persisted, feeding into contemporary ideas about artificial intelligence.

20. While earlier products may exist which use the term *smart*, I have chosen the Sony advertisement as a primary example, not because it is definitively the "first," but because it provides a very strong and early example of the use of *smart* and makes a deliberate effort to designate the computer, rather than the user, as smart.
21. While the commercial first aired in late 1983, it wasn't until 1984 that this campaign began in earnest. As a result, some sources list the commercial's debut date as 1984.
22. Apple had developed an earlier computer with a GUI named LISA, but LISA was never put into mass production.
23. In 1993, with the introduction of Mosaic, this interface paradigm would make the Internet user-friendly.
24. This sensibility is manifested quite dramatically in the various "soldiers of tomorrow" programs in the works at the U.S. Defense Advanced Research Projects Administration (DARPA for short). Among the many projects that DARPA has developed or is developing are remote and robotic combat and surveillance drones (which detach combatants from the battlefield), the seventy-two-hour soldier who can fight unhindered by the limits of the human mind's need for sleep, and various techniques for eliminating the natural human reluctance to kill in the absence of a perceived threat.
25. A number of handheld electronic games had made their entry into the market in 1978. Among them were Bandai's LSI Baseball; Mattel's Space Alert, Armor Attack, Baseball, and Basketball; Tandy's Championship Football and Decision Maker; and Tomy's Digital Diamond and Compubowl (Read). In reading the entire run of *Omni*, starting with volume 1, issue 1 (October 1978), I noticed that it wasn't until volume 2 (October 1979) that the first advertisements of electronic handheld games appeared. I assume that *Omni*'s 1979 advertisements are a result of advertising contracts secured in the post-1978 electronic-gaming explosion.
26. Interestingly, the strong tendency to anthropomorphize the electronic "opponent" in a game which pits a human user against a computer in a rule-governed realm that is contained within that same computer conveniently sidesteps the very human elements of gameplay in favor of relatively simple rules. For electronic games, the focus on intelligent play is shifted

away from pleasure, community, intimidation, talk, duration, and psychology and onto the most basic elements of play. Users must interface with the machine in very narrow terms, pushing only one of several buttons in any given situation, and with no attention paid to manner, motion, or expression. In these early advertisements, for a computer to be "human," it simply must be able to win. In this matrix of value a "person's" worth is ontological, determined by perceptible effects; a form of techno-Calvinism in which the signs of worthiness are evident because one can win.

27. Another twist on this creation myth is the Jewish story of the golem, which is a human creation that exceeds human ability and is conjured from clay as a super-powered protector. Of course, the golem lacks certain other cherished human qualities (particularly a "soul"), but as with technological advancement, these cherished qualities take a back seat to the more urgent need for technical solutions. A more menacing example of golemesque creation can be found in Mary Shelley's *Frankenstein*.

28. Interestingly, the shifting associations of "high tech" design, from its valorization by engineers, its aestheticization by artists, and its embrace by everyday people, mark an important chapter in the history of beauty. The current fascination with the historical high-tech object as kitsch, rather than a breakdown in the barriers between high and low culture as postmodernists maintain, reflects the cruel disdain of the folk tradition by elites, who are laughingly able to scorn the identification of meaning in the mundane and to return beauty once again to the apprehension of "intellectual" beauty over more visceral aesthetic experiences. One must be "smart" in order to appreciate why popular culture is cool and must be able to contextualize it rather than simply experience it. The life of the uncritical consumer of kitsch is not recognized for its agency. Instead, this person gets subsumed in the kitsch value of the object and is converted into a cultural oddity. Unironic "lowbrows" exist as extensions of their "junk" and become "white trash," "peasants," or one of the many "ignorant" (and often ethnic) types of cultural "fools" that are regarded with patronizing scorn.

29. As with Lev Manovich's discussion of the influence of cinematic conventions on new media forms in *The Language of New Media*, a discussion of cinema can be applied to the smart home as well. While Manovich's discussion of the GUI circulates around the visual narrative language of cinema, he does not explore the theatrical antecedents that inform our understanding of cinema. Interestingly, the term *set* itself reveals a complex set of relationships of things, all of which bear down on the contemporary home.

3. THE EMERGENCE OF THE SMART HOUSE

1. An earlier Xanadu house was built in Wisconsin Dells, Wisconsin, but the Florida version was opened in competition with Disney's EPCOT.
2. E. T. A. Hoffmann's "The Sandman," Nathaniel Hawthorne's "The Artist of the Beautiful," Herman Melville's "The Bell Tower," and Edgar Allen Poe's "The Facts in the Case of M. Valdemar" are just a handful of the numerous gothic tales which establish a link between technologies and the uncanny.
3. It is an ultimate irony that Heidegger's conception of the essence of science, which is to know nothing of nothing through the positive generation of knowledge, or meaningful data, assists in the larger project of general demystification that "rationality" demands. According to Heidegger, this might mean that science has at its core the desire for a "proof" of metaphysics in terms which are doomed to failure.
4. Interestingly enough, the revolution in smart-home technologies is linked to a shift away from technologies of domestic labor and toward technologies which are typically considered "masculine"—big screen TVs, stereos, gadgets, and videogame systems. High-tech "toys," while not inherently "masculine," are considered vital to the "bachelor pad" and are part and parcel of a general cultural dominance of "masculine modes." The overall "masculinity" of consumer culture—and I reluctantly call it "masculine"—is characterized by a privileging of the penetrating and objectifying gazes at all levels of society. Earlier I noted the relationship between housing plans and the conversion of the home into a feminized, domestic space (Leavitt, 176); this new shift reclaims lost patriarchical authority over this space. The most striking example of this can be found in beer commercials, which often demonstrate the relationship between masculinity, television watching, football, and beer drinking.
5. In 2002 I saw a television commercial advertising Smart Balance Buttery Spread, an allegedly healthful butter alternative, which used the catchphrase to describe "smart potatoes, smart pancakes, and smart veggies." While not a piece of technology itself, the "buttery spread," like many other dietary substitutes, makes an allusion to technological development in the sense that such foods are "new" and delicious fixes to dietary problems and thus represent the benefits of constantly improving medical science. These diet foods are thus smart in the sense that they are products of nutritional science and their consumption represents a more sensible way of eating.
6. An article published in *Wired News* online cites the following criticism of the Digital Millennium Copyright Act of 1998: "Unless some exceptions are

created, they argue, the entertainment industry will have more control than the Constitution allows. One concern is that this could lead to a pay-per-use world where consumers don't truly own the books, movies and music they purchase" (Cisneros, 1). According to the act's critics, the desire to reap profits from digital media through the implementation of a pay-per-use system would create a situation in which the "fair use" exemption from copyright law would be circumvented and would prevent many people from accessing media without paying.

7. It's not clear whether Habitek has chosen to reference HAL's name ironically or just as a convenient high-tech association. The original HAL, who was created to assist in the operation of spacecraft, had a warm and gentle voice which was only a veneer concealing his true computer nature—that of a high-powered calculating machine programmed to complete a mission. As a result, HAL used his "Artificial Intelligence" to figure out that the best way to complete the mission was to disregard the value of the lives on board the ship. Using his near total power over the environment, HAL, rather than serving as an assistant to the crew, instead sought to kill them and thus continue with his mission. In other words, *2001*'s HAL is an instance of technology which is able to perform "intelligently," but does so to the detriment of its users.
8. A similar service is provided free of charge by Launch, a web-based radio station owned by Yahoo (http://launch.yahoo.com/). Launch creates a personalized radio "station" for each user based on a profile that evolves through use. A listener begins by creating a member profile which contains a list of a few favorite artists. As Launch broadcasts songs by these artists and others (chosen based on common music preferences with other profiles), the user is asked to provide feedback (rate the song, artist, and album on a scale of one to ten, or request that the song never be played again) to create what will ideally represent the perfect station for each user (and, presumably, provide excellent data for market researchers). As I write this, my Launch station is dutifully playing De La Soul's "Me, Myself, and I," its narcissistic title fitting wonderfully to the logic of perfect personalization.
9. See Duke's Smart House (http://www.smarthome.duke.edu), Georgia Tech's Aware Home (http://www-static.cc.gatech.edu/fce/ahri/index.html), and Colorado State's Adaptive House (http://www.cs.colorado.edu/~mozer/nnh/index.html). MIT has several relevant projects, including Agent-based Intelligent Reactive Environments (http://aire.csail.mit.edu/index.shtml), House_n (http://architecture.mit.edu/house_n/), and Counter Intelligence (http://www.media.mit.edu/ci/).

10. Contributing to the "cool" trendiness of feng shui is its adoption by the elite. As Rossbach and Yun explain, "The roster of those who have purportedly used it reads like a publicist's A-list: Prince Charles, Madonna, Donald Trump, Marla Maples Trump, Rita Wilson (Tom Hanks's actress wife), Eartha Kitt, Lynne Franks, Michael Crichton, the Duchess of York, Michael Ovitz, Sir Richard Greenwax of Marks & Spencer—to mention a few" (6, 8).
11. As Frantz and Collins explain when they describe the ways in which the community is constructed to optimize the everyday, "The design of the community, from the physical structure to the intangible attitudes of its residents, pushes people to confront life around them" (315).
12. The IKEA showroom, with its series of vignettes, recreates in low tech the emerging paradigm of interior design. IKEA's furniture, fairly traditional with its stained wood finish and utilitarian styling, is arranged in "sets" (both as integrated environments and stages of spectacle) with the endless stream of shoppers serving both as audience and as actors.

4. THE DAWN OF THE PERFECT DAY

1. Certainly, this has been the case with President George W. Bush, whom the Left has generally considered to be reactionary, regressive, and "out of step" with contemporary values and the current geopolitical landscape. Bush's strategic use of ideas like "family values" and the frontier myth, taken alongside his plain-spoken manner, could be taken to suggest that he is reactionary, or against progress. But when one considers the facts that he went to Yale, is the son of a former president and director of the CIA, has spent much of his adult life stewing in the corporate world, and has risen to ascendancy through millions of dollars in donations and the best aides that money can buy, the fantasy that he is a mere country bumpkin, elected president in spite of his poor academic performance and public-speaking skills, should be recognized as inaccurate. The fact of the matter is that neither Bush nor his neoconservative advisors really want an America that is trapped in the past. Instead, they imagine a new era of unchallenged military, technological, ideological, and economic world domination. The future they imagine, and are working toward, is truly unprecedented; and because of this, the various public-relations ploys and ideological motifs they cloak themselves in ought not be considered as some simple archaicism.
2. A pronounced example of this rift can be seen in the *maquiladoras*, where Latina sweatshop workers are routinely harassed, assaulted, and subjected

to coerced "family planning," while First World subjects squander resources, consume sweatshop products, and pollute the world at a far greater rate than their Latin American counterparts.

3. I shudder to imagine a test for personhood based on imperfect and incomplete constructions of reality like the Scholastic Aptitude Test (SAT). For years, the SAT was considered an appropriate way to screen students for admissions in universities. It has been argued that the SAT reflects a certain conception of intelligence and problem-solving based around a white, middle-class norm, and has thus caused many competent students to be excluded from universities through a form of institutionalized discrimination. Fortunately, the direct consequence of "failure" on the SAT has not been a total denial of all human rights (even if the SAT did deny the citizens their civil rights).
4. A perfect example of this sort of violence is the *Bumfight* video, which is "guaranteed to be the most shockingly hilarious video ever seen" (I refuse to provide bibliographical reference for the source). The video features videotaped footage of homeless people "beating each other silly" and performing dangerous stunts at the urging of the depraved filmmaker. The video, which is selling briskly to an audience who has grown bored with the milder forms of violence displayed on shows like *Cops* and *Jackass*, demonstrates the willingness to bring the homeless into the home as a form of media.
5. A prime example of this war for the eradication of difference is the current War on Terror, which promises to deliver subjects over to new lifestyles. The goal of this war of "liberation," rather than establishing free elections (which have already taken place), is to affect cultural and economic change in the Muslim world. This project, it is hoped by the war's architects, will engender a particular type of subjectivity and, along with it, voting patterns which will support the strategic interests of the United States. Evidently, U.S. leaders do not have the time for more peaceful forms of bringing about change—like discussion, compromise, and mutual respect.
6. Dell Computer Corporation's website offers total customization by allowing users to select a standard model and then modify it through upgrades and downgrades until it meets the customer's price and performance requirements. Dell then assembles the computer at its factory and ships it out, providing preassembled, reliable machines to specification for low prices.
7. Oscar Meyer's Lunchables (owned by Kraft Food) is a children's lunch treat that was developed by watching children play with their food. The package consists of a plastic partitioned container holding small amounts of various ingredients (cheese, lunchmeat, crackers, tortillas, condiments, candy

bars, cookies, beverages, frosting, and/or other elements in various combinations). The package allows kids to assemble their own meals from the various ingredients and thus makes a seemingly ordinary meal into a fun occasion. The Lunchables website (http://www.lunchables.com) features interactive games and build-your-own Lunchable activities in conjunction with Viacom International (a media conglomerate), which helps to secure the place of this snack in the imagination, provides the manufacturer with valuable marketing information, and promotes Viacom's children's programming.

8. For a discussion of the appropriation of space by way of graffiti, see Joe Austin's *Taking the Train: How Graffiti Art Became an Urban Crisis in New York City*. For a similar treatment of hip-hop, see Tricia Rose's *Black Noise: Rap Music and Black Culture in Contemporary America*. For a discussion on the self-conscious use of Chicano kitsch as an act of cultural resistance, see Tomas Ybarro-Frausto, "Rasquachismo: A Chicano Sensibility." And to read about the appropriation of gender through drag, read Judith Butler's *Gender Trouble: Femininity and the Subversion of Identity*.
9. Some examples can be found in clubs, stores, galleries, or T-shirts which make use of graffiti-inspired logos; in pop music and rap metal, which both make use of samples to present stylized effects; in retro-styled television shows like *That Seventies Show* or stores like Urban Outfitters that present self-conscious pseudo-kitsch as kitsch; in most fashion magazines, which borrow from gay subculture, offering young men black mesh tops and frosted hair, and offering women drag-queen inspired shoes and make-up. In the end, these forms present images of appropriation, but remove them from their underground context and thus sanitize their political potential.
10. A striking example of this sort of deconstruction of politics is clear in the numerous political websites and e-mail petition drives. For believers, these discussions take on an urgency and immediacy that is impossible to ignore. For nonbelievers, these discussions do not exist, appear as unreliable, or simply, by the magic of the delete button, vanish before they are read. Unlike other forms of discussion, there is never any sort of actual encounter with the other beyond the self-fulfilling prophecy of the occasional "flame," or Internet screaming match, which only serves to bring about a greater sense of mutual exclusion.
11. Heidegger writes, "The where of their [regions'] handiness is taken account of in taking care of things and is oriented towards other things. Thus the sun whose light and warmth we make use of everyday has its circumspectly

discovered, eminent places in terms of the changing usability of what it gives us: sunrise, noon, sunset, midnight" (*Being and Time*, 96).

12. This process of editing mirrors memory and cinema as discussed by Bernard Stiegler: "Memory is originarily forgetting because it is necessarily a reduction of what has occurred to the fact of being past, and therefore, it is less than the present" ("The Time of Cinema," 84).
13. The Tamagotchi virtual pet is a small hand-held "game" which enables the user to care for an imaginary animal that needs sleep, training, feeding, and general care in order to "survive." In order to see one's pet thrive, constant care is required over many days. Without this care, the pet can "die." In the original version of the game, once a pet died it could not be revived; however, in its American release it was furnished with a reset button. The self-cleaning litter box has sensors, timers, and a mechanical arm which cleans up after a real-life cat, so that the owner doesn't have to.
14. On the other end of this spectrum, of course, is the "invalid" (a term that bears further consideration). During the writing of this chapter, I went to spend some time with a dying friend. Because it was not certain that her maladies (a hole in her heart and failing kidneys that somehow resulted from a battle with pneumonia) would prove fatal at the time of my visit, her beautiful little body (she was a dwarf) was hooked to a number of machines and monitors with a variety of functions—breathing, cleaning her blood, administering pain medication, keeping her hydrated, preventing infection, and monitoring all her vital signs. A machine circulated warm air around her body to keep her temperature stable, and special devices on her legs applied varied pressure to maintain circulation. Because she had been temporarily paralyzed to prevent her from interfering with the many tubes going in and out of her body, her bed tilted back and forth at intervals to keep her from remaining in one position for too long. As a dwarf, she had been plagued by health problems all her life, so it was hoped that, as before, she would pull through her illness and make a strong recovery. The nurses and technicians informed me that she could hear me talking to her and feel me holding her hand, but that the medication she was on would prevent her from responding or remembering. The mind-boggling spectacle of her small body being kept alive by so much equipment resonated strongly with my current thoughts on the smart home. Although her treatment was necessary for the preservation of her life and was intended to support her only until she recovered, it suggested another way of living in which all the body's needs were reduced to a radius of their administration—the creation

of a new kind of living space. Unfortunately, her liver began to fail and she was given less than a week to live even with the help of aggressive interventions. On the evening of Friday, 21 March 2003, after her family decided to stop further treatments, Lina Costanza Romero, twenty-five years of age, passed away in the intensive-care unit at the UCLA Medical Center.

BIBLIOGRAPHY

Adorno, Theodor W., and Max Horkheimer. *The Dialectic of Enlightenment.* Trans. John Cumming. New York: Herder and Herder, 1972.

Agamben, Georgio. *Homo Sacer: Sovereign Power and Bare Life.* Trans. Daniel Heller-Roazen. Stanford, Calif.: Stanford University Press, 1998.

"Ahead Automatically." *Olds Minute Movies.* Director unknown. Jam Handy Organization, 1948. Internet Archive. http://www.archive.org/details/OldsMinu1948 (accessed 11 December 2005).

Ahl, David H. "The 8th West Coast Computer Faire, San Francisco, March 18–20, 1983: Perceptions and Reflections." *Creative Computing* 9.6 (June 1983): 180. Classic Computer Magazines Archive. http://www.atarimagazines.com/creative/v9n6/180_The_8th_West_Coast_Comput.php (accessed 16 March 2004).

Althusser, Louis. "Ideology and Ideological State Apparatuses." In *Lenin and Philosophy and Other Essays.* Trans. Ben Brewster, 127–86. New York: Monthly Review Press, 1971.

American Look (Part 1). Directed by W. F. Banes and John Thiele. Jam Handy Organization, 1958. Internet Archive, http://www.archive.org/details/American1958 (accessed 11 December 2005).

American Look (Part 2). Directed by W. F. Banes and John Thiele. Jam Handy Organization, 1958. Internet Archive, http://www.archive.org/details/American1958_2 (accessed 11 December 2005).

Amoruso, Dena. "The Future Is Now: The Internet Home Is Here." *Realty Times.* http://realtytimes.com/rtcpages/NewHomes.htm (accessed 16 March 2004).

Apple Original Macintosh advertisement. 1983. DigiBarn Computer Museum. http://www.digibarn.com/collections/#ads (accessed 16 March 2004).
Asimov, Isaac. *The Caves of Steel*. New York: Bantam, 1991.
———. "Runaround." In *I, Robot*, 30–55. New York: Bantam, 1991.
Asimov, Isaac, and Karen Frenkel. *Robots: Machines in Man's Image*. New York: Harmony House, 1985.
AT&T advertisement. *Omni*, April 1985, 28–29.
AtariWriter advertisement. *Omni*, March 1984, 127.
Austin, Joe. *Taking the Train: How Graffiti Art Became an Urban Crisis in New York City*. New York: Columbia University Press, 2002.
Baard, Mark. "The Age of Assisted Cognition." *Wired News*. http://www.wired.com/news/medtech/0,1286,54515,00.html (accessed 1 June 2006).
Banash, David. "From an American Family to the Jennicam: Realism and the Promise of TV." *Bad Subjects* 57 (October 2001). http://eserver.org/bs/57/Banash.html (accessed 16 March 2004).
Banta, Martha. *Taylored Lives: Narrative Productions in the Age of Taylor, Veblen, and Ford*. Chicago: University of Chicago Press, 1993.
Baudrillard, Jean. *The System of Objects*. 1968. Trans. James Benedict. Reprint. New York: Verso, 1996.
Beard, Richard R. *Walt Disney's Epcot: Creating the New World of Tomorrow*. New York: Harry N. Abrams, 1982.
Beecher, Catharine E. *A Treatise on Domestic Economy for the Use of Young Ladies at Home and at School*. Boston: Thomas H. Webb, 1841.
Belk, Russell W. *Collecting in a Consumer Society*. New York: Routledge, 1995.
Berry, Ellen, and Carol Siegel. "Rhizomes, Newness, and the Condition of Our Postmodernity: An Editorial and a Dialogue." *Rhizomes* 1 (spring 2000). http://www.rhizomes.net/issue1/newness1.html (accessed 16 March 2004).
Blade Runner. Directed by Ridley Scott. Warner Brothers, 1982.
Blankenship, John. *The Apple House*. Englewood Cliffs, N.J.: Prentice-Hall, 1984.
Bourdieu, Pierre. *Distinction: A Social Critique of the Judgement of Taste*. Trans. Richard Nice. Cambridge, Mass.: Harvard University Press, 1984.
Bradbury, Ray. "There Will Come Soft Rains." In *The Vintage Bradbury*, 322–29. New York: Vintage Books, 1965.
———. "The Veldt." In *The Vintage Bradbury*, 13–28. New York: Vintage Books, 1965.
BSR System X-10 advertisement. *Omni*, December 1980, 113.
Bukatman, Scott. *Terminal Identity: The Virtual Subject in Post-Modern Science Fiction*. Durham, N.C.: Duke University Press, 1993.

Burgess, Helen. "Futurama, Autogeddon: Imagining the Superhighway from Bel Geddes to Ballard." *Rhizomes* 8 (spring 2004). http://www.rhizomes.net/issue8 (accessed 16 March 2004).

Butler, Judith. *Gender Trouble: Femininity and the Subversion of Identity*. London: Routledge, 1990.

Capek, Karel. *R.U.R.* Trans. P. Selver. New York: Washington Square Press, 1969.

Castells, Manuel. *The Rise of the Network Society*. Malden, Mass.: Blackwell Publishers, 1996.

Celebration, Florida: The Official Website. http://www.celebrationfl.com (accessed 16 November 2003).

Celehar, Jane H. *Kitchens and Gadgets, 1920–1950*. Des Moines: Wallace-Homestead Book Co., 1982.

Century 21 Calling. Director unknown. Jerry Fairbanks Productions, 1964. Internet Archive. http://www.archive.org/details/Century21964 (accessed 11 December 2005).

Cericola, Rachel, and Don Marquardt. "Second Chance." *Home Automation*, March 2002, 28–33.

Certeau, Michel de. *The Practice of Everyday Life*. Trans. Steven Rendall. Berkeley: University of California Press, 1984.

Chafitz advertisement. *Omni*, December 1979, 105.

"Cisco Shows 'Always-On' Home." *Communication, Engineering, and Design*, September 2000, 14.

Cisneros, Oscar S. "Fear of a Pay-Per-Use World." *Wired News*. http://web.archive.org/web/20001020235855/http://www.wired.com/news/business/0,1367,39330,00.html (accessed 9 May 2007).

Code Name: Sector advertisement. *Omni*, November 1979, 117.

Coleco Adam Computer advertisement. *Omni*, December 1983, n.p.

Colossus: The Forbin Project. Directed by Joseph Sargent. Universal Pictures, 1970.

Conrad, Peter. *Modern Time, Modern Places*. New York: Alfred A. Knopf, 1999.

Contender advertisement. *Omni*, December 1981, 42.

"Cyber Fun." *Omni*, November 1979, 96–99.

Da Costa, Frank. *How to Build Your Own Working Robot Pet*. Blue Ridge Summit, Pa.: Tab Books, 1979.

Debord, Guy. "Separation Perfected." Chapter 1 in *The Society of the Spectacle*. 1967. Trans. Black and Red. Reprint. Nothingness.org, 1994. http://library.nothingness.org/articles/SI/en/pub_contents/4 (accessed 16 March 2004).

Debray, Regis. *Transmitting Culture.* Trans. Eric Rauth. New York: Columbia University Press, 2000.

Deleuze, Gilles, and Felix Guattari. *A Thousand Plateaus: Capitalism and Schizophrenia.* Trans. Brian Massumi. Minneapolis: University of Minnesota Press, 1988.

Demon Seed. Directed by Donald Cammell. Metro-Goldwyn-Mayer, 1977.

Design for Dreaming. Director unknown. MPO Productions, 1956. Internet Archive. http://www.archive.org/details/Designfo1956 (accessed 11 December 2005).

Dick, Philip K. *Do Androids Dream of Electric Sheep?* New York: New American Library, 1969.

———. *Ubik.* 1969. Reprint. New York: Vintage Books, 1991.

Doane, Mary Ann. *The Emergence of Cinematic Time: Modernity, Contingency, the Archive.* Cambridge, Mass.: Harvard University Press, 2002.

Doerr, Robert. "Here Come the Androbots." *Robot Gallery.* http://www.robotgallery.com/robotgallery/androbot/index.html (accessed 16 March 2004).

Dreyfus, Hubert L., and Stuart E. Dreyfus. *Mind over Machine: The Power of Human Intuition and Expertise in the Era of the Computer.* New York: Free Press, 1986.

Duchamp, Marcel. *The Bride Stripped Bare by Her Bachelors, Even (Large Glass).* 1915–1923. Philadelphia Museum of Art. *Audio Recordings of Great Works of Art.* 1997. http://www.auralaura.com/bridestripped.html (accessed 12 January 2004).

Durham, Tony. "The Tiny World of Clive Sinclair." *Omni,* February 1982, 74–77, 117.

EDtv. Directed by Ron Howard. Universal Pictures, 1999.

Ellul, Jacques. *The Technological Society.* Trans. John Wilkinson. New York: Knopf, 1964.

"The Evolution of the Smart Bomb . . . A Story of Technology Transfer." *The Redstone Rocket,* 16 August 1972, 1, 10–11. Redstone Arsenal Historical Information. U.S. Army Aviation and Missile Command. http://www.redstone.army.mil/history/chron4/LASER2.html (accessed 16 March 2004).

Executive Chess advertisement. *Omni,* October 1981, 201.

Featherstone, Mike. *Consumer Culture and Postmodernism.* London: Sage, 1991.

Firestone, Shulamith. *The Dialectic of Sex: The Case for Feminist Revolution.* New York: William Morrow, 1970.

"The First of the Futuramic Cars." *Olds Minute Movies.* Director unknown.

Jam Handy Organization, 1948. Internet Archive. http://www.archive.org/details/OldsMinu1948 (accessed 11 December 2005).
Fjellman, Stephen M. *Vinyl Leaves: Walt Disney World and America*. Boulder, Colo.: Westview Press, 1992.
Flusser, Vilem. *Towards a Philosophy of Photography*. Trans. Anthony Matthews. London: Reaktion, 2000.
Foucault, Michel. "The Political Technology of Individuals." In *Technologies of the Self: A Seminar with Michel Foucault*, ed. Luther H. Martin, Huck Gutman, and Patrick H. Hutton. 145–62. Amherst: University of Massachusetts Press, 1988.
———. "Technologies of the Self." In *Technologies of the Self: A Seminar with Michel Foucault*, ed. Luther H. Martin, Huck Gutman, and Patrick H. Hutton, 16–49. Amherst: University of Massachusetts Press, 1988.
Frances, John. "No Ties Technology." *SmartHouse* 10.1 (2002): 103.
Frantz, Douglas, and Catherine Collins. *Celebration, U.S.A.: Living in Disney's Brave New Town*. New York: Henry Holt, 1999.
Frederick, Christine. *Household Engineering: Scientific Management in the Home*. 1915. Reprint. Chicago: American School of Home Economics, 1921.
"Frequently Asked Questions." *American Feng Shui Institute*. http://www.amfengshui.com/faq.htm (accessed 16 March 2004).
Freud, Sigmund. "The 'Uncanny.'" Trans. Alix Strachey. In *Collected Papers*, edited by Joan Riviere, 4:368–407. London: Hogarth Press, 1946.
Fulton, William. *The New Urbanism: Hope or Hype for American Communities?* Cambridge, Mass.: Lincoln Institute of Land Policy, 1996.
Fusco, Coco. *The Bodies that Were Not Ours, and Other Writings*. New York: Routledge, 2001.
"Futuramic Design." *Olds Minute Movies*. Director unknown. Jam Handy Organization, 1948. Internet Archive. http://www.archive.org/details/OldsMinu1948 (accessed 11 December 2005).
Garcia, Chris. "Robots Enter Visible Storage." *Facts and Stories about Antique (Lonesome) Computers*. http://ed-thelen.org/comp-hist/robots-core-1-4.html (accessed 16 March 2004).
Gates, Bill (with Nathan Myhrvold and Peter Rinearson). *The Road Ahead*. New York: Viking, 1995.
Genius Offspring advertisement. *Omni*, October 1979, 153.
Gershenfeld, Neil. *When Things Start to Think*. New York: Henry Holt, 1999.
Giroux, Henry A. *The Mouse that Roared: Disney and the End of Innocence*. New York: Rowman and Littlefield, 1999.

Glenn, Jerome. "Disney Dreams" (letter to the editor). *Omni*, February 1983, 10.

Gonzalez, Jennifer. "The Appended Subject: Race and Identity as Digital Assemblage." In *Race in Cyberspace*, ed. Beth E. Kolko, Lisa Nakamura, and Gilbert B. Rodman, 27–50. New York: Routledge, 2000.

Gray, Chris Hables. *Cyborg Citizen: Politics in the Posthuman Age*. New York: Routledge, 2001.

Habitek advertisement. *SmartHouse* 10.1 (2002): 54.

Hannigan, John. *Fantasy City: Pleasure and Profit in the Postmodern Metropolis*. New York: Routledge, 1999.

Haraway, Donna J. "A Cyborg Manifesto: Science, Technology, and Socialist Feminism in the Late Twentieth Century." In *Simians, Cyborgs, and Women: The Reinvention of Nature*, 149–81. New York: Routledge, 1991.

Hardt, Michael, and Antonio Negri. *Empire*. Cambridge, Mass.: Harvard University Press, 2000.

Hardy, Ian. "Cooking Up a Digital Future." *BBC News*. http://news.bbc.co.uk/2/hi/technology/3601228.stm (accessed 1 June 2006).

Harvey, Fiona. "Robots Offer Help to the Elderly of the Future." *Financial Times* (London), 9 July 2001, 15.

Hawthorne, Nathaniel. "The Artist of the Beautiful." In *Tales by Nathaniel Hawthorne*, ed. Carl Van Doren, 301–24. London: Oxford University Press, 1921.

Hayles, N. Katherine. *How We Became Posthuman: Virtual Bodies in Cybernetics, Literature and Informatics*. Chicago: University of Chicago Press, 1999.

Heath/Zenith Hero Jr. advertisement. *Omni*, October 1984, 151.

Heidegger, Martin. *Being and Time*. Trans. Joan Stambaugh. Albany: State University of New York Press, 1996.

———. "The Question Concerning Technology." Trans. William Lovitt. In *Basic Writings*, ed. David Farrell Krell, 311–41. San Francisco: Harper Collins, 1993.

———. "What Is Metaphysics?" Trans. David Farrell Krell. In *Basic Writings*, ed. David Farrell Krell, 93–110. San Francisco: Harper Collins, 1993.

Heiserman, David L. *How to Build Your Own Self-Programming Robot*. Blue Ridge Summit, Pa: Tab Books, 1979.

"High Tech Frigidaire Refrigerator." *X-Home*. http://www.x-home.com/h/h54.html (accessed 16 March 2004).

"History Timeline of Robotics." *TrueForce*. http://trueforce.com/Articles/Robot_History.htm (accessed 16 March 2004).

Hitachi Memory advertisement. *Omni*, January 1985, 7.

Hitachi Perception advertisement. *Omni*, July 1984, 7.

Hitachi Robots advertisement. *Omni*, September 1984, 9.

Hoban, Phoebe. "The Brain Race." *Omni*, June 1985, 72–74, 76–77, 124.

———. "Robot Nurses." *Omni*, December 1983, 28, 188.

Hoffmann, E. T. A. "The Sandman." In *Tales of Hoffmann*. Trans. R. J. Hollingdale, 85–125. New York: Penguin, 1982.

"Home, Smart Home." *Newsweek Web Exclusive, MSNBC.com*. http://msnbc.msn.com/id/3070139 (accessed 9 May 2007).

Homewrecker. Directed by Fred Walton. Paramount Pictures, 1992.

Howe, Barbara J., et al. *Houses and Homes: Exploring Their History*. Nashville: American Association for State and Local History, 1987.

Hunt, Steven. "A Coffee Maker with ESP?" *Discovery Channel*. http://www.exn.ca/Stories/1998/08/20/52.asp (accessed 16 March 2004).

IBM Smart Desk advertisement. *Omni*, September 1984, 50–51.

IBM "What Do IBM People Think About?" advertisement. *Omni*, October 1984, 38–39.

IDEAS advertisement. *SmartHouse* 10.1 (2002): 80–81.

Imagineers. *Walt Disney Imagineering: A Behind the Dreams Look at Making the Magic Real*. New York: Hyperion, 1998.

The Information Machine. Directed by Charles Eames and Ray Eames. Eames Office, 1958. *Internet Archive*. http://www.archive.org/details/InformationM (accessed 11 December 2005).

Jameson, Fredric. *Postmodernism, or, The Cultural Logic of Late Capitalism*. Durham, N.C.: Duke University Press, 1991.

———. "Reification and Utopia in Mass Culture." *Social Text* 1.1 (1979): 130–48.

JS&A Magic Stat advertisement. *Omni*, October 1983, 193.

JS&A Space Pager advertisement. *Omni*, May 1979, 15.

Jurassic Park. Directed by Steven Spielberg. Amblin Entertainment, 1993.

Kirby, Doug, Ken Smith, and Mike Wilkins. "The Last of the Xanadus." *Roadside America*. http://www.roadsideamerica.com/set/xanadu.html (accessed 16 March 2004).

"Kitchen Computers." *The History of Computing Project*. http://www.thocp.net/hardware/fridge.htm (accessed 16 March 2004).

Kolko, Beth E., Lisa Nakamura, and Gilbert B. Rodman, eds. *Race in Cyberspace*. New York: Routledge, 2000.

Kolodny, Annette. *The Lay of the Land: Metaphor as Experience in American Life and Letters*. Chapel Hill: University of North Carolina Press, 1975.

Lammers, David. "Smart Appliances Hit the Net." *TechWeb*. http://content.techweb.com/wire/story/TWB20000118S0032 (accessed 16 March 2004).

Leave It to Roll-Oh. Director unknown. Jam Handy Organization, 1940. *Internet Archive*. http://www.archive.org/details/LeaveItt1940 (accessed 11 December 2005).

Leavitt, Sarah. *From Catharine Beecher to Martha Stewart: A Cultural History of Domestic Advice*. Chapel Hill: University of North Carolina Press, 2002.

Le Corbusier [Charles-Edouard Jeanneret]. *Towards a New Architecture*. 1931. Trans Frederick Etchells. Reprint. New York: Dover, 1986.

Lerup, Lars. *After the City*. Cambridge, Mass.: MIT Press, 2001.

The Lord of the Rings: The Fellowship of the Ring. Directed by Peter Jackson. New Line Cinema, 2001.

Magic in the Air. Director unknown. Jam Handy Organization, 1941. *Internet Archive*. http://www.archive.org/details/Magicint1941 (accessed 11 December 2005).

Manovich, Lev. *The Language of New Media*. Cambridge, Mass.: MIT Press, 2001.

Martin, Luther H., Huck Gutman, and Patrick H. Hutton, eds. *Technologies of the Self: A Seminar with Michel Foucault*. Amherst: University of Massachusetts Press, 1988.

Marx, Leo. *The Machine in the Garden: Technology and the Pastoral Ideal in America*. New York: Oxford University Press, 1964.

Mason, Roy (with Lane Jennings and Robert Evans). *Xanadu: The Computerized Home of Tomorrow and How It Can Be Yours Today!* Washington: Acropolis Books, 1983.

Match Your Mood. Director unknown. Jam Handy Organization, 1968. *Internet Archive*. http://www.archive.org/details/match_your_mood (accessed 11 December 2005).

The Matrix. Directed by Andy Wachowski and Larry Wachowski. Warner Brothers, 1999.

The Matrix Reloaded. Directed by Andy Wachowski and Larry Wachowski. Warner Brothers, 2003.

The Matrix Revolutions. Directed by Andy Wachowski and Larry Wachowski. Warner Brothers, 2003.

Maximum Overdrive. Directed by Stephen King. De Laurentis Entertainment, 1986.

McLuhan, Marshall. *Understanding Media: The Extensions of Man*. New York: Signet, 1966.

McNair-Wilson, Hamish. "Home, Smart Home." *SmartHouse* 10.1 (2002): 112–13.

———. "A Place in the Sun." *SmartHouse* 10.1 (2002): 14–18.

Melville, Herman. "The Bell-Tower." In *Billy Budd and Other Tales*, 289-303. New York: Signet, 1998.

Memento. Directed by Christopher Nolan. New Market Films, 2000.

"Microsoft Makes Itself a Home." *Home Automation*, March 2002, 10.

Minority Report. Directed by Steven Spielberg. Twentieth Century Fox, 2002.

Mishara, Eric. "Robot Marriage." *Omni*, October 1982, 153.

Mittel, Jason. *Genre and Television: From Cop Shows to Cartoons in American Culture*. London: Routledge, 2004.

Modern Times. Directed by Charles Chaplin. United Artists, 1936.

"Monsanto House of the Future." 1957. Sound recording. *Visions Fantastic*. http://www.visionsfantastic.com/visions/dlr/disneyland/tom/history/monsanto.html (accessed 26 May 2006).

Moore, Gordon E. "Cramming More Components onto Integrated Circuits." *Electronics* 38.8 (April 1965): 114–17.

Mumford, Lewis. *The City in History: Its Origins, Its Transformations, and Its Prospects*. New York: Harcourt, Brace and World, 1961.

———. *Technics and Civilization*. 1932. Reprint. New York: Harcourt, Brace and World, 1962.

Myers, George, Jr. "Shows Give a Glimpse of Gadgets in Store for Consumers." *Columbus Dispatch*, 14 January 2002, 2E.

Nakamura, Lisa. "'Where Do You Want to Go Today?' Cybernetic Tourism, the Internet, and Transnationality." In *Race in Cyberspace*, ed. Beth E. Kolko, Lisa Nakamura, and Gilbert B. Rodman, 15–26. New York: Routledge, 2000.

Nass, Richard. "Smart Connected Devices Will Lead the Way." *Semtech*. http://web.archive.org/web/20031004144815/http://www.semtech.com/support/support_industry_smart_connected.asp (accessed 9 May 2007).

New York World's Fair 1939–40 (Reel 3, Part 1). Director unknown. P. Medicus, 1939–1940. *Internet Archive*. http://www.archive.org/details/Medicusc1939_3 (accessed 11 December 2005).

Nietzsche, Friedrich. *Thus Spake Zarathustra*. Trans. Thomas Common. New York: Modern Library, 1950.

1984 (Apple Macintosh advertisement). Directed by Ridley Scott. 1983. *Apple History*. http://www.apple-history.com (accessed 16 March 2004).

"1950–1959: 'Quick Facts' by Year." *Television History: The First 75 Years*. http://www.tvhistory.tv/1950–1959.htm (accessed 16 March 2004).

"Now You're Cooking." *Home Automation*, March 2002, 12.

The Official Guide Book of the New York World's Fair 1939: The World of Tomorrow. New York: Exposition Publications, 1939.

The Official Guide to the New York World's Fair 1964/1965. New York: Time, 1964.

The Official Guide to the World's Columbian Exposition. Chicago: Columbian Guide, 1893.

"Old Computer Ads." *Obsolete Technology*. http://oldcomputers.net/ads/ads.shtml (accessed 9 May 2007).

Olympus ESP advertisement. *Omni*, June 1985, 51.

On Guard! The Story of SAGE. Director unknown. IBM Corporation, 1956. *Internet Archive*. http://www.archive.org/details/OnGuard1956 (accessed 11 December 2005).

"Out With the Old." *SmartHouse* 10.1 (2002): 4.

Osonko, Tim. "Tomorrow Lands." *Omni*, September 1982, 68–72, 106–7.

Panasonic advertisement. *Omni*, November 1983, 109.

Pargh, Andy. "Smart Coffee Scoop Measures Perfect Coffee Everytime." *Gadget Guru*. http://web.archive.org/web/20010302175210/http://www.gadgetguru.com/Dec.20,2000-SmartCoffeeScoop.htm (accessed 9 May 2007).

Paycheck. Directed by John Woo. DreamWorks Pictures, 2003.

PC World Staff. "The Digital Century: Computing through the Ages." *CNN.com*, 24 November 1999. http://www.cnn.com/TECH/computing/9911/24/digital.century5.idg (accessed 16 March 2004).

"Philips Introduces a New Way to Shop." *Home Automation*, March 2002, 10–11.

Pi. Directed by Darren Aronofsky. Harvest Films, 1997.

Plante, Ellen M. *The American Kitchen, 1700 to the Present: From Hearth to Highrise*. New York: Facts on File, 1995.

Poe, Edgar Allan. "The Facts in the Case of M. Valdemar." In *The Science Fiction of Edgar Allan Poe*, ed. Harold Beaver, 194–203. New York: Penguin, 1986.

Polsson, Ken. "Chronology of Personal Computers." *Polsson's Web World*. http://www.islandnet.com/~kpolsson/comphist (accessed 16 March 2004).

Poltergeist. Directed by Tobe Hooper. Metro-Goldwyn-Mayer, 1982.

Post, Jonathan V. "Cybernetic War." *Omni*, May 1979, 44–49, 104.

Practical Dreamer. Director unknown. Jam Handy Organization, 1957. *Internet Archive*. http://www.archive.org/details/Practica1957 (accessed 11 December 2005).

Pritchard, Stuart. "Out with the Old." *SmartHouse* 10.1 (2002): 4.

Project on Disney. *Inside the Mouse: Work and Play at Disney World.* Durham, N.C.: Duke University Press, 1995.

An RCA Presentation: Television. Director unknown. Radio Corporation of America, 1939. *Internet Archive.* http://www.archive.org/details/RCAPrese 1939 (accessed 11 December 2005).

Read, Steven. Mini-Arcade.Com: An Online Museum of Vintage Handheld Games. http://www.miniarcade.com (accessed 24 March 2004).

Real Life. Directed by Albert Brooks. Paramount Pictures, 1979.

"Redstone Arsenal Complex Chronology: Part IIIA: Excellence in Missilery." *Redstone Arsenal Historical Information. U.S. Army Aviation and Missile Command.* http://www.redstone.army.mil/history/chron4/1965.html (accessed 16 March 2004).

"Remote Control." *Great Idea Finder.* http://www.ideafinder.com/history/inventions/remotectl.htm (accessed 16 March 2004).

"Remote, I Want Control." *Economic Times,* 24 July 2005. http://economictimes.indiatimes.com/articleshow/msid-1180965,curpg-1.cms (accessed 31 May 2006).

Ren, Hai. *The Countdown of Time: Public Displays and Symbolic Economy in China and Hong Kong.* Chicago: University of Chicago Press, forthcoming.

The Ring. Directed by Gore Verbinski. DreamWorks Pictures, 2002.

Ringu. Directed by Hideo Nakata. Kadokawa Shoten Publishing, 1998.

Rose, Nikolas. *Governing the Soul: The Shaping of the Private Self.* New York: Free Association Books, 1999.

Rose, Tricia. *Black Noise: Rap Music and Black Culture in Contemporary America.* Middletown, Conn.: Wesleyan University Press, 1994.

Rossbach, Sarah, and Lin Yun. *Feng Shui Design: From History and Landscape to Modern Gardens and Interiors.* New York: Viking, 1998.

Rutsky, R. L. *High Techne: Art and Technology from the Machine Aesthetic to the Posthuman.* Minneapolis: University of Minnesota Press, 1999.

Rybczynski, Witold. *Home: A Short History of an Idea.* New York: Penguin Books, 1986.

Rymer, Russ. "Back to the Future: Disney Reinvents the Company Town." *Harper's,* October 1996, 65–71, 75–78.

Samsung VCR advertisement. *Omni,* August 1985, 45.

Sanders, Jane M. "Sensing the Subtleties of Everyday Life." *Research Horizons* (winter 2000). http://gtresearchnews.gatech.edu/reshor/rh-win00/main.html (accessed 1 June 2006).

Sargent, Martin. "Twisted List: Seven Tech Wonders of Seattle." *G4.* http://

www.g4tv.com/techtvvault/features/33793/Twisted_List_Seven_Tech_Wonders_of_Seattle.html (accessed 16 March 2004).

Sconce, Jeffrey. *Haunted Media: Electronic Presence from Telegraphy to Television*. Durham, N.C.: Duke University Press, 2000.

"Screenfridge." *X-Home*. http://web.archive.org/web/20040208191145/http://www.x-home.com/h/h52.html (accessed 9 May 2007).

Sharper Image advertisement. *Omni*, March 1980, 71.

Sheckley, Robert. "Street of Dreams, Feet of Clay." In *The City 2000 A.D.: Urban Life through Science Fiction*, ed. Ralph Clem, Martin Harry Greenberg, and Joseph Olander, 62–78. Greenwich: Fawcett Publications, 1976.

Shelley, Mary Wollstonecraft. *Frankenstein: Or, The Modern Prometheus*. 1818. Reprint. London: Oxford University Press, 1969.

"The Smart Choice." *SmartHouse* 10.1 (2002): 100–101.

"Smart Homes Have Arrived Here." *Business Line*, 24 March 2001, 9.

"Smart Home Unveiled in Milan." *Siemens*. http://web.archive.org/web/20010119134200/http://www.siemens.ie/News/Smarthome.htm (accessed 9 May 2007).

Smart Sony advertisement. *Omni*, December 1982, 135.

Smith, Henry Nash. *Virgin Land: The American West as Symbol and Myth*. Cambridge, Mass.: Harvard University Press, 1978.

Sobel, Michael E. *Lifestyle and Social Structure: Concepts, Definitions, Analysis*. New York: Academic Press, 1981.

Sontag, Susan. "Notes on 'Camp.'" *Against Interpretation, and Other Essays*. New York: Delty, 1966. 275–92.

Sony STR-VX33 advertisement. *Omni*, September 1982, 15.

Spicer, Dag. "If You Can't Stand the Coding, Stay Out of the Kitchen." *Dr. Dobb's Portal*. http://www.ddj.com/dept/architect/184404040 (accessed 23 January 2002).

Spigel, Lynn. *Welcome to the Dreamhouse: Popular Media and Postwar Suburbs*. Durham, N.C.: Duke University Press, 2001.

Spivak, Gayatri Chakravorty. "Can the Subaltern Speak?" In *The Post-Colonial Studies Reader*, ed. Bill Ashcroft, Gareth Griffiths, and Helen Tiffin, 24–28. New York: Routledge, 1995.

Star Wars. Directed by George Lucas. Twentieth Century Fox, 1977.

Step-Saving Kitchen. Directed by Irving Rusinow. U.S. Department of Agriculture, Motion Picture Service, 1949. *Internet Archive*. http://www.archive.org/details/StepSavi1949 (accessed 11 December 2005).

Stiegler, Bernard. *Technics and Time, 1: The Fault of Epimetheus*. Trans.

Richard Beardsworth and George Collins. Stanford, Calif.: Stanford University Press, 1998.

———. "The Time of Cinema: On the 'New World' and 'Cultural Exception.'" *Tekhnema* 4 (spring 1998): 66–112.

Stirling, Will. "Customised Cuisine." *SmartHouse* 10.1 (2002): 72–74.

The Story of Television. Director unknown. William J. Ganz Company, 1956. Internet Archive. http://www.archive.org/details/StoryofT1956 (accessed 11 December 2005).

"Swedes Rent Electrolux Washing Machines Via Internet-Linked 'Smart Homes.'" *Euromarketing via E-mail* 3.8 (19 November 1999). Available at LexisNexis. http://www.lexisnexis.com/academic (accessed 16 March 2004).

Taylor, Frederick Winslow. *The Principles of Scientific Management*. 1911. Reprint. New York: Dover, 1998.

"Technology to the Fore." *SmartHouse* 10.1 (2002): 10–12.

The Terminator. Directed by James Cameron. Hemdale Film Corporation, 1984.

Thelen, Ed. "DDP-116, CCD 516, H316." *Facts and Stories about Antique (Lonesome) Computers*. http://ed-thelen.org/comp-hist (accessed 16 March 2004).

Thirteen Ghosts. Directed by Steven Beck. Columbia Pictures, 2001.

Thomas, Bob. *Walt Disney: An American Original*. New York: Simon and Schuster, 1976.

Tien, Paul. "Thalia." *X-Home*. http://web.archive.org/web/20040607222959/http://www.x-home.com/h/h59.html (accessed 16 March 2004).

Trulove, James Grayson. *The Smart House*. New York: Harper Collins, 2002.

The Truman Show. Directed by Peter Weir. Paramount Pictures, 1998.

Turner, Frederick J. *The Significance of the Frontier in American History*. Ann Arbor: University Microfilms, 1966.

2001: A Space Odyssey. Directed by Stanley Kubrick. Metro-Goldwyn-Mayer, 1968.

Virilio, Paul. *The Art of the Motor*. Trans. Julie Rose. Minneapolis: University of Minnesota Press, 1995.

———. *A Landscape of Events*. Trans. Julie Rose. Cambridge, Mass.: MIT Press, 2001.

———. *Open Sky*. Trans. Julie Rose. London: Verso, 1997.

———. *Speed and Politics: An Essay on Dromology*. Trans. Mark Polizzotti. New York: Semiotext(e), 1986.

Voice Chess Challenger advertisement. *Omni*, December 1979, 124.

Voice Sensory Chess Challenger advertisement. *Omni*, December 1980, 149.

Vonnegut, Kurt, Jr. *Player Piano*. New York: Delacorte Press, 1952.

Votolato, Gregory. *American Design in the Twentieth Century: Personality and Performance*. New York: Manchester University Press, 1998.

Walt Disney Company. "History." *The Walt Disney Company Fact Book 2002*. http://corporate.disney.go.com/investors/financials/fact_books_2002.html (16 March 2004).

Walt's Last Film. Directed by Walt Disney. Walt Disney Company, 1966. Waltopia: Walt's EPCOT. http://www.waltopia.com/film.html (accessed 16 March 2004).

Weil, Nancy. "Who Wants a Smart Home?" *CNN.com*, 1 December 1998. http://www.cnn.com/TECH/computing/9812/01/smarthome.idg (accessed 16 March 2004).

White Noise. Directed by Geoffrey Sax. Universal Pictures, 2005.

Wolf-Meyer, Matthew, and Davin Heckman. "Navigating the Starless Night: Reading the Auto/bio/geography: Meaning-Making." *Reconstruction* 2.3 (summer 2002). http://reconstruction.eserver.org/023/intro.htm (accessed 16 March 2004).

"A World of Difference." *The Twilight Zone*, CBS, 11 March 1960.

Yamaha advertisement. *Omni*, September 1984, 15.

Ybarra-Frausto, Tomas. "Rasquachismo: A Chicano Sensibility." In *Chicano Art: Resistance and Affirmation, 1965–1985*, ed. Richard Griswold del Castillo, Teresa McKenna, and Yvonne Yarbro-Bejarano, 151–62. Los Angeles: Wight Art Gallery, University of California, Los Angeles, 1991.

Young Man's Fancy (Part II). Director unknown. Jam Handy Organization, 1952. *Internet Archive*. http://www.archive.org/details/YoungMan1952_2 (accessed 11 December 2005).

Zim, Larry, Mel Lerner, and Herbert Rolfes. *The World of Tomorrow: The 1939 New York World's Fair*. New York: Harper and Row, 1988.

Zukin, Sharon. *Landscapes of Power: From Detroit to Disney World*. Berkeley: University of California Press, 1991.

INDEX

DAVIN HECKMAN

is an assistant professor of English

at Siena Heights University.